MY JERUSALEM

TWELVE WALKS IN THE WORLD'S HOLIEST CITY

TEDDY KOLLEK

AND SHULAMITH EISNER

PHOTOGRAPHS BY RICHARD NOWITZ

SUMMIT BOOKS

New York   London   Toronto   Sydney   Tokyo

SUMMIT BOOKS
Simon & Schuster Building
Rockefeller Center
1230 Avenue of the Americas
New York, New York 10020

Text Copyright © 1990 by Teddy Kollek and Shulamith Eisner
Photographs (except those mentioned below) © 1990 by Richard Nowitz

Published simultaneously in Great Britain by
George Weidenfeld & Nicolson Ltd.

Summit Books and colophon are trademarks
of Simon & Schuster Inc.

Library of Congress Cataloging-in-Publication Data
Kollek, Teddy, 1911–
    My Jerusalem: twelve walks in the world's holiest city/
    Teddy Kollek and Shulamith Eisner: photographs by Richard Nowitz.
    p.   cm.
    ISBN 0-671-70245-9
    1. Jerusalem—Description—1981—Tours.
    I. Eisner, Shulamith.
    II. Title.
    DS109.15.K65   1990
    915.694′420454—dc20   89-21831
                             CIP

Manufactured in Italy

10 9 8 7 6 5 4 3 2 1

ISBN 0-671-70245-9

Photographs not taken by Richard Nowitz were supplied by or are reproduced by kind permission of the following:
Ben-Dov (Israel Museum): 36; Central Zionist Archives, Jerusalem: 97;
Eisenstark: 138; Tim Gidal: 12; David Harris: 82, 84–5;
Israel Government Press Office: 20, 103; Israel Museum/David Harris: 110, 114, 115;
Jewish National and University Library, Hebrew University, Jerusalem: 43;
Keren Kajemeth Le Jisrael: 51; Garo Nalbandian, Jerusalem: 55;
Eli Ross: 13; Weidenfeld Archives: 75, 81, 129;
Zoom 77/Eli Hershkovitz: 6, 88–9, 127.

TITLE PAGE
Aerial view of Jerusalem with the Old City
in the middle foreground.

CONTENTS

Teddy Kollek walking in the Old City.

INTRODUCTION
AND ACKNOWLEDGMENTS

Jerusalem is a city of striking contrasts. It is a mystical, eternal city of contemplation and withdrawal, but it is also a city where half a million people seek to find their place in the modern world. It is that unique city in which the power of the spiritual past meets the vicissitudes and opportunities of an advanced, modern, technological society. It is a city which must exemplify the way in which religious traditions can flourish in a democratic, pluralistic society. It is a city of joys and a city of sorrows.

And it is a city of beauty, of singular historical and religious sites, of culture and the arts. It is a city which welcomes the visitor to explore and to savour.

This is not a typical guidebook, which catalogues and indexes facts and figures. It is a very personal book, an amalgam of history, local lore and autobiography. The book grew out of my desire to circumvent the laws of physics, the laws of time and motion, which preclude the possibility of my walking through Jerusalem with every visitor to the city. I sought to take your hand and walk by your side, so that you could experience more intimately the city which consumes my every waking moment.

The walks can be walked, or they can simply be read before a visit, after a visit, or – heaven forbid – instead of a visit. There is no stipulation as to the duration of the individual walks though the average one is half a day (except for Walk No. 4, Mount Zion and the Jewish Quarter, which is longer).

The acknowledgments for a book such as this are vast, including as they do the kings and prophets, emperors and sultans, rabbis and bishops and sheikhs, who wittingly and unwittingly left their mark on the city; pilgrims and travellers, who bequeathed to our generation the oral, written and pictorial chronicles of centuries; the people who have shared in the city's development, some of whose names appear on plaques or testimonials and some whose names are lost to history; and most fervently the residents of Jerusalem, for whom the city's joys and sorrows are their daily bread.

My co-author and I owe untold debts of gratitude – to our families, who shared the trials and tribulations of our attempt to run double-time jobs and write a book; and to our colleagues and our staffs, who lent a helping hand whenever called upon. We would like to single out those who had a share in guiding us, in advising us, in reading and re-reading the manuscript: Magen Broshi, Daniel Furman, Rabbi Dr David Hartman, Father Immanuel, Salah Jarallah, Aryeh Kofsky, David Kroyanker, Irene Lewitt, Abraham Rabinovitch, Dr Rehav Rubin, Noemi Teasdale and Yitzhak Yaacovy.

We are particularly grateful to Colin Grant and Linda Osband of Weidenfeld & Nicolson, who edited and queried and were often able to spot what we had missed and who were extraordinarily patient with our regrettable delays and with the vagaries of facsimile communication. And, lastly, our gratitude to George Weidenfeld, who conceived the notion for this book and who was responsible for its realization.

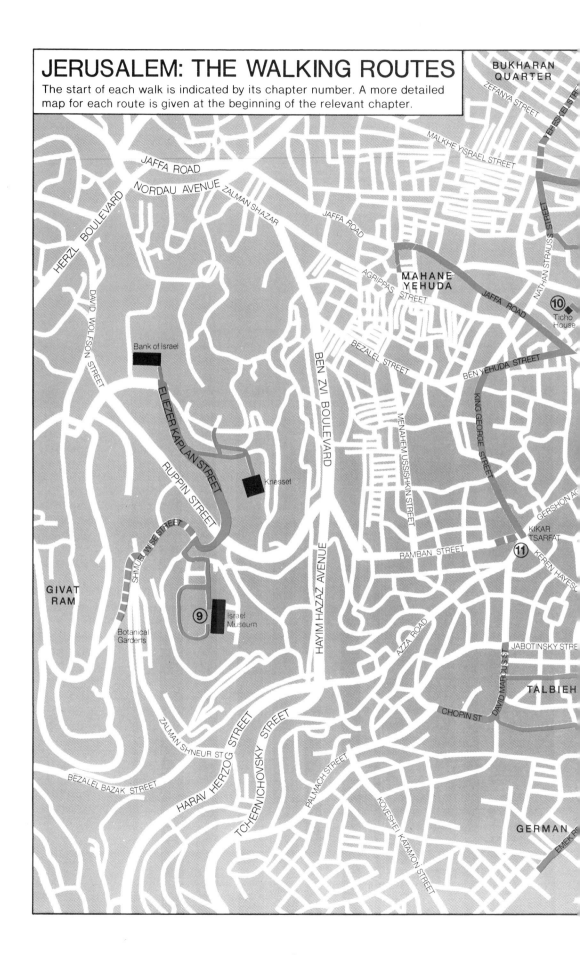

JERUSALEM: THE WALKING ROUTES

The start of each walk is indicated by its chapter number. A more detailed map for each route is given at the beginning of the relevant chapter.

BUKHARAN QUARTER

ZEFANYA STREET

YESHE'EL STR

JAFFA ROAD

NORDAU AVENUE

ZALMAN SHAZAR

MALKHE YISRAEL STREET

NATHAN STRAUSS STREET

JAFFA ROAD

HERZL BOULEVARD

DAVID WOLFSON STREET

AGRIPPAS STREET

MAHANE YEHUDA

JAFFA ROAD

⑩ Ticho House

Bank of Israel

ELIEZER KAPLAN STREET

BEZALEL STREET

BEN YEHUDA STREET

RUPPIN STREET

BEN ZVI BOULEVARD

MENAHEM USSISHKIN STREET

KING GEORGE STREET

GERSHON AG

Knesset

SHMUEL WISE STREET

KIKAR TSARFAT

RAMBAN STREET

⑪

KEREN HAYESO

GIVAT RAM

⑨ Israel Museum

HAYIM HAZAZ AVENUE

AZZA ROAD

JABOTINSKY STRE

DAVID MARCUS ST

TALBIEH

Botanical Gardens

ZALMAN SHNEUR ST

HARAV HERZOG STREET

TCHERNICHOVSKY STREET

PALMACH STREET

CHOPIN ST

BEZALEL BAZAK STREET

KOVESHEI KATAMON STREET

GERMAN

EMEK R

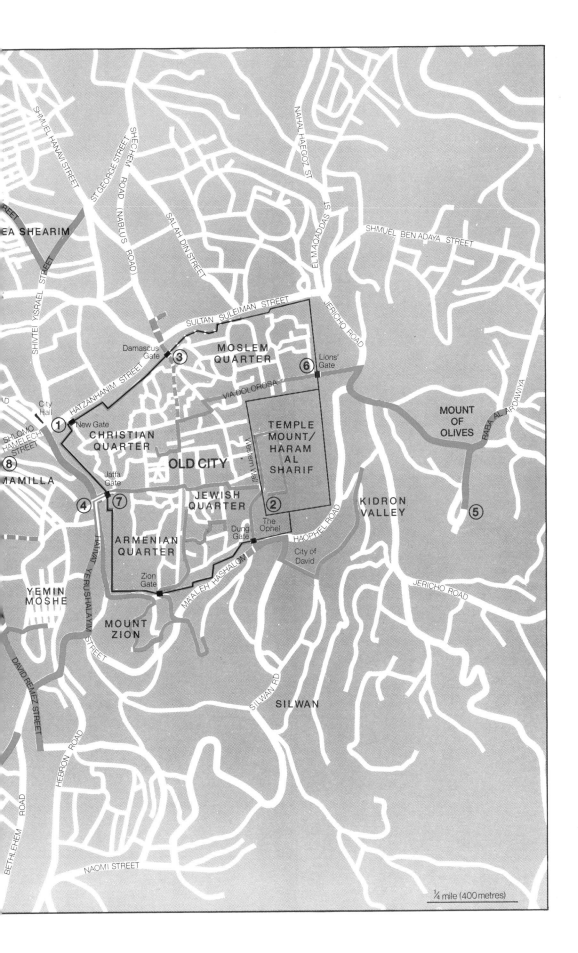

SHMUEL HANAVI STREET

EA SHEARIM

ST GEORGE STREET

SHECHEM ROAD (NABLUS ROAD)

SALAH DIN STREET

SHIVTEI YISRAEL STREET

NAHAL HAEGOZ ST

EL MQADDAS ST

SHMUEL BEN ADAYA STREET

SULTAN SULEIMAN STREET

MOSLEM QUARTER

Damascus Gate

③

JERICHO ROAD

Lions' Gate

⑥

VIA DOLOROSA

City Hall

HATZANHANIM STREET

① New Gate

CHRISTIAN QUARTER

OLD CITY

MOUNT OF OLIVES

RABA AL ARDAWIYA

TEMPLE MOUNT/ HARAM AL SHARIF

SHLOMO HAMELECH STREET

⑧

MAMILLA

Jaffa Gate

④   ⑦

JEWISH QUARTER

②

Western Wall

The Ophel

KIDRON VALLEY

⑤

HAOPHEL ROAD

Dung Gate

ARMENIAN QUARTER

City of David

HATIVAT YERUSHALAYIM STREET

YEMIN MOSHE

Zion Gate

MA'ALEH HASHALOM

JERICHO ROAD

MOUNT ZION

DAVID REMEZ STREET

HEBRON ROAD

SILWAN RD

SILWAN

BETHLEHEM ROAD

NAOMI STREET

¼ mile (400 metres)

I
FROM CITY HALL
TO THE WESTERN WALL

Even in books where one's choice of a starting-point may seem obvious – biographies and histories, for example – it must still be given some careful reflection. For our tour of Jerusalem, the choice of a starting-point was not a simple undertaking. Should we start at the oldest site? The most beautiful site? At one end of the city, or perhaps the other?

My choice of City Hall was neither whim nor arbitrary. It is the hub of the city, flanking the cross-roads of the Old City and the New: one block south, the Citadel is the repository of 2,000 years of history; one block north, the city's Central Post Office abounds with modern telecommunications. City Hall was on the border between Jordan and Israel – the very last building on the Jewish side – in the nineteen years that the city was divided, 1948–67. Arab Jerusalem lay immediately to the east; Jewish Jerusalem to the west. And, indeed, I begin each day at City Hall, a fact not without influence in my choice of our starting-point.

It is perhaps unfair to begin a tour with a site which is not readily accessible to the reader, for while the building is open to the resident who hankers to dispute his tax bill or complain about the lighting in his street, it is hardly a tourist stop. But as City Hall merits a footnote in the history of the modern city, a few words are in order.

Built in 1934, it served the British Mandate as the seat of the Mayor of Jerusalem (always Arab except for a short period of an English Mayor). The doors of the building, which I often am the one to unlock at 6.15 a.m., depict the gates of the Old City and were created by a Jerusalem artisan in the early 1970s. The City Council Chamber is adorned by modernistic stained-glass windows created by the Israeli artist, Avigdor Arikha. And while the double thickness of the glass is ostensibly to keep out the street noise, it serves equally to mask the high decibels of the shouting which is an all-too-regular feature of our City Council meetings. Jerusalem's diversity is not always

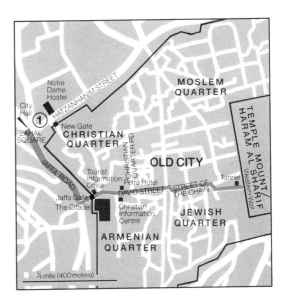

conducive to genteel deliberations.

The Council Chamber evokes a *pot-pourri* of memories. There was the very first meeting I chaired as Mayor, a nervous novice. There were the meetings at which I yelled; there were the meetings at which I was yelled at. There were the people who have passed through my office, not only local citizens with grievances but also visiting delegations of congressmen, businessmen, scientists, sportsmen, academics and even Brooklyn firemen. There were Israeli schoolchildren and foreign teenagers. There was the British Prime Minister, Margaret Thatcher, Queen Beatrix of the Netherlands, Liv Ullmann and Jane Fonda. There was Artur Rubinstein and Isaac Stern. There were Roman Catholic cardinals and Greek Orthodox patriarchs. Jerusalem City Hall is the hub of a city that has a spiritual constituency embracing half the world.

There were occasions on which we honoured statesmen and friends of Jerusalem. Of course, the one that stands out in my mind was David Ben-Gurion's eightieth birthday, when we awarded him the rare distinction of the honorary citizenship of Jerusalem. He had been my mentor, and the ideals which he instilled in me have guided many of my thoughts and perhaps as many of my actions.

The Western Wall (here with the Dome of the Rock behind) and its adjoining plaza now accommodate large numbers of visitors especially at festival times.

When I was elected Mayor in 1965, City Hall was not *on* the border but was *the* border. My predecessor had approved plans for a new City Hall in the centre of Jewish (new) Jerusalem, and the architect's model for this undertaking greeted me on my taking office. My decision to scrap this plan had its rationale. During the mass influx of immigrants to Israel in the 1950s and early 1960s – refugees from the Holocaust and from Moslem countries – numerous newcomers insisted on living in Jerusalem, the focus of their prayers for generations. The hurriedly created housing was along a sometimes dangerous border, which meandered through the city. It seemed to me improper to place families on the frontier while removing the city fathers to a less exposed area.

I had a second reason, more esoteric than pragmatic. I believed that one day – if not in our generation, then in our children's or grandchildren's – the city would be united. And for a united city, City Hall was perfectly situated. My dream, of course, was a reunification by peaceful means.

Between 1965 and 1967, I would often escort

Teddy Kollek looking towards the Old City from the terrace of the City Hall in 1966. Anti-sniper walls stand across the street below leading into the Mamilla Quarter.

visitors to the roof of City Hall to see the 'view'. This was a jarring clash between the beauty of the Old City and the glaring – offensive – barbed wire, tank traps, concrete walls and abandoned buildings which comprised the frontier adjoining City Hall. A photograph of these anti-sniper walls being torn down, taken just after the Six Day War ceasefire, hangs on my office wall, a poignant reminder if one is needed.

Today, standing on the very same roof, one can discern the bullet marks from two wars: Israel's War of Independence in 1948 and the Six Day War of 1967. But one can also see the hustle and bustle of a thriving city, with parks and gardens covering the physical scars of the division. Spiritual wounds heal more slowly.

A postscript to the buried plans for the new City Hall. With the doubling of the city's population and with municipal authority covering responsibilities which had been under the jurisdiction of the Mandate Government, the British-built City Hall hurriedly proved inadequate. Staff doubled up in cramped quarters. Departments moved to new addresses as far away as the city entrance. A resident's municipal transactions often included a forced tour of the city, while inter-office functioning could only become less efficient. A new City Hall was no longer a luxury.

The present location was a prerequisite for any

*Toppling anti-sniper walls after the Six Day War
in 1967.*

plan and the buildings you see to the right and to
the left (an architectural treat if not covered by the
necessary evil of scaffolding) will be incorporated
into the new complex. The town square included
in the plans is undoubtedly an outgrowth of my
European childhood. It will comprise restored old
buildings with carefully inserted new ones – and
the town square. The new City Hall will cover ten
acres from the present City Hall to the Russian
Compound. A place for ceremony and celebration
(and, undoubtedly, demonstrations) will aug-
ment the democratic quality of the city. The goal is
to create functional buildings and public spaces
for a better-functioning municipality – all to be
enjoyed by my successor . . .

The architect, Jack Diamond, stated that he
views City Hall Square as the culmination of his
career. He sees this site as 'a texture revealing historical continuity and eclectic evolution. . . . When
King David made Jerusalem the capital of his
kingdom some three thousand years ago, he
probably put up a tent somewhere so that people
would have a place to come with their complaints.
That was the first City Hall.'

Let us leave City Hall and walk southward
around the building towards the Old City. Traffic
is heavy and this may be the appropriate time to
add a warning about Jerusalem's drivers: they are
not always the most polite, even when it is the
pedestrian's right of way in a carefully laid-out
cross-walk.

The westernmost corner of the Old City is a few
metres away. A glance over our left shoulder
reveals the St Louis Hospital, for terminally ill
patients, and the beautiful, newly restored Nôtre
Dame pilgrims' hostel. Before 1967, tourists – for a
fee – could ascend to the roof of the building and
look across the border to the Temple Mount. It
was very reminiscent of childhood warnings: you
can look, but you cannot touch! Today Nôtre
Dame's fame rests on its fine restaurant.

It may be a bit premature to burden you with
the complexities of life in Jerusalem, but to understand the city, one must be aware of how a commonplace municipal or even commercial decision
can cause international ramifications. The story of
the Nôtre Dame Hostel reflects these
complexities.

The year was 1969. While Nôtre Dame was no
longer a border outpost, and while much of the
rubble from the surrounding areas had been
removed, it was not yet considered a lucrative
commercial property. The Assumptionist Fathers, who owned the then monastery, opted to sell
this huge nineteenth-century building for which
it had been difficult to recruit both monks and ser-
vants. The Hebrew University, seeking dormitory
space, was a ready buyer. All legal contracts were
drawn up and signed. The price was paid. The
sale was final.

But not quite. The Assumptionist Fathers had not sought or received the approval of the Vatican to sell Church property in the Holy City. When news of the sale reached Rome, the Holy See's hue and cry was easily audible in Jerusalem. It was not a simple matter as the sale was legally binding. And yet the transfer of this building would cause untold harm to Israel's relations with the Catholic Church.

I was approached by the Apostolic Delegate in Jerusalem, Monsignor Pio Laghi. Much goodwill was at stake. I became convinced of the wisdom of returning the property, but the proposed annulment of the sale entailed persuading a host of others, including the Prime Minister. Opposition was rampant: why return a valued landmark, newly acquired, to foreigners? The final outcome was the return of the building at its original price, though its free-market value had more than quadrupled. This is but one example of how a simple transaction can take on the burden of centuries.

The small gate in the Old City wall opposite Nôtre Dame, which leads to the Old City's Christian Quarter, was built in 1889 and bears the name 'New Gate'. (In Jerusalem, what is merely a century old is labelled new.) The Turkish Sultan, Abd al Hamid II, had given the French Government the parcel of land to build Nôtre Dame, in appreciation for French support of the Turks against the Russians in the Crimean War. The New Gate was to be its link with the Christian Quarter.

The walk towards Jaffa Gate is one of greenery and flowers. Although I would like to take credit for the concept of a green belt around the Old City wall, it was an idea conceived, soon after General Allenby's conquest of Jerusalem in World War I, by Sir Patrick Geddes, perhaps the first modern town planner. He had this dream, but the British authorities were unable to fund it. We found the plans and took up his dream – half a century later.

Surely we were less affluent than the British Colonial Office? Even before the city was reunited, pressing needs with which we were confronted were met with threadbare pockets. Jerusalem's tax base is hardly substantial and trying to make City Hall a viable economic concern is akin to miracle-making. Well over two thousand tax-exempt institutions – synagogues, churches, monasteries and mosques; government ministries and institutions; universities and museums; diplomatic missions – are not helpful in filling municipal coffers. I can only envy my counterpart in Tel Aviv, whose ledgers list banks and commercial and industrial enterprises.

Thus we learned early on that with all our diligence and dedication, what was needed would not happen without outside help. Soon after I was elected Mayor, friends in New York, perhaps more realistic than I about the challenges ahead, suggested the creation of a fund which would enable friends abroad, for whom Jerusalem is the font of their spiritual strength, to lend a helping hand. Starting in a nook of my office in Jerusalem – and in a cubicle of a friend's shirt company in New York's garment district – the Jerusalem Foundation came into being. Beginning with a pocket park here and a basketball court there, it has since become a flourishing partnership with friends of Jerusalem on every continent and its logo is a familiar sight even in the most obscure corners of our city.

While one side of the road towards Jaffa Gate is a medley of flowers, the other side is a cacophony of abandoned buildings. Plans for the renovation of this area have now been finalized after much argument and anguish.

At times progress is hindered by local civic groups who fight to preserve anything and everything, often with no serious consideration as to what merits preservation. Preservation at times actually depends on demolition. During the latter part of the nineteenth century, the very first – brave – souls ventured to live outside the Old City wall; but there were middle-of-the-roaders in the courage department, who built their homes right against the wall. These homes and shops had lain in the no-man's-land of the divided city and were uninhabited when the city was reunited. It was only by tearing them down that the beauty of the wall could be fully exposed and Sir Patrick Geddes's green belt created. These abandoned buildings – one can still discern the markings – were mainly Church property and we paid extensive compensation.

We rapidly reach Jaffa Gate. Even before entering the Old City we encounter hawkers who are the frontispiece to the Arab market. The sesame bagels are well worth their price and one should be sure to ask for the accompanying spice, *zaatar* (hyssop), elegantly wrapped in yesterday's newspaper.

We can enter Jaffa Gate either through the pedestrian gate or through the vehicular entrance. The massive opening in the wall was made by the Ottomans in 1898, when the wall was breached and the moat filled so that Kaiser Wilhelm could enter the city on horseback, and the Empress by carriage, with the appropriate pomp and circumstance. I try to imagine world reaction were we to attempt a similar breach. Jerusalem today is always under the microscope of the international media. If we move a stone, it becomes headlines. But the Ottomans did not have to be concerned with wire services, the *New York Times*, *Sixty Minutes* or a threatened session of the United Nations Security Council. When they needed a break in the wall, they made it.

We pass the entrance to the Citadel and this may be a good time for a visit, even though I place

Jaffa Gate, the western entrance to the Old City, with the Citadel, or David's Tower, on the right, and the flowers of the 'green belt' that now surrounds the Old City in the foreground.

it in the context of our walk along the Cultural Mile (see p. 79). Even the first-time visitor will recognize the distinctive form of the Citadel's tower, a fifteenth-century minaret, which for generations has been Jerusalem's uncopyrighted trademark.

While I had been to Jaffa Gate before 1948, my clearest memories are those of June 1967. Adjoining no-man's-land, Jaffa Gate had been walled off during the nineteen years of the city's division. When I reached here, I was confronted with the barriers which prevented access, and my first entry to the Old City was through the Lions' Gate (St Stephen's Gate) on the opposite side of the city, in the footsteps of our soldiers. The barriers blocking Jaffa Gate were removed within days.

The name Jaffa Gate is self-evident because the road from here led and still leads west to the ancient port of Jaffa. The Arabic name for this Gate is Bab al Khalil, the Gate of the Friend, referring to Abraham who is buried in Hebron (Khalil) to which this road also leads in the opposite direction. The Crusaders called it Porta David and it is so marked on Crusader maps.

As we go into the L-shaped pedestrian entrance, we can see markings where the axles of carts and carriages rubbed the side of the wall before the breach gave vehicles a less cumbersome entry.

Jaffa Gate is also a possible point of ascent for the walk atop the Old City wall – the Ramparts Walk – which we will take at a later time (see p. 37). It is surely worth overcoming one's acrophobia.

THE OLD CITY
The open area in which we are standing is Omar ibn al Khattab Square, named for the seventh-century Moslem conqueror of Jerusalem. The euphoria of the early days following the Six Day War catalysed numerous suggestions for the renaming of this square, ranging from historic Jewish figures to contemporary Israeli heroes. We felt strongly that the integrity of such sites should be maintained and the only change made was the addition of Hebrew to the Armenian plaque commemorating the name of this great caliph.

Immediately to our left on entering the Old City is a small enclosed area, with two tombstones. A rather far-fetched legend, which our tourist guides have made into lore, relates that these are the tombs of the two architects commissioned by Suleiman the Magnificent in the mid-sixteenth century to build the Old City wall, the wall which we know today. On returning to Jerusalem, Suleiman learned that the architects had left Mount Zion outside the wall and he had them summarily

15

beheaded. If only Mayors today could do the same . . .

Adjacent to the little graveyard is the general Tourist Information Office, which can help solve all and sundry quandaries.

On our left is the Christian Quarter, easily identifiable by the names of the streets we pass: Latin Patriarchate Road, Greek Catholic Patriarchate Road (ironically a short detour along the Greek Catholic Road brings you to a small museum of the Greek Orthodox Patriarchate), and there is even a Copts Road, noting the presence of Egypt's native Christian church. At the far corner of this square is a building housing the Christian Information Centre, noted prominently across the building's façade. Before 1914, when European powers had extensive rights throughout the Holy City, this was the Austrian Post Office.

The Christian Information Centre, administered by the Catholic Custodian of the Holy Land, is a treasure trove of information concerning Christian holy places, holidays and religious services, a plethora of detail if one considers that Jerusalem has more than forty different Christian denominations. For example, the Anglican Christ Church nearby not only has divine services for visiting pilgrims but also chamber concerts, which attract both tourists and non-Christian Jerusalemites.

People-watchers might find themselves tempted to try the Turkish coffee at the café adjacent to the Information Centre. One can choose the 'terrace area' (a porch) of either the Citadel Bar and Restaurant or the Moses Café.

One has the feeling of being at the centre of the world, as Jerusalem was commonly depicted on maps of the fifteenth and sixteenth centuries. (I once gave a print of the most famous of these maps, Jerusalem at the centre of a cloverleaf, as a gift to the visiting head of the Russian Church, Metropolitan Filaret. His first reaction was that Russia did not appear at all on the map, but he was immediately assuaged when I pointed out that neither did the United States.)

The world passes by: the black-garbed Hassidim and the T-shirted backpackers, the long-frocked Armenian and Greek priests, the Ethiopian monks and the shorts-and-sandals kibbutzniks, the sensibly shod American Baptist pilgrims and the veiled Moslem women. An occasional soldier or policeman. And an occasional sheep on its way to becoming lamb chops.

With coffee in hand, we can view the majestic Citadel and its drawbridge-like entrance, which elegantly traverses a Crusader moat. Laden with ancient history, it has a touch of modern history as well, for it was here in 1917 that General Allenby, having (unlike the Kaiser) dismounted and entered the city on foot, accepted the surrender of the Turks from second-level city officials.

The Turkish Mayor, having surrendered the city to junior officers twice before General Allenby's arrival, was hoarse and down with a cold.

An amusing item of history followed this surrender. When the British Military Governor handed over his command to the first British High Commissioner, Sir Herbert Samuel, the military officer, in true good form, asked Sir Herbert for a receipt. 'Received from Major-General Sir Louis Bols, one Palestine, complete', was what Sir Herbert signed. The receipt bore the notation 'E. & O.E.' – errors and omissions excepted, a common formula on official British documents. The British can always be counted on for the necessary formalities.

Beyond the Citadel entrance is the 'Kishle', built as barracks by the Turks, and used as a police station and prison by the British and then by the Jordanians. In a similar tradition, it now serves as an Israeli police station. One day we shall dig below it and perhaps find the remnants of Herod's Palace, which was located here.

This is also a point of crucial decision-making for the continuation of our walk. The Christian Quarter is to the north and the Armenian and Jewish Quarters to the south, but we shall take up the inviting sounds, sights and aromas of the suq, the market, which beckons ahead.

THE SUQ

We enter the market at David Street, which is basically the east–west axis of the Old City, the Roman Decumanus. On one of our later walks, we shall go along the Cardo, the north–south axis and actually the main street as in any Roman city or encampment.

Often when I enter this market, I reflect on the first days of the 1967 ceasefire. Even before the fighting had ended, untold tasks faced us, not an easy proposition with a dearth of able-bodied men, all of whom had been called up by their reserve units. We had to arrange proper burial for the dead, to supply water, bread and milk for the Arab civilian population, and to ensure that emergency supplies reached where they were most needed.

The urgency of this work did not afford the time to consider, or even notice, the deteriorated state of much of the Old City. But very soon this became our jurisdiction and very soon these were problems which we had to solve. Admittedly, the Old City was filthy and unsanitary, reflecting the bad press accorded Jerusalem in the nineteenth century in Mark Twain's *The Innocents Abroad*: 'Rags, wretchedness, poverty and dirt . . . abound . . . Jerusalem is mournful, and dreary, and lifeless. I would not desire to live here.'

Greek Orthodox Patriarchate Street in the Old City.

16

But the modern populace was not to blame. Jerusalem had been ignored by the Jordanian administration, which concentrated all resources on the new capital in Amman. Few improvements or repairs were made in Jordanian Jerusalem following 1948. Ninety per cent of the houses had no running water; those which did were allocated water once or twice a week. The private cistern of rainwater collected during the winter months was the water source for the majority.

Our first major undertaking, therefore, was to bring running water into the houses of the Old City and other Arab neighbourhoods. But this opened a Pandora's Box, leading us into new problems: sewage. The sewage and water pipes of the Old City had been laid by various authorities from Roman to Ottoman times – true museum pieces – but most homes were served only by cesspools. These quickly proved insufficient to deal with the increased amounts of water we supplied and we had to lay an entirely new sewage system. As we had to rip up the ground, we used the opportunity to restore the dilapidated pavements. We dug up and retained the very cobblestones used in centuries past, though earlier generations were more concerned with horses' hooves than the high heels of the twentieth century.

At the entrance to the market, one might consider a brief interruption and take a quick run into the Petra Hotel on one's left. While today it resembles any other cheap hotel, it was very much a centre of Jerusalem Bohemia immediately after the city's reunification. Just as a century earlier it was the courageous who lived outside the Old City wall, in the late 1960s it was 'in' to live inside the Old City. Painters and writers joined young American and British immigrants in creating a one-building Greenwich Village or Soho in the Petra Hotel. These young people have long since dispersed, but the ease with which they traversed the two worlds still lingers. From the roof of the Petra Hotel, one can glimpse Hezekiah's Pool below. Another project on our planning boards is to restore this ancient pool to its former glory and to make it accessible to visitors.

I act like the parent who does not permit his children to enter any of the tempting stores they pass until he is ready to do so. Because before you now is an array of shops, stores and stalls which will tempt you with their sheepskin slippers, mother-of-pearl jewellery boxes, Armenian pottery, embroidered shirts and dresses, carpets, jewellery, glass and leatherwork. Handiwork in straw is about a block down and up a few stairs to your right. Bargaining is expected and comparison shopping is advised. You will be told that you are getting a good price because you are the first sale of the day – or perhaps the last (either claim made unabashedly even at midday).

I have a particular weakness for antiquities, having started collecting small objects in the late 1940s and early 1950s, when there were few takers and rare relics were often cheaper than everyday tourist trinkets. Visits to Turkey, Iran and Cyprus infused in me an early interest in the archaeology of neighbouring cultures. But I shall resist the temptation to stop in at one of the local antiquities shops, for in the presence of millennia, I easily lose track of mere hours. While an aficionado of antiquities may have a good eye for what is real and what is a bit less real, the novice might have to be a bit more wary. If the price is good, the artefact might be less so.

A possible detour is Christian Quarter Road, the first left turn on David Street, a main shopping street of the market. In the early months after the city's reunification, the Armenian shoe stores on this street were as popular a tourist site as second-century tombs. In Arabic, this street has been known as the Patriarch's Street since the Crusader period.

Further along David Street on the left is a fruit and vegetable market – in a twelfth-century Crusader building. Passing here, I am reminded of a prose poem by Yehuda Amichai, one of our foremost Israeli poets:

> Once I sat on the steps by a gate at David's Tower, I placed my two heavy baskets at my side. A group of tourists was standing around their guide and I became their target marker. 'You see that man with the baskets? Just right of his head there's an arch from the Roman period. Just right of his head.' 'But he's moving, he's moving!' I said to myself: redemption will come only if their guide tells them, 'You see that arch from the Roman period? It's not important: but next to it, left and down a bit, there sits a man who's bought fruit and vegetables for his family.'

We should not entirely fill our baskets with the tempting fruit and vegetables because we must give equal time to the bakers with their dozen kinds of pita, the flat Arab bread, and rolls. We have already made any lunch stop entirely redundant.

At the end of David Street are three streets which centuries ago were specific markets. The first is the Butchers' Market – Suq al Lahamin – which, unlike the others, is still very much a meat market. One is likely to pass sheep's heads and animal carcasses hanging freely as in centuries past. The difference is the newly acquired refrigeration as dictated by city ordinances and the absence of the flies which used to thrive in this market. The next market is the Spice Market – Suq al Attarim – which does carry stalls of spices but perhaps less than the nearby Street of the Chain. The third market is the Jewellers' Market – Suq al

The vegetable market in David Street, with some of the vaulted areas which date from Crusader times.

Khawajat – and again while one can still find jewellery here, it is not in any greater concentration than other areas of the suq.

The French who arrived here with the Crusades had their own name for this area, '*Mal Cuisinat*' (Bad Cooking), their frank opinion of the smell of the meat fried here. The fact is, with due and proper deference to the French, the unadorned cubbyhole restaurants in the Old City have some of the best skewered lamb you will ever taste as well as the best salad – chopped very fine as is the local custom – from stem-ripened vegetables, probably picked that very morning.

The history of Jerusalem is always subtly evident. On some of the buildings in these markets, one can see markings of the past: T for the Templars, SA for the Church of Saint Anne, which was supported by the income from these shops.

It is said that Bashoura's billiards room may have been the site of the Tetrapilon, the crossroads of the Decumanus and the Cardo, the two axes of the city. In any case, it is a possible stop for the billiards aficionados.

And here again one has a choice as to which direction to continue: right to the newly uncovered Cardo and the Jewish Quarter (see p. 50), left through the markets to Damascus Gate (see p. 33), or straight – actually a right and an immediate left – along the Street of the Chain, to the Western Wall. We shall choose the latter.

En route one should generally note the architec-ture of the thirteenth–fifteenth-century Mameluke buildings. There is often a black-and-white striped pattern with a touch of red; the arched pattern gives a stalactite effect. Here, too, we found a job for the city's engineering department, as foundations were crumbling and had to be strengthened. And here, as always, we had to allay the suspicions of the residents, to assure them that we had only their welfare in mind and that our work was not part of some nefarious (Zionist) plot.

THE WESTERN WALL

There are signs indicating the direction to the Western Wall, but the flow of the crowd will show the way even more effectively. A few minutes' walk will bring us to the steps leading down to the Western Wall and the surrounding plaza.

It is not only the first-time visitor who tends to stand at the top of this staircase, look before him and reflect on what his eye beholds. The Western Wall, in actuality an outside retaining wall, has been a treasured site for Jews since the destruction of the Second Temple in AD 70. It is the focus of dreams, it is the focus of hopes, it is the symbol of Jerusalem and redemption. While the Hebrew name, Hakotel Hamaravi, translates as the Western Wall, the tears shed over generations transmuted the name to the Wailing Wall, le Mur des Lamentations.

For centuries the Wall has inspired prayers, poems, songs, legends, paintings and photographs. 'Hakotel' has as its refrain: 'There are people with a heart of stone, and there are stones with the heart of man.'

The Western 'Wailing' Wall in the late nineteenth century, showing the narrow enclosed alley available for worshippers until 1967.

The Western Wall is a powerful symbol of the unity of the Jewish people. For all Jews, the Western Wall symbolizes the eternal drama of Jewish history and the centrality of Jerusalem in Jewish consciousness. Yet no one who approaches the Western Wall is told how and in what way to offer prayers and express hopes (though there have been incidents when attempts by women to hold a prayer service incite the wrath of the ultra-Orthodox). Each can listen to the past and dream of the future in one's own particular way. No uniform worship is imposed.

People today behold a vast plaza, where the curious intermingle with the devout. When I first came to the Wall, in 1937, a very different sight greeted me.

I had arrived in Haifa from Vienna almost a year previously. But between my adjusting to kibbutz life in the Galilee and struggling to survive successive bouts of typhoid fever, a good deal of time passed before my first visit to Jerusalem. In fact, it was my fifth bout of typhoid fever which provided the circumstances for this visit, as I had been sent to a convalescent home in Motza, a Jerusalem suburb.

Finally regaining a little of my strength, I set out with a friend for Jerusalem. We reached the Western Wall in a narrow alleyway, almost indistinguishable from other narrow alleyways, part of a crumbling slum, yet awesome.

In my most fervent imagination, I could not have known that, three decades later, I would be implementing a decision, taken mere hours after the 1967 ceasefire, to raze this quarter. The British in the 1920s had prepared plans to destroy this slum for humanitarian reasons, but for us there was an added consideration: to allow access to the Western Wall for the tens and hundreds of thousands of worshippers who had been denied this access for nineteen years.

It was late on Saturday night, 10 June 1967. That evening Jerusalemites, who had spent the week huddled in shelters, gathered in the Binyanei Ha'ooma concert hall to hear Zubin Mehta, Daniel Barenboim and Jacqueline du Pré. It was an esoteric intermingling of joy and sadness. The war and the victory had taken their toll. As the last strains of music faded and most Jerusalemites went home, I drove to the Western Wall. There a group of our local building contractors waited, their bulldozers at hand. It took several hours to clear the area. As the dawn hour neared, we found ourselves in front of the Western Wall as it had stood centuries before.

Even before the ceasefire, those who had once prayed daily at the Wall and had been denied this right for nineteen years, and those who had only dreamed of praying there, were clamouring to reach the Wall. A few hardy souls even risked their lives to do so despite the sniping of the Jordanian legionnaires.

It was too soon to open the entire city freely to both sides, but we sensed that the long-dreamed visit to the Wall could not be delayed. Thus, one week later, on the festival of Shavuoth (Pentecost), from the first glimmer of dawn we enabled access to the Western Wall. It was a dreadfully hot day and, though the route laid out was a circuitous one, 300,000 people wended their way to the Wall. The barrier which today separates men from women had not yet been erected – indeed, none had existed before 1948 – but the occasion was such that black-robed Hassidim prayed freely alongside teenage girls.

The age-old custom of writing a wish on any available chit of paper and sticking it in the crevices of the Wall was resumed. Christian pilgrims can be seen following this custom as well. I was at the Wall early one morning following a particularly heavy rain and the slips of paper had been washed to the ground. I watched as an elderly man gently gathered them together and reverently buried them in the nearby earth.

There are a few rules for visitors to the Western Wall, which are prominently displayed. Modest dress is required, although pieces of material are available to provide hastily produced skirts and shawls for those improperly dressed. Men must have their heads covered, but cardboard *kippot* (skullcaps) are also provided. One cannot take photographs on the Sabbath, which begins at sunset on Friday and ends at sunset on Saturday.

Visitors will often be confronted by the outstretched palms of people seeking alms. Not beggars in the accepted sense, they seek money for an ailing mother of ten or an indigent bride, for this synagogue or that *yeshiva* (Jewish religious school). People find these approaches annoying, particularly as the number proliferates, and complaints reach City Hall, though the proper address is the Ministry of Religious Affairs which has jurisdiction here.

Because it is the holiest site for Jews, it has become customary to celebrate a son's Bar Mitzvah – his coming of age at thirteen – at the Western Wall. (It is technically more complex to celebrate a daughter's equivalent Bat Mitzvah.) While Bar Mitzvahs are commonly celebrated on the Sabbath, the ceremony can take place on Mondays and Thursdays when the Torah, the Bible, is read during the morning prayers. For observant families, this may be preferable since they would not countenance travel on the Sabbath for this purpose. Thus, on Monday and Thursday mornings, a visitor to the Wall will encounter groups of celebrants, festively noting this happy occasion. It is customary to throw sweets at the Bar Mitzvah boy, so the visitor should be wary of oncoming trajectories.

While parents from the Western, Ashkenazi, tradition surely love their children as much as do the Sephardi, the pomp and circumstance of the latter cannot be equalled: the Bar Mitzvah boy is often dressed in colourful ethnic robes and carried aloft to the Wall, and the entire procession is accompanied by horns and drums.

The story of today's Western Wall would be incomplete without a look to the past. Archaeology is a mainstay of life in Jerusalem. Our archaeologists are not part-time hobbyists who unearth an occasional arrowhead, but scientific explorers for whom inch-by-inch discovery is as crucial as the excitement of unexpected finds.

THE WESTERN WALL TUNNEL

The Western Wall area teems with remnants of the past and you will have an unfettered encounter in the next walk (see p. 23). But the Western Wall tunnel has its place here and, in the hope that public access will precede this book's publication, I shall include it. Entry will be at the far side of the Wall.

Bar Mitzvah celebrations at the Western Wall.

School textbooks always present historical periods simplistically, a neat little chart with neat little boxes. Archaeology often conveys this equally obscurant perception: neat little horizontal layers. Would that it were so simple. One day's truth engraved in stone becomes the next day's misconception and the following day's clarification.

A brief glance backward brings us to the thirteenth century, the Mameluke era. The Mamelukes were early-day mercenaries as indicated by their name, 'ruled by'. But by 1250, having assumed increasing power, they saw no reason to continue their service to Saladin's descendants and rebelled. By 1260, they ruled most of the Middle East, excepting Acre which remained in Crusader hands until 1291. Originally non-Moslem, they converted to Islam.

They had attained power but acknowledged its ephemeral nature. The ladder was two-directional and gaol and strangulation were familiar fates. Thus, after creating the enormous substructures which you will see, they donated their property to the Waqf, the Moslem religious council, which afforded a modicum of protection.

The tunnel extends from the Western Wall to the Via Dolorosa, 440 metres in length. It was discovered in the nineteenth-century by the archaeologist Charles Warren, although he came upon it from the northern side through the Convent of the Sisters of Zion – Ecce Homo (see p. 69), and did not explore its entire length. The opening of the whole tunnel was carried out in the 1970s and 1980s by archaeologist Dan Bahat, who can give you a treatise on each and every stone.

Gigantic stones were used to cast weight on the structure. You will pass a stone which is 12.5 metres long, 3.25 metres high and 3 metres deep, weighing 37 metric tons. It was quarried at the apex of the valley and slid down into place.

We reach a concrete wall, which is the intersection of this tunnel and an oblique tunnel leading from the Herodian level to the Temple Mount, which served as a cistern. During the excavations – which in general were opposed by the Moslems, who feared the weakening of their structures above the tunnel – Rabbi Goren, a former Chief Rabbi, deemed this as the main synagogue area of yore and blew the ram's horn in celebration. This trumpeting inflamed Moslem apprehensions and led to an out-and-out clash. The concrete wall resulted from this confrontation.

We pass several cistern openings, recognizable by the rougher appearance of the stones and by the waterproof plaster affixed by the Mamelukes. After all, these were cisterns: practicality had to take precedence over aesthetics.

Just beyond a pillar lying on its side is an open area, which is actually a Herodian street, evidenced further on by the columns found in place. In all probability, an arcade was planned but never completed because of Herod's death.

The far wall of the tunnel is the very same wall seen from the other side in the Convent of the Sisters of Zion.

That we are still facing difficulties in opening the tunnel to the public is once again a result of political sensibilities. Because the tunnel is narrow, it can safely comprise only one-way traffic, thus necessitating an exit in the area of the Via Dolorosa, a bare few metres from one of the Temple Mount access gates. In July 1988, the Ministry of Religious Affairs attempted a test opening of the tunnel on the Via Dolorosa though city officials felt that, because of the already-existing tensions, this should not be done without consultation with the ever-suspicious Moslem authorities. The resulting clash was immediate and intense. The call from the minarets was to defend the area and hundreds descended on the site hurling rocks and bottles. The confrontation was violent – and uncalled for. Negotiations are under way to attain agreement to complete the opening of this tunnel. Once this is achieved, an exciting addition will be made to Jerusalem's archaeological map.

This walk, sans tunnel, ends at the Western Wall, giving the walker a range of choices: a quick taxi ride home, a less quick bus ride or an even slower walk. If it is early enough in the day and the mosques are still open, the hearty can take on the next walk. If the mosques are closed, the second half of the next walk, beginning with the excavations of the southern wall, is a possibility.

Once the tunnel is open, the walk will end in the vicinity of the Via Dolorosa (see p. 69).

2

THE TEMPLE MOUNT, THE OPHEL AND THE CITY OF DAVID

Nomenclature can be more than just a name. The terms one uses are not always arbitrary and the baggage borne by their nuances may be light and inconsequential – or fundamental and weighty.

There are those who attribute political nuances to the choice of the reference Temple Mount or Haram al Sharif, when in fact the nuances are historical and religious. The Temple Mount refers to the First and Second Temples and the holiness of this site in Judaism; the Haram al Sharif refers to the Al Aqsa Mosque and the Dome of the Rock and the holiness of this site in Islam.

The walk begins at the Western Wall, the access for non-Moslems to the Temple Mount – the Haram al Sharif. The visitor is greeted by an official admonition of the Ministry of Religious Affairs indicating that it is forbidden for Jews to ascend to the Temple Mount. Orthodox Jews abide by this admonition proscribed by Maimonides. In days of yore, the most sacred site in the Temple was the Holy of Holies, which the High Priest alone could enter, once a year, on Yom Kippur, the Day of Atonement. As we cannot know with exactitude the location of the Holy of Holies, we might inadvertently tread on its site. Rabbi Goren claims that there is a definable corner of the Temple Mount which could not possibly have been the Holy of Holies and he has given his consent for ascent to that single spot.

The word 'haram' means closed, forbidden, taboo; the Haram al Sharif is the Noble Sanctuary. It continues to be administered by the Waqf, an unusual decision we took in 1967 because of our understanding of Moslem sensibilities towards an area which is the cardinal Moslem symbol and possession in Jerusalem.

This understanding was evident from the very day of the 1967 ceasefire. Though battle-weary, General Moshe Dayan, Minister of Defence, ordered the removal of an Israeli flag which a soldier had affixed to the top of the Dome of the Rock. A few days later Major-General Chaim Herzog, the area commanding officer (and subsequently Israel's sixth President), met with Moslem and Christian dignitaries, assuring them of respect for their rights. Prime Minister Levi Eshkol, heading a unity government which included opposition leader, Menachem Begin,

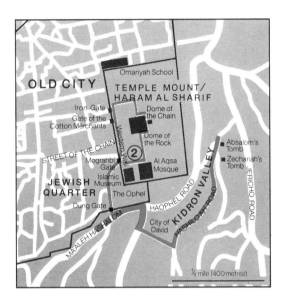

reiterated these promises.

Our decision to grant this functional sovereignty to the Waqf was not universally accepted by the Jewish population and difficulties yet arise. Nationalist Jewish groups such as 'The Faithful of the Temple Mount' claim the right to pray there, although the Government has issued regulations, upheld by the Supreme Court, forbidding these prayers.

The sanctity of the Temple Mount to Judaism may be a reason for the Moslem fear of encroachment. Moslems cannot envision themselves, were the situation reversed, allowing infidels to hold a Moslem holy place and thus do not entirely trust our acceptance of Moslem administration over an area so holy to the Jews.

Jerusalem, called in Arabic Al Kuds (the Holy), is the third holiest site in Islam, after Mecca and Medina. When Mohammed went on his night journey to heaven, the Koran relates that he went first to 'al masjid al aqsa', the farthest house of prayer. This was accepted to be Jerusalem.

This site has been holy to the Jews for millennia as, according to tradition, it is the biblical Mount Moriah on which Abraham was called to sacrifice his son Isaac. It was the hill on which Solomon built his Temple, to be destroyed by Nebuchadnezzar of Babylon. It was the hill on which the

Second Temple was built, to be destroyed by Titus and the Roman legions in AD 70. In AD 135, Hadrian built a Temple to Jupiter, which was then destroyed by the Byzantines after the empire became Christian.

In 362, the Byzantine Emperor Julian, called the Apostate, devised a plan enabing the Jews to reconstruct their Temple, but the idea died with him. The area then lay desolate, possibly serving as a huge garbage dump, and no trace of it is marked on the Madaba map, a sixth-century mosaic on the floor of a church in Madaba, Jordan. This mosaic, discovered in the nineteenth century, can qualify as Jerusalem's Rosetta Stone, supplying crucial missing pieces to an unfinished puzzle.

According to Moslem lore, it was from this Mount and from this rock that Mohammed ascended to heaven, travelling from Mecca to Jerusalem and from Jerusalem to heaven, evidence that any journey to heaven, its starting-point notwithstanding, entails a stopover in Jerusalem.

In 638, the Arabs conquered Jerusalem. The most imposing structure they found was the Church of the Holy Sepulchre, and the Moslem conquerors undertook to build a more spectacular edifice, not only to proclaim the supremacy of Islam, but also to ensure that the followers of Islam would not be tempted by Christianity. Legend has it that the Caliph Omar asked the Jews where the Temple had stood and he chose this site for the grand mosque. But it was the Omayyad Caliph, Abd al Malik, who, in 691, built the Dome of the Rock (mistakenly called the Mosque of Omar).

The unimposing doorway to the Haram al Sharif, the Mograhbi Gate or Gate of the Moors, is a misleading introduction, for one almost feels the astonishment of Alice in Wonderland as she followed the rabbit through the hole in the hedge. You are unexpectedly awestruck by the world you have entered, a world of caliphs and sultans, of mosques, minarets, archways and fountains.

It is useful to learn a few terms at the outset. The minaret is the tower from which the muezzin calls the faithful to prayer. Technology has taken its hold and the muezzin no longer climbs the minaret's narrow staircase five times a day to fulfil his duty. Today's muezzin uses a loudspeaker system and often the call to prayer is emitted from a pre-recorded tape.

The mihrab, a prayer niche, indicates the direction of prayer towards Mecca, very similar to the 'Mizrah' (East) which gives Jews throughout the world the direction of prayer towards Jerusalem. The mihrabs are not only inside the mosque but are also scattered atop the Haram, so that those who cannot find room inside the mosque know in which direction to pray. Outdoor prayer areas are marked by stone platforms. The minbar is the stepped pulpit from which the sermon is preached, often a political rallying call.

A mini-course in the architecture of the minarets will tell you that the square ones are Mameluke, dating from the fourteenth century, while the round ones, like that of the Citadel, date from the later Ottoman period.

Visits to the Haram al Sharif are prohibited on Fridays, the Moslem holy day. How typical of life in Jerusalem that while we have a one-day weekend, we actually have three weekends: the Moslems rest on Friday, the Jews on Saturday and the Christians on Sunday.

AL AQSA MOSQUE

Our first visit is to the Al Aqsa Mosque on the right. While there is no fee for entry to the Haram, there is a fee for visiting the mosques and a small museum. There is a ticket booth for this secular transaction.

The Al Aqsa Mosque was built by al Walid, the son of Abd al Malik, and it is the house of worship on the Haram. Five thousand supplicants can pray – and kneel – at a single time. Within the mosque, the minbar is easily discernible. The carpeted areas were often to create a semi-private space to protect notable supplicants. But this protection was not afforded to King Abdullah, King Hussein's grandfather, who was assassinated in front of the mosque on 21 July 1951. A bullet mark on the second pillar on the left bears witness to this event.

One can easily distinguish the old section of the mosque, on the right, from the new section, on the left, completed in 1938 after an earthquake a decade earlier. The pillars were imported from Italy and the arches newly constructed. The original ceiling is made of cedarwood imported from Lebanon. President Sadat, during his historic visit to Jerusalem in November 1977, prayed at the Al Aqsa Mosque and actually pledged funds towards the restoration, but he was assassinated before making good on this pledge. King Faisal of Saudi Arabia habitually expressed to foreign reporters his desire to pray there as well and I often conveyed, through these same reporters, our invitation for him to come and do so. He never did.

If I still experience tremors during visits to Al Aqsa, it is the residue of the havoc which I witnessed in August 1969, when a mentally deranged Australian Christian, Dennis Rohan, set fire to the mosque causing extensive damage. The news of this attack spread faster than the fire itself. Initial rumours described the assailant as an Israeli, possibly even an Israeli soldier. Hysteria

The Al Aqsa mosque on the Temple Mount during Ramadan.

24

fanned the flames of rumour and a spontaneous demonstration erupted, the first with which we were confronted.

I perceived it as my duty to try to mitigate the tensions, despite premonitions of the dangers. A policeman was assigned to accompany me and we went up to the Temple Mount. Within a minute or two, the policeman lost me in the incensed crowd, and for a moment my decision seemed foolhardy. But I pressed on. And I explained that it had not been an act of nationalism on the part of a Jew, but an act of insanity on the part of a non-Jew. I explained and people eventually listened to what I was saying.

Before the fire could be contained, Al Aqsa's dome was ruined and had to be repaired in its entirety. As all photographs and engravings of the last century portray the dome, as well as the Dome of the Rock, as black, rather than the silver and gold domes created by the Jordanians, we suggested to the Waqf that they revert to the original colour. The new lead domes are also far more dependable in keeping out the rain. The smoke damage can still be seen in the cupola, which remains ensconced in the scaffolding of repair work.

The damage perpetrated by this demented sheep shearer extended beyond the physical damage and even today, as visitors from all over the world wander around the Haram, a residue of apprehension lingers.

In recent years, psychologists have identified a phenomenon termed the 'Jerusalem syndrome', referring to a short-term emotional 'incident' affecting Christians, usually Protestants. The intensity of the experience of being in the Holy Land and following in the footsteps of Jesus catalyzes messianic or hysterical reactions, among heretofore upstanding, normal citizens. It affects perhaps a dozen people a year and the police have become adept at handling the white-robed Messiahs who arrive in their precincts. The syndrome is short-lived and disappears long before the victim disembarks in his home town.

Dennis Rohan's arson might have been prevented, as he had been spotted hanging around the Haram, arousing suspicions, and there was negligence on the part of the Waqf security force. Our policy of non-interference in the administration of the Haram by the Waqf had backfired in this instance. In consequence we insisted on stationing a tiny but well-trained police force in the area and we carried out necessary improvements, including a water system linked to the city's water supply rather than the underground cisterns of the Haram. These precautions proved crucial when, years later, a plot by a 'Jewish underground' of extreme nationalists to blow up the mosques was uncovered. Their aim was to hasten the coming of the Messiah by liberating the site so that the Temple could be rebuilt.

Since the time of the arson, visitors to the mosques must leave all their belongings outside. It can be a hardship to one who travels singly because, though this is a holy place, it is not advisable to leave one's belongings, except one's shoes, unguarded. It is best to search out an honest-looking fellow traveller to exchange mutual guard duty.

The staircase to the east of the mosque entrance, which seemingly leads to nowhere, was once a functional staircase leading to an area of arches from the Herodian period, probably storerooms, and ultimately to the Hulda Gate outside the wall (see p. 31). The early Moslems blocked the city's entrances in an unsuccessful attempt to ward off the Crusader attacks.

Under Crusader rule, the mosque became a royal palace for the European Crusader kings. The underground vaulted area, used by the Knights Templar to stable their horses, was erroneously named Solomon's Stables.

It was Saladin who reconquered Jerusalem in 1187 after his historic victory over the Crusader armies at the Horns of Hittim in the Galilee and who restored the mosques to the glory of Islam. In more recent times, the Waqf eliminated the remnants of Crusader elements, replacing twelfth-century Crusader capitals and columns with copies of Moslem architecture.

Between Al Aqsa and the Dome of the Rock, there is a Mameluke ritual fountain called *al kas* (the cup), where devout Moslems wash their hands, face and feet before prayer. The fountain is for Moslems only and all temptations to divest oneself of the dust of the day should be eschewed unless you number among the faithful. There is a Moslem guard who miraculously materializes when any rule or regulation is transgressed. A couple who may casually take one another's hand will be admonished forthwith.

Ascending the main staircase towards the graceful arched gateway, you can see an outdoor minbar on the left as well as a mihrab.

There is a Moslem tradition that when the resurrection of the dead takes place in Jerusalem one's good deeds and one's sins will be weighed. It is supposed that good deeds done in Jerusalem carry double weight. The arched columns are known as the Arcade of the Scales as these columns will hold the scales to weigh good deeds (and bad) as an archangel presides over the weighing in of the souls at each cardinal point. One of the arches was built by a slave from Khotan, an oasis on the Silk Road in Central Asia, who became Governor of Jerusalem.

The interior of the Dome of the Rock showing the dome and the rock.

THE DOME OF THE ROCK

The word magnificent is surely overused in our lexicon, but no other word effectively describes the Dome of the Rock, its beauty, its grace, its stateliness, its delicacy. It was built by Byzantine craftsmen imported by the Arabs who, as desert dwellers, had little architectural experience. The dome was said to have originally been moulded of real gold, though the one depicted in the nineteenth-century model of the city (see p. 82) is of lead. The present gold, anodized aluminium dome was financed by Saudi Arabia and other Arab League countries.

To visit the Dome of the Rock, shoes and belongings again have to be relinquished.

The interior is decorated with mosaics and gold leaf, and verses of the Koran are beautifully written on the ceiling circumference. The dome is 20 metres high and 10 metres in diameter. You see the Foundation Stone, the centre of the world, where Abraham, according to tradition, prepared to sacrifice Isaac and from which Mohammed was said to have ascended to heaven. It is protected by a wooden fence to prevent pilgrims from chipping away souvenir pieces of the rock as was the practice in centuries gone by. It is said that the hole in the rock was made by the angel Gabriel, who held tightly to the rest of the world so that it would not follow the Prophet. The handwoven carpets were a gift of Mohammed of Morocco, the grandfather of the present King Hassan. A relic of the beard of the Prophet Mohammed is preserved in the crevice. As this is not a place of public worship, there is no minbar.

At a press conference some years ago, I was confronted by a query as to whether or not it was true that we intended destroying the mosques in order to rebuild the Temple. I explained: 'The

The southern approach to the Temple Mount and the Dome of the Rock.

Temple will be rebuilt when the Messiah comes – and that is a chance you have to take.'

To the east of the Dome of the Rock, the structure which resembles an architect's on-site scale-model, covered interminably by repair scaffolding, is called the Dome of the Chain. It is said that King David stood in judgement on this site and by pulling a chain would ascertain guilt or innocence.

A walk to the eastern edge of the Haram is an absolute must for an unequalled view of the Garden of Gethsemane across the Kidron Valley.

Descending the steps at the north-west corner, to the right we see the wall of a building which is actually bedrock, with quarrying marks easily discernible. This is the back wall of the Omariyah School, built on the site of the Antonia Fortress where Jesus was condemned (see p. 69).

During the rule of the Mamelukes, the borders of the Haram area were surrounded with a series of *madrassas*, Moslem schools of learning, which still exist today. The Waqf is also headquartered here. Along the western arched edge, we pass a series of gates including the Prison Gate (the Ottomans had their prisons here, hence the name), the Iron Gate and the Gate of the Cotton Merchants. It is worth taking a peek through this gate at the massive enclosed market area, the Suq al Qattanin, built by the Sultan in 1336 and reconstructed by the Waqf in 1974. But do not stray into the market, as this gate is only an exit and you will be unable to return to your original route.

The cotton market area was long under dispute. The British maintained that it was the property of the Government and not of the Moslems and refused permission to restore the crumbling elements. After 1967, the Jerusalem City Council voted to permit this restoration, against the opposition of the Likud councillors who maintained it would justify Moslem claims to their rights in the market. I supported the decision because I valued the involvement of the local populace in restoring their own environment.

Though subsequently the single criticism levied by Professor Lemaire of Louvain University in Belgium, the UNESCO representative overseeing our restoration work, was that this undertaking fell short of the quality of work elsewhere in the city, I continued to consider the local initiative itself noteworthy.

Retracing our steps we visit the small museum included in the entry fee to Al Aqsa and the Dome of the Rock. Besides the voluminous Korans, the cauldrons used in the past to feed the poor, and the ornamental doors and crescents, there are remnants of the minbar presented by Saladin to the Al Aqsa Mosque, which had fallen prey to Dennis Rohan's arson. Saladin had presented gifts of hand-crafted mahogany and mother-of-pearl minbars, interlocking wood without a single

The Gate of the Cotton Merchants.

nail, both to Al Aqsa and to a mosque in Hebron. This exact minbar could not be replaced as there are no longer artisans with this ancient talent, but as close a copy as possible is slowly being crafted.

We leave the Haram through the gate at which we entered, the Mograhbi Gate. The slum area which adjoined the Western Wall and which we razed immediately following the ceasefire (see p. 20) was called the Mograhbi Quarter. We return to the Western Wall Plaza and the newly built elaborate gateway, and walk down towards Dung Gate and the southern wall excavations.

THE OPHEL
Immediately before Dung Gate, to the left, is the entrance to the excavations. I find it difficult to remember that this was once a barren expanse, with barely a hint of the ancient structures secreted beneath it. Today it is an ecumenical *pot-pourri*, with the intermingling of Jewish, Christian and

The Ophel excavations by the south-eastern wall of the Old City.

Moslem civilizations perhaps nowhere as salient.

While there are no remains of the First or Second Temples themselves, besides the outer (retaining) Western Wall, we are well versed in the lore of this period. It was once claimed that on the three Jewish holidays on which it was customary to make a pilgrimage to Jerusalem: Passover, Shavuoth and Succoth (Tabernacles), this city of 250,000 residents accommodated 250,000 pilgrims, but today's historians tend to give lower numbers. Even so, with all our modern hotels, I cannot begin to conceive of such a mass influx of outsiders reaching the city at one time, with all their needs provided for. Of course, the pilgrims brought their own tents and food and camped outside the gates.

Walking down into the excavated area (after paying the required entrance fee), we reach the south-west corner of the outside wall of the Temple Mount and walk to our left. We pass under Robinson's Arch, named for a nineteenth-century American archaeologist, Edward Robinson, founder of modern scholarly research into the geography of the Holy Land. This is a remnant of a series of arches across the valley in which you are standing, named the Tyropoeon Valley or Cheesemakers' Valley. On the second row of

stones, you can make out a Hebrew inscription from the Book of Isaiah, carved by an early pilgrim, our version of fourth-century graffiti.

The grooves which are prominent at the corner of the wall were built for water pipes, probably for the Omayyad palaces whose remains are scattered throughout these excavations. The construction of these palaces often included Herodian stones lying around from the Roman destruction.

In general, there was always a pressing need for water in this area, whether for ritual baths or for grand palaces. It should be remembered that during the time of the holiday pilgrimages of the First and Second Temple, each pilgrim brought a sacrifice and that just cleaning it and draining away the sacrificial blood required massive amounts of water.

At the end of this wall, you find yourself transfixed when attempting to comprehend the enormity of the construction feat which is before you, in truth no less wondrous, even if less dramatic, than Egypt's Pyramids. There are stones which weigh 400 tons. Modern cranes can barely lift this weight.

Herodian masonry – known as dry masonry – is distinctive. The large stones, called ashlars, have a frame around the edge, wider at the top, with recognizable chisel marks. The stones for this wall were all quarried before being set in place, using an interlocking method. Each stone was set back an inch so that the wall is pitched slightly, architectural methods valid even today. And while on the outside it seems as if the stones are close-fitting, inside there are spaces to allow seepage and even to prevent massive damage in the event of earthquakes.

At the end of the wall, on the right, are remnants uncovered by early archaeologists who used a shaft system. The Herodian stones here are in even better condition, protected as they were from the elements. It should be noted that there are fourteen more levels until bedrock.

On the left (indicated by no. 5) are remains from the main street in Herodian Jerusalem. The paving stones together with the kerb-stones are from the Temple period and were covered by the actual stones which had toppled from the wall during the destruction of the Temple.

Much of what is known of this area is culled from the writings of Flavius Josephus. Born Joseph ben Matthias in AD 37, of a priestly family, he became a soldier, orator and historian. He was appointed Governor of Galilee but, when his stronghold fell to Vespasian, he subsequently took on Vespasian's name Flavius and served the Romans with unswerving devotion, becoming a Roman citizen and ending his days as an imperial pensioner. But it is for his work as a historian of this period that he is best remembered. Archaeological finds have confirmed the veracity of Josephus again and again.

Retracing our steps to the corner of the wall, we now make a left turn along the outer wall of the Al Aqsa Mosque. Looking up, we first see the larger Herodian and Omayyad stones, then the Crusader and Mameluke stones and, finally, the stones with the little bosses typical of Ottoman builders of the sixteenth century.

We can walk freely through the remains of a restored Byzantine house (no. 9) or go through the excavation gate opened in 1970 to allow passage to the eastern entrance to the Omayyad Caliph's palace. Passing through this gate, we find ourselves outside the city wall. Here, too, I find it hard to recall that in 1967 this was a mound of dirt, but photographs exist to confirm my recollection.

To the left, we pass a series of ritual baths, public as well as private ones. In the monumental stairway leading to the Temple Mount the steps were each of different heights so that the ascent to the Temple would have to be deliberate. The pilgrim could not race up wantonly. In the restoration, we maintained this anomaly.

The staircase leads to an Omayyad triple gate, replicating the earlier Hulda Gate. Named for the prophetess Hulda, this triple gate afforded access to the Temple. Entry was through the triple gate while the double gate, hinted at towards the left, was used as an exit. It is said that lepers, mourners and outcasts customarily did the opposite – went in the double gate and left by the triple gate – so that they could be easily identified.

The Ophel excavation is a family affair, having been started by the premier archaeologist, Benjamin Mazar, and continued by his granddaughter, Eilat. When these excavations were initially proposed, they were opposed by the ultra-Orthodox groups. Moreover, the opposition was not limited to the Jewish community, for the Moslems also objected, fearing that the excavations would undermine the foundations of the Al Aqsa Mosque. These fears were ultimately assuaged.

Retracing our steps through the Ophel, we return to Dung Gate, which served just that use. The original structure, even in the mid-twentieth century, was a small postern, barely meriting the designation as a gate. The Jordanians ultimately were forced to widen it for vehicular traffic with an ugly iron beam at the apex. To renovate it, we enlarged the design of the original gate, thus restoring the original beauty while not losing the traffic advantages, our attempt at having our cake and eating it.

While the official continuation of our walk is downhill to our left, a minuscule detour to the right will give me the opportunity to emphasize once more the trials and tribulations of trying to run a modern city in the confines of an ancient one. For several years, the only road from the Dung Gate was eastward, a circuitous route for the motorist intent on reaching either Zion Gate or the southern part of the new city. Logic dictated building a road which would link up with the Pope's Road (see pp. 47–9). And so we began work.

Our twentieth-century road builders uncovered the work of their first-century predecessors with the discovery of a portion of a Roman road, and we were faced with the quandary of how to proceed in building the new road without destroying the old one. The solution was a low, bridge-like and costly construction over the earlier road.

The entire area to the right is an archaeological garden restored by the Jerusalem Foundation, with noteworthy finds clearly marked. These include a corner of the Nea, a grandiose Byzantine church built by Justinian in the sixth century, probably the largest structure of its time in this part of the world. Other remains of the Nea have been found within the Jewish Quarter inside the Old City walls, which can only give an inkling as to its size. Procopius, a sixth-century chronicler of the history of his era, left behind a precise description of the Nea and the difficulties of its construction because of the steep slopes. The arches built to form level ground have been excavated.

THE CITY OF DAVID

The entrance to the City of David excavations is at the bottom of the hill, with a sign indicating a right turn at the parking lot.

In the early part of this century, a scion of the French branch of the Rothschild family bought this piece of land in order to seek the true burial place of King David. Baron Edmond de Rothschild, known as 'Hanadiv' ('the generous one'), had been extensively involved in the early settlement of the country, but this was his personal obsession. The land was purchased in 1911 and excavation work carried out until 1914, resuming in 1920.

The British designated this entire area as an archaeological site and thus prohibited all building. When it became Jordanian territory, this prohibition was disregarded. Much of the area, undoubtedly covering millennia of ancient artefacts, was built up and became the Arab village of Hilweh. But as the Jordanians preserved property rights, the land bought by the Rothschilds was held by the Jordanian administrator as enemy property and remained untouched. Thus the City of David was a magnet for archaeological interest. Suppositions were rampant as to what might be awaiting revelation.

Archaeologists, individual explorers and more formal expeditions had flocked to Jerusalem from about the 1860s. They searched for remains of the Temple, of palaces and tombs. Some sought to confirm biblical sources; others to disprove these same sources.

While modern-day archaeology has at its disposal the wonders of twentieth-century technology, it is probably a field which resembles its century-old predecessor more than any other. And the passion of today's archaeologists equals that of old.

Our desire to dig and our need for funds juxtaposed with the desire of a devoted South African Jew, Mendel Kaplan, to impart his Zionism to his children. How could he foster a lasting bond? He feared it might not sprout without encouragement. His sponsorship of the City of David excavations became the track for fulfilling this quest, for his children and their friends became the volunteer corps for this dig. And he himself became more expert on the City of David than many historians.

Zechariah's Tomb, in the Kidron Valley.

The finds were as exciting as anticipated. In one house alone, fifty-one bullae – clay pellets used for sealing papyrus documents and dating to the seventh and early sixth centuries BC – were found, most of them stamped with Hebrew biblical names like Azaryahu the son of Hilkiyahu. The layer of ashes covering the floors of the houses is witness to the destruction of Jerusalem by Nebuchadnezzar in 586 BC. Pottery artefacts and figurines helped map the site's history.

Beneath the remains of seventh–sixth-century BC buildings, attesting to the excellent workmanship of the time, is a stepped stone structure dating from the tenth-century BC, found in what was termed 'Area G'. Area G was to become a household name, for it was the site of a bitter dispute between the ultra-Orthodox Jews and the archaeologists. The ultra-Orthodox, with bits of bones to support their position, claimed that Area G had been a Jewish cemetery and thus opposed excavation there. They generally oppose any change; moreover, from time to time they seek trouble to strengthen their appeal to overseas benefactors.

As you read through this book, you will find such confrontations occurring again and again. But Area G stood out for the violence it brought in its wake, with not only verbal attacks on Yigal Shilo, the resident archaeologist, and his team (see p. 127), but also the physical abuse which accompanied it. A sad portrait caught by the media wires was that of Israeli policemen called in to stop the violence, with headlines spotlighting 'Jew against Jew'. But as often happens with each such occurrence, it disappeared as suddenly as it appeared.

The visit to the City of David excavations includes Warren's Shaft, named for the by-now-familiar Charles Warren. Water was always a cause for concern for Jerusalem, as it is today. During the First Temple, three systems, all emanating from the Gihon spring, supplied water to the city. Warren's Shaft was one of these, dating to the tenth–ninth centuries BC, and the entire system is detailed at the site. (Hezekiah's Tunnel, which can be pinpointed exactly to 701 BC, can also be visited, but candles or a flashlight, rubber shoes, a warm day and a little courage are prerequisites.)

If the climb down and up Warren's Shaft has not entirely exhausted you, one more stop on this walk could be the tombs of the Kidron Valley, a short walk down from the City of David in the direction of the Mount of Olives. These distinctive structures, hewn into the hillside, are called the Tomb or Pillar of Absalom and the Tomb of Zechariah, although neither Absalom nor Zechariah are buried here. Their splendour does, however, suggest that they served as burial grounds for people of distinction.

3
DAMASCUS GATE
AND THE RAMPARTS WALK

If only walls could talk . . . Of the corners of Jerusalem which have trod in tandem with the history of the city, no kinship has been as intimate as that of Damascus Gate. The splendour of this gate alone would have entitled Suleiman the Magnificent to his sobriquet.

A gate existed on this site long before Suleiman. It had not only seen Jerusalem pass from hand to hand, but it had assumed aliases to satisfy each of its rulers. There was a gate at the time of King Agrippa, who ruled in the middle of the first century BC, although its name has been lost to posterity. Documentation on the period of the Roman Emperor Hadrian (Publius Aelius Hadrianus) is far more complete as he had the foresight to employ a court historian. Hadrian, having vanquished the Jewish revolt of Bar Kochba in AD 135, not only razed the city but expunged its name. He renamed the city Aelia Capitolina, commemorating his family name as was the custom.

In later centuries, the Arabs called the city Iliya. While theories abounded as to the meaning of this name – perhaps Iliya was the woman who built the city or Iliya referred to the house of Allah – a more logical assumption is that it was a distortion of Aelia.

Hadrian was a prolific builder and his opus on this site was a large middle gate with two smaller gates on each side, contiguous with two towers. He named it Porta Neapolis as the road from here led north to Neapolis, the 'new' city he built on the site of biblical Shechem.

In the fourth century, the spread of Christianity inspired the next rechristening. Porta Neapolis became St Stephen's Gate, commemorating the first Christian martyr who was stoned to death nearby. On Crusader maps, this name is used. After the second conquest of Jerusalem by the Moslems in 1187, the Christians transferred St Stephen to the present-day Lions' Gate.

The Moslem Omayyad period in the seventh–eighth centuries brought the name Bab al Amud, the Gate of the Pillar, the Arabic name still in use. Hadrian had installed a massive pillar in the centre of the gate's inner square with, it is surmised, a bust of himself gracing its pinnacle. It is distinctly delineated on the sixth-century Madaba map, but in all likelihood it was destroyed or moved during the Crusader period.

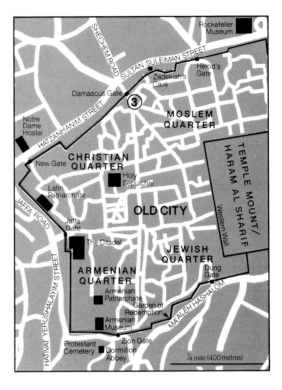

The name Damascus Gate, probably in use since the seventeenth or eighteenth century, attests to the flourishing of Damascus in that period, for the road from here leads north to Damascus (in theory, of course, since it comes to an abrupt halt at the Syrian–Israeli border). The road leads north via Nablus, a major Arab city of 100,000 inhabitants built on the ancient city of Shechem, hence the Hebrew name, the Gate of Shechem. Nablus is the descendant of Hadrian's Neapolis, but fell prey to the Arab inability to pronounce the letter 'P', which becomes 'B'. Thus the visitor to the Old City will often be greeted with 'Bleased to welcome'.

Because of its extraordinary beauty, Damascus Gate intrigued eighteenth- and nineteenth-century pilgrims and travellers to the Holy Land. Roberts and Turner painted it; Bonfils and Salzmann photographed it; Bartlett wrote about and drew it. Since these scenes and photographs hang on the walls of my office and home, I have ample

33

time to contemplate them, becoming a second-hand witness to periods in which the environs of the gate remained unchanged and periods in which change was rampant.

The gate has a rare delicacy intertwined in its massiveness. It is the most impressive structure of Islamic architecture in Jerusalem, second only to those on the Haram al Sharif, which was the product of hired Byzantine architects.

What we found in 1967 was a deteriorating structure. Water had seeped into the cracks and the stones were loose and crumbling. Shacks were wantonly affixed to every available crevice, inside and outside the gate. Any attempt to seek tranquillity in the shadow of this structure was futile because the entire entrance was blocked by a bevy of taxi-cabs with the attendant clamour and din of their eternal honking.

Here, too, we were faced with the task of replacing the Turkish water and sewage system. It was a formidable undertaking, since within the gate we were dealing with a densely occupied residential area. Anyone who has ever remodelled a home without moving out will need no further explanation.

It was also a delicate undertaking, not only because of the physical and archaeological nature of the task at hand but also because of the human aspects. There is little we do in Jerusalem that does not entail political complications. One of the blights on the aesthetics of the Old City panorama was the multitude of television antennae. We sought to remove these unsightly antennae and replace them with a central antenna, beginning with the heavily populated Moslem Quarter, where the growth of the antenna forest was notably dense. But our motives were suspect. Surely we intended blocking the Moslem population's access to Jordanian television transmissions?

We thus began work in the Christian and Jewish Quarters, where there was a modicum of trust. By the time the residents of the Moslem Quarter accepted that, if anything, the central antenna allowed clearer reception, the till was empty and we no longer had the funds available. It thus remains in our ledger of unfinished business.

At Damascus Gate, we surmised that here and there we would find an artefact or two of archaeological value. But once we uncovered huge flagstones inside the city wall and the potential loomed enticingly before us, we decided to go for broke (both figuratively and literally). Our resolve here was rewarded with the uncovering of paving stones from the Roman period, ridged to prevent horses' hoofs from slipping. These are easily evident throughout the Old City and are usually marked accordingly.

Once work began, we decided not only to fix up the kitchen but the entire house. The crowded entry to the city was our initial venture. While the British had destroyed the concrete shops outside Damascus Gate, which blocked its beauty, makeshift structures had subsequently sprouted in their place.

Work began from three directions: inside, out-

34

Damascus Gate and the Old City walls, with the golden Dome of the Rock on the left and the grey domes of the church of the Holy Sepulchre on the right.

side and atop the gate's ramparts. Wishful thinking flourished amidst the pickaxes: if only a fragment of the Roman gate would emerge. The first eureka came from the top of the ramparts. Workers demolishing a blocked opening revealed a staircase descending into the city wall. Workers on the outside shared equal good fortune, uncovering not merely remnants of the Roman gates but one of the original gates, which had been covered in the course of time and was now below ground level.

We were compelled to continue. But we were now faced with a new brick wall: funding, a wall thicker than those Herodian or Hasmonean. If it seems as if I am for ever walking around with my hand outstretched, it is a somewhat accurate description. But I want to make it clear that I am merely following in the footsteps of an illustrious predecessor. Sir Ronald Storrs was the first British Governor of Jerusalem and the President of the Pro-Jerusalem Society, which he founded in 1919 because 'there were, and always will remain, many aspects of civil life, more especially in this unique city, in which no Military Administration, no Civil Government even, could, without thwarting civic and individual effort, occupy itself, however sympathetically inclined. The objects of the Society . . . are the preservation and advancement of the interests of Jerusalem, its district and inhabitants.' The Society was truly the forerunner of our Jerusalem Foundation.

Sir Ronald tells of a fund-raising trip in 1923: 'Early last year I travelled to the United States

with the object of enlisting the interest, sympathy and assistance of that generous nation. I have to record with gratitude the chivalrous reception accorded to my remote and unusual quest, in so much that a sojourn forcibly limited to twenty days resulted in subscriptions and donations amounting to several thousand pounds.'

Despite his success, some of his projects remained unsponsored. Thus for £20 you could sponsor: 'Seats in Palestine marble or other good stone for the Society's parks and gardens. The donor's name will be carved upon the seat.' A lesser gift of £2–5 would fund 'Seats in wood or iron at convenient points in the Rampart Walk or in the gardens. The donor's name will be cut or painted on the seat.' A larger gift of £2,000 would cover repairs to the Citadel, while repairs to the gates of Jerusalem were a reasonable £50 each. If only we could offer such bargains today . . . .

Despite our higher rates, we found the funds to continue work at Damascus Gate. The green light occasioned major upheavals. There were fourteen shops and six storerooms within the gate. Twenty-two contracts were signed in which we undertook to move the shops temporarily and, once excavation work was completed, to rebuild the shops anew, maintaining their indigenous architecture.

35

Damascus Gate as it was in the 1920s.

Work took two years. We rebuilt the shops on today's ground level and renovated the Mosque of Ibn-Omar, which had been non-functioning for years. We also widened the square on the upper level of the ramparts. There had been a sizeable carpentry workshop owned by Muhammed Hafez abu al Dabath, but the square was begging for a café. Abu al Dabath readily agreed to trade his workshop for two shops and a café (true Middle Eastern bargaining), which he presently runs with great panache as do his two neighbours.

Clearing the inner rooms of the Roman gates and towers was a daunting enterprise. The job was painstaking: baskets filled with dirt were removed with donkey power. It took eight months, working three shifts around the clock.

One day Yitzhak Yaacovy, the man in charge of this undertaking, was showing work-in-progress to a visiting journalist, Chris Walker of the London *Times*, who was writing an article for his paper's Christmas edition. The mostly Bedouin workers had nearly reached ground level of the eastern tower and were loading the last baskets of rubble on to the donkeys. The donkeys suddenly abandoned their posts and bolted to a corner of the room, discovering a Turkish feeding trough where some seeds remained. The donkeys forged ahead for a stale, 400-year-old dinner, while everyone around tried to grab a few seeds for the sake of science. Science lost.

It is now surmised that the towers had been in use up to the Omayyad period. One of the discoveries made on this site solved an age-old puzzle: why was a main road in the Old City market called in Arabic Tariq Bab Khan es-Zeit, the Road of the Gate of the Oil Press? The Butchers' Market had butchers; the Jewellers' Market had jewellers; but no oil press was known. The solution lay in the newly excavated eastern tower of Damascus Gate, where seven presses were found, revealing a major olive oil industry.

On the eastern wall of the eastern tower, a small chamber was revealed, probably the office of the gatekeeper. This was an influential position as the gatekeeper's decision determined whether or not you could enter the walled city and the security it afforded. No one would take responsibility for your fate if you had to stay the night outside the walls.

We soon became greedy. The success of the excavations kindled the hope that we might discover Hadrian's pillar. We did find what may have served as the base, but no more than that. We thus decided to make use of twentieth-century technology and create a hologram of the pillar, which we placed near the base – until the real pillar is discovered.

Our decision to repair the gate had been dictated by a no-alternative situation: it was deteriorating. We applied the 'no-alternative' dictum to another objective: removal of the taxi-cabs from the gate's entrance. It was too jarring a note even in our modern times. Safety was also a concern as divine intervention was too often called upon to prevent fatalities. The mass exchange of people – and donkeys and mules – in either direction, amidst the assortment of hawkers assiduously seeking customers, was not meant to compete with a vast garrison of vehicles.

We sought a plan which would be mindful of the diverse needs of a diverse population: peddlars could peddle their wares, tourists could rest their weary bones and enjoy unhindered views (and photographs) of the gate, Old City residents could reach their homes and shops without danger to life and limb, the Jewish residents of nearby neighbourhoods would have greater ease in reaching the Western Wall as would Christian pilgrims in reaching the Via Dolorosa. We chose an unencumbered concept: an amphitheatre-like approach.

The changes had to be completed almost as soon as they were started, for hampering access to Damascus Gate is akin to blocking Piccadilly Circus or Times Square. The absolute numbers may be less, but the disarray would be similar. Work was indeed completed at supersonic speed, which was surely another instance of divine intervention.

The future of Damascus Gate and its environs not only intrigued the Jerusalem city fathers, but became a class project for a group of aspiring young architects from Harvard University. These students came to Jerusalem under the stewardship of Moshe Safdie, the Israeli architect who first achieved fame with his Habitat creation at the 1967 Montreal Expo. They quickly experienced one of life's important lessons, not learned in any academic setting: it is not only pure architectural notions which must dictate decisions, but the existing human mosaic as well. It may well be years or even decades before a planning enterprise of this magnitude can be undertaken, so I shall leave the creativity of these students as a further legacy to my successors.

THE RAMPARTS WALK

Next on our list of 'things-to-do-today' was the Ramparts Walk to enable people to walk atop almost the entire circumference of the wall, excepting the area of the Temple Mount and the mosques. This idea also followed that of Sir Ronald Storrs, who envisioned a Ramparts Walk.

One step taken by the British was the dismantling of a clock tower, which had been constructed above Jaffa Gate to commemorate the thirty-third year of the reign of Sultan Abd al Hamid. While it was a hideous creation, again one can only imagine the international castigations had we even contemplated such a move. The British carried this out with nary an outside whimper.

The British did make some appreciable progress towards the creation of their Ramparts Walk, but this was obliterated by the Jordanian legionnaires who converted the ramparts into army positions. We had to start anew. As atop Damascus Gate, water had seeped into the cracks of the crenellations, creating a precarious situation. There were hardly any railings and the Turkish steps to the ramparts were in a state of ruin. This damage had to be repaired. Where possible, the Turkish steps were restored; where necessary, new steps were built. Railings were set at a comfortable height, with narrow slats to ensure protection for small children.

The Ramparts Walk is a medley of sights and sounds. One criss-crosses centuries as if in a game of checkers: here, remnants of the Roman period; here, an Arab family in a domed stone house sitting down to lunch; here, a glance through the parapets to the traffic jams of the modern city; there, the shaded courtyard of the Spafford Children's Home.

While today the ramparts are imbued with peaceful overtones, their past was far less amiable. Intruders to the walled city were greeted by scalding oil poured from the machicolations, the overhanging channels in the ramparts, an effective way of discouraging unwanted guests.

The walk extends $3\frac{1}{2}$ kilometres. One can ascend at several points (Damascus Gate and Jaffa Gate) and also descend at several additional gates (Lions' Gate, Herod's Gate, Zion Gate and Dung Gate). As we are already at Damascus Gate, we shall begin the Ramparts Walk here, walking west towards Jaffa Gate (see p. 14).

For the ambitious and for those not pressed for time, a detour in the opposite direction should be considered, even though the walker will eventually have to retrace his steps. An alternative to retracing one's steps is walking to Herod's Gate on the Ramparts, descending there and walking back on ground level. This has the advantage of permitting a visit to Zedekiah's Cave, but the disadvantage that one cannot ascend again at Damascus Gate on the same ticket but would have to walk up to Jaffa Gate (or pay a second time).

The Ramparts Walk towards Herod's Gate overlooks the Moslem Quarter, often in arm's reach. Because of its proximity to the Haram al Sharif, this area has always been a Moslem enclave as it is today.

In the late nineteenth and early twentieth centuries, there were a handful of Jewish families and institutions in the Moslem Quarter. One of the issues we face today is the attempt by several Jewish groups to resettle here.

During the 1980s, two *yeshivot* moved into the Moslem Quarter occupying buildings which had once been owned by Jews. The students yearned to be as close as possible to the Temple Mount, where, it is believed, the Messiah will appear at the End of Days. One of the schools is particularly fanatical in its philosophy and is a source of tension with its Moslem neighbours.

In December 1987, General Ariel Sharon, an Israeli war hero, also moved into the Quarter. His express purpose was to make a political statement to all and sundry that Jews had the right to live anywhere, including the Moslem Quarter. This move aroused Arab fears and suspicions that the Jews who had come to live among them had come as trespassers intent on methodically driving out the Arabs, one building at a time, from the Old City.

Some years earlier, the Israeli Government had prevented an Arab family, who had owned a house in the Jewish Quarter prior to 1948, from rebuilding their home in the reconstructed Jewish Quarter. The Supreme Court upheld the Government's decision, claiming that homogeneous neighbourhoods had always been a historic fact in Jerusalem. The Arabs – and a group of Israelis of which I was part – found it hard to understand why this ruling did not similarly apply in the Moslem Quarter.

We reach one of the smaller gates on the northern side of the Old City, Herod's Gate, the main entry to the Moslem Quarter. In fact, there are two entrances by this name: the original, smaller gate facing east, which was closed for most of the last 150 years, and the larger gate, facing north. Both the Hebrew name, Sha'ar Haprachim, and the Arabic name, Bab al Zahireh, translate as Gate of the Flowers. It is thought that the name is a bastardization of the Arabic phrase 'Es Sahirat' (the Awakened), referring to the Day of Judgement, because of the Moslem cemetery situated behind this gate.

The restoration of Herod's Gate again entailed moving a taxi-stand, but by then we were already experienced at this. The major enterprise to be tackled was the reopening of the original gateway, which had been sealed by the Turks.

Standing on the tower of Herod's Gate, the visitor should allow a few minutes for an appraisal of the view. To the left, in the distance, is the new city with the green cupolas of the Russian Church in the Russian Compound. Below the gate is the modern Arab shopping quarter and a modern post office. In the distance, to the right, is the terraced Mormon University building (see p. 77), as well as Mount Scopus and the Hebrew University campus to the left and the Mount of Olives to the right.

Just across the road, the white imposing structure is the Rockefeller Museum, or, as officially titled, the Palestine Archaeological Museum. Its exhibits mirror those in the Bronfman wing of the Israel Museum (see p. 115) – though compared to the latter's spacious and artistic display, the arrangements of antiquities here is stiff and even oversimplified, typical of displays in the heretofore, when creative museum design was in its infancy. There are exceptional artefacts displayed, but even for those who do not share a mania for archaeology, the architecture itself is worth a visit. The galleries surround a cloistered pool and one can wend one's way through the galleries to the open courtyard and back again.

The Rockefeller Museum was funded by the Rockefeller family, specifically a gift of $2 million made by John D. Rockefeller Jr in 1927. He gave the funds for the collection, conservation and preservation of all manifestations of man in this part of the world from earliest times. Designed by a British architect, Austin Harrison, and planned so as to accommodate both the museum and the British Mandate's Department of Antiquities, it was opened to the public on 13 January 1938. It was administered by an international committee until 1964, when the Jordanians unilaterally nationalized it. Thus, with the reunification of the city, it was transferred to the jurisdiction of the Israeli Government.

Following the city's reunification, Israeli archaeologists converged on the Rockefeller Museum, which had been out of bounds since 1948. One of the archaeologists found a note in her handwriting in a showcase: 'Temporarily Removed. R. A. [her initials]'. The temporarily had lasted nineteen years.

For some years, the parking area opposite the Rockefeller Museum was transformed each Friday morning into a sheep market. Sheep and goats from outlying districts were transported on trucks, in cars and even on foot for sale here. The squeals indicated a singular lack of co-operation on the part of the animals. Litanies of traditional bargaining led to the final transactions, usually completed in Jordanian dinars. The scene was a picturesque one and an occasional tourist could be spotted here. Some stood to the side while the more adventurous, or those with foresight to wear washable shoes, would join the *mêlée*. Often, when I stopped by, I was sure the sheep dealers looked at me as the 'one who never buys'. The market was not the delight of the city veterinarian and it had to be closed on health grounds from time to time. It is presently not functioning and we are seeking an appropriate site (next to the slaughterhouses, which is the ultimate fate of these animals) for the resumption of the market.

Just metres away is a Moslem cemetery and a monument to the Jerusalem Arabs who fell in the Six Day War. This monument represents for me probably the most difficult, and surely the most vociferous, battle I ever fought in City Hall.

In 1968, I was approached by the elders of the Arab community. Their dead in the Six Day War had been buried helter-skelter, often on the spot

The Rockefeller Museum from the air with the Old City walls behind it. Above and to the left is the Mount of Olives, with the Jewish cemetery, and on the right is the Temple Mount.

they had fallen, and the elders wanted to build a memorial adjoining the main cemetery. The opposition on our City Council was vehement. 'Did the French allow a monument to the Germans killed in World War II?' Unquestionably, the fear was that this monument would inspire violent demonstrations in the Arab community, if not a full-scale revolution.

I was not oblivious to the complexity of this issue. The wounds of the war in Jerusalem, a war which we had tried so hard to avoid, were still raw. We had losses and many disabled young men. And yet one could not equate the situation in Jerusalem with that in France after World War II. The Arabs were an intrinsic part of this city and they, too, had suffered losses.

The opposition City Councillors filibustered through the night – and I nearly lost not only the battle but also my job. But the decision was taken and the fallen were gathered and reburied in one place. The monument was erected and has never been the source of a single anti-Israel act. Moreover, I feel that the existence of this memorial may have helped ensure respect for the memorial tablets which we erected, many of which are in Arab neighbourhoods where the fighting had taken place.

A visit to Zedekiah's Cave is a possibility for

Looking along the Old City walls towards the Citadel and beyond to the Notre Dame Hostel on the far left.

those who descend at Herod's Gate – or even for those who want to visit here before they go to Damascus Gate. It is about midway between the two gates.

Zedekiah's Cave was discovered in 1854 by the archaeologist Dr J. T. Barclay, who wrote of it in his book *The City of the Great King*. Legend has it that King Zedekiah fled the armies of Nebuchadnezzar through this cave. Its alternative name, King Solomon's Quarries, was affixed by Charles Warren, a freemason who began the tradition of masonic gatherings in the cave. The quarry is probably slightly more recent, seventh–sixth century BC, as evidenced by a cherub excavated here, though it was Herod who made the most use of the quarry for his building activities.

For those who have retraced their steps along the Ramparts, and for those who opted instead for a rest at one of the cafés at Damascus Gate, we shall now resume our original walk. The Ramparts Walk westward passes the Christian Quarter, easily identified by the church steeples and crosses.

We pass the Franciscan School, where we had encountered a stumbling-block in the Ramparts planning. There had been steps which led from outside the wall directly to the Franciscan School, a veritable private entrance to the Old City. The Franciscans at first refused to allow passage there, fearing passers-by could, and would, jump into their open schoolyard. We negotiated and negotiated – and negotiated. Finally we succeeded in resolving the problem, by building a small bridge over the ramparts for their use and by ensuring that the fences in this section were higher than elsewhere.

We reach New Gate, where across the main road is the Notre Dame Hostel and Jerusalem City Hall and at the corner is a Crusader tower.

We follow the turn of the wall, always taking a minute or two to glimpse the kaleidoscope of views, and eventually reach Jaffa Gate. The British had intended constructing a bridge over Kaiser Wilhelm's breach, so that the visitor would not have to descend and ascend the stairway, but they never did it and thus far neither have we. So descend and ascend it is.

We cross the breach in the wall and walk across the outside court of the Citadel, reaching the spot at which we can re-ascend the Ramparts. As we continue, we pass the Armenian Quarter on our left. The modern building houses the Armenian Seminary, where clergy are trained.

The Armenian Patriarchate is within the walled compound which is off limits to visitors, although there is a small museum displaying some of the Armenian treasures. Soon after the city's reunification, we suggested to the Armenian Archbishop, Shahe Ajamian, the possibility of having the Israel Museum arrange an exhibition, at the Patriarchate, of Armenian treasures – ancient manuscripts, jewellery, ceremonial art – which were rarely, if ever, displayed. The result was a magnificent show, which gave both Israelis and tourists, including Armenians from abroad, an appreciation of the rich heritage of this community. Unfortunately, the Armenians felt uneasy about having these riches displayed and soon returned the majority to the vaults. The current exhibition is a limited version.

At the corner of the wall, on our right, we pass the Protestant cemetery and then the Dormition Abbey (see p. 44), which brings us to Zion Gate (and the possibility of descending into the next chapter).

Continuing onwards, we overlook on our left the Garden of Redemption, Gan Hatekumah (see p. 50), situated in a deep geological rift between the Jewish Quarter and the outer city wall. The initial archaeological pickings uncovered a few remnants of Justinian's Nea Church. Continued excavations brought us to massive water reservoirs and, ultimately, a tablet in Greek where the Emperor Justinian is mentioned. A group of friends from New Jersey, all survivors of the Holocaust, wanted to create a project in memory of those who had perished. They sought a project in close proximity to the Western Wall and thus was born the Garden of Redemption.

The Ramparts Walk (or jog) is unquestionably better exercise than any treadmill machine. Even American President Jimmy Carter did two laps around, with bodyguards in tow!

The Ramparts Walk ends at the Dung Gate, allowing the walker a visit to the Western Wall (see p. 19), the mosques (see p. 24), the Ophel or City of David excavations (see p. 29 and p. 31), a walk towards the Valley of Kidron (see p. 32), or a bus/taxi ride back to town and an iced coffee on the Pedestrian Mall (see p. 136).

Easter celebrations in the Armenian Quarter.

4
MOUNT ZION
AND THE JEWISH QUARTER

Someone once said to me that 'Mount Zion is a difficult hill'. The reference had little to do with the physical attributes of the ascent – though, if one uses the stepped approach built in the years of the divided city, it might seem an appropriate epithet. The engineering had had little to do with the topography but apparently resulted from the planner's wish to have 150 steps, the number of chapters in the Book of Psalms. I can only be happy that I was not Mayor at the time these steps were built; it is a heavy enough burden to bear responsibility for the Film Centre steps (see p. 87).

The 'difficult hill' referred to the intermingling of the religions which share this hill. With the Solomonic interventions of religious and political leaders, relative quiet has reigned in recent years. But there is the recurring question of the very hazy delineation of ownership boundaries; the recurring pressure by the Greek Orthodox Church to restrict access to their properties, which would virtually make Mount Zion inaccessible to others; and the recurring inter-religious power plays.

The history of Mount Zion is not easily determined. The biblical Mount Zion was the ridge to the east of the City of David but, by the Byzantine period, the name devolved upon the hill at the south-west corner of the Old City. Although

some worship it as the site of the tomb of King David, archaeologists claim that the tomb, if it still exists, is somewhere inside the other ridge. With a better claim to historical likelihood, the Christians see this hill as the site of the Last Supper (the Coenaculum – literally, the supper room of an ancient Roman house).

While one can begin one's tour of Mount Zion at the foot of the Mount (and up the 150 chapters of the Psalms), we shall begin at Jaffa Gate, which affords us a leisurely stroll along the western side of the Old City wall, a walk we shall do again (although on the opposite side of the road) in our visit to the Cultural Mile (see p. 79).

A word of warning: this is a long walk, not necessarily in mileage but in the wealth of sites along the route. Thus the possibility should be weighed of doing Mount Zion in one session and the Jewish Quarter in another. It is not a decision which need be made now; one can check one's energy level midway.

Leaving Jaffa Gate, we walk southward to the continuation of the National Park around the wall. Today's panorama is of a majestic wall, 12 metres high, but, until a decade ago, half this height was obscured. The residents of the Old City had had a rather novel method of garbage disposal, which entailed neither removing the garbage, nor compacting it, nor incinerating it, but merely tossing it over the wall, which, while it surely made the work of the eighteenth- and nineteenth-century City Hall simpler and cheaper, did have its drawbacks. The accumulation of this debris over centuries created its own landfill and obscured metres of the wall. Countless truckloads were needed to remove it and we watched, day by day, as the stones were revealed.

For some years the demarcation line halfway up the wall was distinct, with the lower half a lighter colour than the upper part, which had been exposed to the elements over centuries. Today the difference is hardly discernible, but we did leave a single mound of earth and a single tree midway up the wall as a testimonial to the past.

I did, one day, regret the efforts we had invested to expose the entire wall. To celebrate the opening of the 1984 Israel Festival in our city, the Japanese troupe Sankai Juku performed its

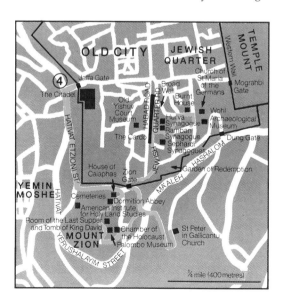

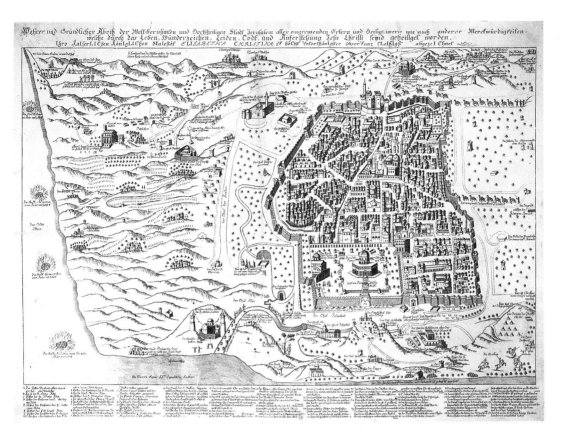

A map of Jerusalem produced in Vienna in 1728.

famous act, scaling the entire wall with ropes. I would have been less nervous had they to travel only half the distance.

MOUNT ZION

As we approach Mount Zion, we encounter a mixture of historical remains. There is a sign noting remains from the Israelite period, probably a seventh-century BC workshop. The metal box is twentieth century, but the corner above it is Hasmonean. The stairs further on are Herodian and the remains near the bushes are late Roman and Byzantine. The top of the wall is sixteenth-century Ottoman.

We reach a well-preserved tower, built by the nephew of Saladin, Al Malik al Muallam Isa, the Sultan of Damascus. (The sign, unless I succeed in having it changed, incorrectly consigns Al Malik's sultanate to Egypt.) He was a messianist and scholar, surrounded by many scholars writing sychophantically about him. Two inscriptions were found during excavations of the site attesting to the work of Al Malik; eight additional inscriptions are known.

His is a strange tale. In the very early thirteenth century, he rebuilt the walls of Jerusalem, a seven-year construction job. But in 1219, fearing a possible Crusader invasion, he pulled these walls down, an unmitigated scorched-earth policy. Anything was preferable to a territorial agreement with the Crusaders. It is said that with the destruction of the city walls, the Moslem women gathered at the mosques and tore out their hair until the entire Haram was covered with hair.

Though hard to conceive, the walled city remained unwalled for 320 years. The Moslems, unaccustomed to life without the protection of the walls, temporarily evacuated the city. The thirteenth-century Crusaders also found it difficult to live in Jerusalem.

At the corner of the tower, we turn left, climbing a non-Psalmist set of stairs. The unique ecumenicism of Mount Zion, beyond the array of religious sites, is nowhere more pronounced than in the profusion of its burial sites. On the right, we reach a gated Catholic cemetery used only for the burial of priests. The burial site for lay Catholics is on the far slope of Mount Zion, where there was also a Sephardi Jewish cemetery. There is also a Protestant cemetery (see p. 41), a Greek Orthodox cemetery and an Armenian cemetery.

While one cannot enter the Catholic priests' cemetery, a peek through the gate to the far wall brings into view two metal squares. Because of the scarcity of space, burial is now done in drawers, which permits a multi-level use of the land available.

Just opposite this gate, one can discern a portion of the city wall which is disfigured, a black-

43

ened concavity at knee-height. During the War of Independence, the Palmach, the elite pre-state Haganah fighting unit, attempted to blow a hole in the wall in order to relieve the besieged Jewish Quarter. The plan, as is evident, did not succeed. Suleiman's contractors should be commended.

ARMENIAN CEMETERY
The next gateway is that of the Armenian cemetery and here one can enter freely. The site is also that of an unoccupied convent.

On the left is a partially built structure. The Armenians had planned to build a cathedral which would be higher than the nearby Dormition Abbey, as height was frequently adjudged a parameter for importance. We objected to the addition of any new intrusive structures to the skyline and a lower-scaled compromise was approved. But funds ran out in mid-project and the cathedral remains 'under construction'. The partially built walls encompass a series of tombstones, mainly of priests, as in the Armenian tradition it is an honour to have one's headstone entombed in a holy site.

The main cemetery is to the right. For one who knows Armenian, the cemetery is a chiselled history book. One tombstone, for example, notes that the deceased was an Armenian monk in his twenties, who was killed by a Greek monk.

Leaving the main cemetery, we reach the area of what is thought by the Armenians to be the House of Caiaphas, where Jesus spent his last night. The remains of a medieval church mark the site. A glance at your feet will reveal that the terrace on which you are treading is an extension of the cemetery, with burial dates as recent as this century. The more elaborate decorations denote the graves of patriarchs and archbishops.

A bit of wandering in either direction will yield its rewards. If we turn left, we discover a Byzantine mosaic, an ancient cistern and a burial statue, whose inscription in French indicates the tomb of a family whose members died in 1885, 1887 and 1889. A five-foot stairless doorway leads to a narrow alley with the Byzantine ruins thought to be the House of Caiaphas.

If we turn right, up a flight of stairs, we encounter remains of what was evidently a kitchen. Climbing additional stairs, one reaches a nonrailed roof, which affords a telescopic view of Mount Zion and beyond.

Returning to where we entered this complex – inevitably late as I am, I have to forgo the offer of a good cup of Turkish coffee from Mahmoud, the custodian, but your schedule might be more accommodating – we continue on, turning right opposite Zion Gate and walking until we reach a Y intersection. The building at the intersection is Franciscan, easily identifiable by the Franciscan crosses and the hands of St Francis with stigmata.

Turn right before the church and walk a minute until reaching another Y. The signs clearly indicate the way, right to the Dormition Abbey and left to the Coenaculum. We bear right to the Dormition Abbey.

DORMITION ABBEY
The earliest church on this site was a Judeo–Christian structure designated as the Mother of all Churches, constructed with huge stones from a demolished Herodian building. In 380, the Byzantines built a church north of this, the Church of the Pillars, which had a pillar from the House of Caiaphas inserted in its colonnade. In 415, this church was remodelled into the Basilica of Hagia Sion by Bishop John II.

The Hagia Sion was probably destroyed by the Caliph el Hakim in 1009, as he could be relied upon to destroy anything non-Moslem. The Crusaders rebuilt it, combining it with the remains of the Church of the Apostles and calling it 'Sancta Maria on Zion'. This church was destroyed by the Sultan of Damascus, with only the Room of the Last Supper and one chapel surviving. The latter ultimately suffered a similar fate, being destroyed by the Moslems in 1468.

To trace the history of the modern church entails a jump of four centuries to the year 1898. The Emperor Wilhelm II, during his journey to the East, succeeded in obtaining this plot of land from Sultan Abd al Hamid. In April 1899, H. Renard, the cathedral architect of Cologne, began work and, on 31 March 1904, in the presence of a large German pilgrimage, the crypt was dedicated. The church itself was consecrated on 10 April 1910.

The Benedictines pursued their religious life unhindered throughout World War I, but, in November 1918, the British interned a number of the German monks. They were taken captive to Egypt and eventually repatriated to Europe until 1921, when they were allowed to resume their custody.

World War II brought internment of nearly the entire contingent of German priests, though they were allowed to return to the monastery towards the end of the war. But their solace was shortlived, as the Dormition was ill-placed during the fighting of 1948. The monastery was evacuated and the Benedictines began a series of sojourns in various church institutions. Only in 1951, after protracted negotiations, could they return to the church then bordering the no-man's-land dividing the city. For several years there were soldiers rather than bats in the belfry, as the tower dominated the Jordanian army positions on the ramparts of the Old City wall below.

In 1967, the Dormition was again in the line of fire and I have a vivid memory of its melted roof, with the nude spokes of the triangular structure

The Dormition Abbey, built on Mount Zion at the turn of the century.

resembling a cheap umbrella which was not storm-proof. While one could not be sure to whom the blame should be meted, the Jordanian army or the Israel Defence Forces, we accepted responsibility for the repairs.

Jerusalem lore tells that the Dormition spire was built to portray a Prussian general. Indeed, if one looks at the illuminated spire at night, one can identify the spiked casque and the bearded face. It is almost too convincing to be easily dispelled and accorded to mere chance.

The Dormition tower bears a four-directional clock reminiscent of that described by Günter Grass in his book *Cat and Mouse*, noting a church clock which provided 'the time of day, enabling Protestant as well as Catholic factory workers and office workers, salesgirls and schoolboys to reach their schools or places of work with interdenominational punctuality'.

In recent years, the Dormition Abbey has assumed a unique role in the musical life of our city, indeed our country. Concerts in the church, mainly of sacred music, are sold out as soon as they are publicized. The beauty of the church, its acoustics, the spirituality of Mount Zion, and the fine musicians and singers who perform here, are an unbeatable combination. During the period of the springtime Israel Festival, as well as the Christmas week Liturgica series, music resounds throughout the church.

The Dormition Abbey houses one of Jerusalem's colourful personalities, Father Immanuel, a slight, bearded man, who moves effortlessly among a half-dozen languages. I often find myself envying his seemingly unlimited fount of energy, which during the period of the Dormition concerts allows him to be an impresario until long past midnight and yet be at matins at 5 a.m.

ABOVE *The Room of the Last Supper.*   BELOW *The Tomb of King David.*

THE ROOM OF THE LAST SUPPER AND THE TOMB OF KING DAVID

Returning to the last intersection, we now follow the left fork into a religious hodge-podge. Several of the buildings we pass were taken over by the Diaspora *Yeshiva*, whose students are generally 'born-again Jews' from abroad. On the left we pass through an entry with a Moslem inscription and the signature of the Sultan and walk up a flight of steps to the Room of the Last Supper. Here we meet a combination of Crusader and Moslem architecture. It is rare to reach here and not encounter groups of Christian pilgrims. The hymns which they sing in their native tongues echo the hymns of centuries of pilgrimages.

Leaving the Room of the Last Supper, we continue straight and reach the so-called Tomb of King David, again a Crusader structure, thus built two millennia after David was buried. This tomb is mentioned in the writings of Benjamin of Tudela, a pilgrim to the Holy Land in 1172.

Before 1948, this area was owned by a Moslem family named Djanni and Jews were forbidden entry. This may be an appropriate place to clarify a significant point. Even before 1948 and the division of the city, Jews were not permitted to visit either the Haram al Sharif/the Temple Mount (see p. 23) or the Church of the Holy Sepulchre (see p. 71). Jews who attempted such visits tell of the hefty blows they encountered. Thus, when we talk of the free access which has become the byword of the reunified city we are speaking of a new Jerusalem phenomenon.

While the Western Wall is again the focus of Jewish pilgrimage, during the years of the divided city, when the Wall was off-limits, the Tomb of King David assumed this role. In the foyer is a room belonging to the Breslav Hassidim. Every Thursday night, a group of 150–200 Hassidim come here and pray through the night; some leave at midnight to pray at the Tomb of Rachel in Bethlehem.

Following the signs, we reach the Chamber of the Holocaust, a memorial to the six million Jews killed during the Nazi period. Pre-dating the establishment of Yad Vashem, the national museum of and monument to the Holocaust (see p. 144), the Chamber of the Holocaust was created by the Ministry of Religious Affairs and is presently administered by the Diaspora *Yeshiva*. Proposals to transfer and integrate this material into Yad Vashem have been submitted, but have encountered opposition. My position is that the material should not be transferred but placed under the care and jurisdiction of Yad Vashem, the appropriate authority.

Nearby is the Palombo Museum, commemorating a Jerusalem sculptor known pre-eminently for his creation of the powerful gates of the Knesset building. He lived on Mount Zion and was tragically killed when, returning home on his motorscooter one Saturday night, he crashed into the chain placed across the road to prevent traffic on the Sabbath. The chain was to have been removed at sunset.

A frequent quandary as I guide you on these walks is to the just treatment of buildings and sites which are not open to the public. I do not feel comfortable placing a candy within sight but out of reach, yet I hesitate to delete mention entirely. To skip the story of the Rose House on the eastern slope of Mount Zion, adjoining the Palombo Museum, would be a disservice to Mount Zion and to the Roses.

Real estate is a risky business, but never as risky as when the property doubles as a frontier outpost. The Roses, immigrants from South Africa, were house-hunting when they spotted this building. It was well-built, no leaky roofs, a lovely garden – just what every potential homeowner seeks – except that its location was on a mined border. Yet the Roses deemed it perfect.

They tended their English garden as if they were living in the centre of Hampstead. Their affinity with Jerusalem was almost metaphysical though connected so closely with the physical, their Mount Zion home. Their hospitality was legendary and the Municipality should undoubtedly have re-zoned the site as a (non-paying) boarding-house.

The Roses, growing old in the tranquillity of this house – its border status ceased to exist in 1967 – were anxious as to its future and bequeathed it to the city of Jerusalem. After much deliberation as to how the building should be used (the official mayoral residence was one of the proposals), we resolved that it should serve visiting artists and created the Centre for Visual Arts. Regrettably, it is not open to the public.

ST PETER IN GALLICANTU CHURCH

For those interested in visiting the St Peter in Gallicantu Church across the main road, this is the closest point to do so. Gallicantu – the cock's crow – commemorates the statement made by Jesus to Peter that 'before the cock crow thou shalt deny me thrice'. This church is a modern structure built on the remains of Byzantine and Crusader churches, which have been uncovered in archaeological excavations, a physical hierarchy which will repeat itself time and time again in the churches in Gethsemane and along the Via Dolorosa (see ch. 6). Underneath the modern church is a cave thought to be the prison where Jesus was incarcerated.

For years, the single route from west to east was the private road of the church, never intended for use as a thoroughfare. We accepted the church's contention that a new road was essential and bought the land to build it. The contract stipulated

that, as soon as the new road was constructed, traffic would be banned on the church road. But, as often is the case, Jerusalem's past disrupted its present. Because of archaeological finds, the road was delayed again and again. The new road was not getting built. I decided that it was time to intervene. With pressure on every municipal and government body – and with the construction of a bridge over the archaeological finds (see p. 31) – we finally saw the completion of this road and one more source of tension was averted.

We return to Zion Gate, either on the main road, where a sign indicates the turn off (to the left) or, perhaps easier, we can retrace our steps through the complex of King David's tomb. (Through the open area there are utilitarian, if not especially attractive, restrooms.)

A point of sociological interest, indicating a disparity in people's habits in the 1960s and the 1980s: at the far exit to this complex – the single point of entry when the city was divided – is a sign which, though painted over, can be deciphered, indicating that visiting hours were from 6 a.m. or 7 a.m. Today entry is permitted from 8 a.m. The pioneering spirit is sleeping later.

Just beyond King David's tomb, there is a flight of ascending steps which leads to an observation point. For nineteen years, people would stand here and look towards the Old City. Signs denoted a frontier area, taking photographs was prohibited, and tourists were admonished not to point because there was always the possibility that a legionnaire would mistake a finger for a gun and take a potshot.

Other institutions on Mount Zion open to the public include the American Institute for Holy-land Studies in the Gobat School. The Institute had been the target of harassment by the Diaspora *Yeshiva* students, as one of the aims of the Diaspora *Yeshiva* has been to ensure an enduring Jewish presence on Mount Zion, where, over the centuries, churches have proliferated. The *Yeshiva* students' fight for this conviction led to increasing tensions, which had to be – and occasionally still have to be – adjudicated.

Back at Zion Gate, the Hebrew plaque notes that the Palmach broke through here on 19 May 1948 during the War of Independence; the bullet marks authenticate the veracity of the plaque. When the Palmach had failed in its plan to breach the wall further to the west, to relieve the Jews still holding out in the Jewish Quarter, entry through the gates was the last resort. The success of this attack was short-lived and the Jewish Quarter fell.

We pass through to the Old City, an easier feat for the pedestrian than for the motorist as the former is more adept at making right-angle turns.

An Arab entering the Old City through Zion Gate.

A street in the Jewish Quarter.

The Old City was never intended for motorized traffic and, even where it is allowed, it often entails tricky manœuvring. Parking is another problem which Suleiman the Magnificent did not foresee. We once considered a plan for underground parking in the Zion Gate area. In one of the memorable exchanges at meetings of the Jerusalem Committee (see p. 95), San Francisco architect Larry Halprin presented this plan. The fiery reaction of the Italian architect Bruno Zevi was surely heard in his native land: 'I cannot see making decisions of such a crucial nature on account of people's aversion to walking a few metres. If Venetians can walk for the privilege of living in Venice, Jerusalemites can walk for the privilege of living in the historic Jewish Quarter.'

His oratory at the time was convincing, but when my daughter Osnat lived in the Jewish Quarter and I had to drive around for half an hour trying to park, lofty ideals crumbled and I found myself squarely in Larry's corner.

Continuing straight and bearing left with the

49

road, we overlook the Garden of Redemption (see p. 41). The entrance is down to the right; just follow the sign.

Within the walled city, the finite supply of living space is eternally grappling with a non-finite demand. Open public space is sparse, nearly non-existent. The extensive green area of the Garden of Redemption should be viewed in this context, a welcome rarity. It is breathing-space for the occasionally stifling nature of the burden of history, which is carried by all Old City residents as the inner lining of an overcoat. And the garden beckons the visitors who have taken on this chapter as a single walk so that they can rest their weary bones/heads/feet.

THE JEWISH QUARTER

Our walk continues straight ahead, through the farther parking lot, to the Jewish Quarter Road, along which we will eventually enter the Jewish Quarter. But a detour to our right and down the stairs will bring us to the complex of four Sephardi synagogues, marked with a single tile.

This may be an opportune time to give an overview of the guidelines devised for the restoration of the Jewish Quarter, a seventeen-year project undertaken by the Company for the Reconstruction of the Jewish Quarter.

When we reached the Quarter in 1967, it was a shambles, with more rubble than buildings. The Quarter had been ravaged and nearly sixty synagogues destroyed. It seemed that every trace of the once-thriving Jewish community here had been purposefully obliterated.

The question was: what should be our next step? The ideas bandied about at the time were endless, ranging from leaving the Quarter untouched to razing it entirely and rebuilding it anew. We chose a middle-of-the-road approach. We knew it would not be the same Jewish Quarter. It would not have the same houses, the same sounds, the same smells – even the same aspirations. Yet we would preserve what could be preserved and rebuild what could be rebuilt, adhering to its style and ambience.

One guideline remained tantamount: that we were rebuilding a living organism, not a museum. Strict regulations ensured that those who purchased homes would actually live in them. We did not want absentee landlords, who could boast a holiday home with a Jacuzzi overlooking the Western Wall.

We also had to attend to archaeological considerations. Every inch of land was a treasure trove of ancient lore and, if every ancient site uncovered were to be preserved, we could shelve all ideas of a living quarter. Our alternative was selective preservation: all sites would be excavated, studied and marked, but only those with major significance would remain exposed.

A system was devised to indicate finds which were ultimately to be concealed. Red floor tiles indicate finds of the First Temple period; black tiles, finds of the Hasmonean period.

The four Sephardi synagogues, though seemingly demolished, had actually remained intact, owing their survival to an Ottoman law which had proscribed the building of any house of worship higher than the city's mosques. The desire of the Sephardi communities to have a majestic house of worship led to an architectural resolution of the dilemma and the synagogues were built deep into the ground, thus providing height while acceding to the Ottoman dictates.

Thus the synagogues survived, but this is not to say that they were undamaged. We sought synagogues; we found donkey stables. The rubble in the buildings literally reached the ceilings. It took over a year merely to clear out the rubble, before we could even consider the extensive restoration required. But once work was started, the momentum and the inspiration did the rest.

The synagogues were not yet officially opened when the eminent American opera singer, Richard Tucker, visited here. As countless opera singers before him, he had started his career as a *chazan*, a synagogue cantor. I stopped at his hotel late on a Friday afternoon and proposed taking him to the Sephardi synagogues for an impromptu prayer service. A handful of people huddled in the corner of the unfinished synagogue, we were transformed in one magical moment as the space filled with age-old cantorial music and a singular voice. Passers-by, returning from services at the Western Wall, were drawn by the magic of what they heard and, before the last Amen, there was an overflow audience. In that single moment, I could physically sense the past grandeur of these synagogues.

Of the four synagogues in the complex, the oldest is the Eliyahu Hanavi Synagogue (Elijah the Prophet), followed by the Yohanan Ben Zakai. The Istanbuli and the Emtzai (Middle) are later additions, possibly having originally served as the women's sections for the earlier houses of worship. Travellers speak of the synagogues as early as 1625; it is known that by 1790, all four synagogues existed, though the community underwent extensive hardships in the second half of the eighteenth century, following an Arab revolt against the Turkish Governor in Jerusalem. Christian travellers of the period conveyed a gloomy picture of the synagogues, though the spiritual life of the community continued unabated. The nineteenth-century saw the community flourishing once again.

To reach the heart of the Jewish Quarter, we return to Jewish Quarter Road. A glance to the left gives you a chance to see how Arab pita bread is made (and a chance for a quick snack as well). The open Cardo area soon comes into view followed by the closed Cardo. We shall later walk through the Cardo from the opposite end, unless you lose the battle with temptation and do so sooner.

To the left, between the open and closed Cardo, is a small flight of steps. At the top of the steps, to the left – follow the signs – is the Old Yishuv Court Museum in the Weingarten House at 6 Or Hahayim Street. Rabbi Weingarten was the president of the Jewish Quarter before 1948, but beyond his official titles and duties, he had true leadership qualities. He participated in the surrender of the Jewish Quarter though it proved to be an amputation of his soul.

His daughter Rivka and I met following the city's reunification and, while she had been part and parcel of life in the Jewish Quarter and I had been at best an outsider, we were equally imbued with the dream of preserving a semblance of life as it was. And thus we collaborated on this tiny, imaginative museum, which commemorates a way of life and the people who lived it.

A right turn at the Cardo steps leads to the office of the Archaeological Seminars, 34 Habad Road. I shall be accused of aiding the competition, but I would be doing a disservice if I did not mention the excellent walking tours of the Old City which the Archaeological Seminars organizes. Each tour begins with a short lecture which places the walk in its historical and geographical context, equally useful for the Jerusalem expert as well as the Jerusalem novice.

THE HURVA SYNAGOGUE

We return to the Jewish Quarter Road. On the right, at no. 7, was the nineteenth-century Hurva Synagogue built on the site of an earlier one.

This brings us to the saga of Rabbi Yehuda Ha-Hassid, who in 1700/1701 left his home in Eastern Europe and, with several hundred followers, descended on the Holy City. It was a messianic, Kabalistic pilgrimage with no realistic economic base for survival. The synagogue they envisioned remained partially built, a 'hurva' – the ruin. By the time of the Rabbi's death, the community was in dire straits. Those who could flee did so; the remainder took on the yoke of the community's debts. The situation was so critical that, for more than a century, no Ashkenazi Jew could enter Jerusalem because he would immediately be saddled with responsibility for the debts of his predecessors – plus interest. The only alternative was to masquerade as a Sephardi Jew.

The actual Hurva was built in the nineteenth century after a building permit had been obtained, with much difficulty, from the Ottoman Sultan with the combined help of Sir Moses Montefiore in England and the British Consul in Constantinople. The official name of the synagogue was Beit Yaacov, for the Baron James Jacob Roth-

The Hurva Synagogue before its destruction in 1948.

schild. The cornerstone for this synagogue, which was 24 metres high, was laid in April 1856; the dedication took place in September 1864.

It was once assumed that the Hurva had been destroyed in the fighting of the War of Independence, though we later learned from local off-the-record sources that it had been blown up by the Jordanians. In 1967, soon after the dust had settled, the restoration of the Hurva Synagogue was pondered. The Hurva was not merely a place of worship but also a symbol of the once-flourishing Jewish community in the Jewish Quarter. In the euphoria of the newly united city, renewing the Hurva seemed the logical first step towards renewing the Jewish Quarter.

The first impetus came from a Haifa lawyer, Yaacov Salmon, whose ancestors had settled in Jerusalem in the early nineteenth century and had been instrumental in the building of the Hurva. He commissioned plans from Louis Kahn, an architect of world repute and a founding member of the Jerusalem Committee. Kahn was enthralled with this commission and soon presented his design for a massive, modern edifice. The plans are displayed in the Hurva courtyard; the inner courtyard depicts the internal structure of the original synagogue.

Kahn died before this project was realized and no architect dared touch the master's plans. There was also discomfort with the modernity of the proposed building and it was felt that the new Hurva should be conceptually closer to the original.

Soon after, Yaacov Salmon died. But the dream did not die with either Kahn or Salmon. A promi-

*The Hurva Square with the remains of the Hurva
Synagogue and the rebuilt arch behind.*

nent Englishman, Sir Charles Clore, took up the
reins and agreed to provide the funds on one condition: that the synagogue be completed within a
specified number of years. Clore was not a young
man and he wanted to witness the rebuilding of
the Hurva.

The commission was given to an eminent
English architect, Sir Denys Lasdun. Though Jewish, he had little knowledge of Jewish tradition
and thus worked in partnership with a local architect, an observant Jew who lived almost in the
shadow of the Hurva ruins. Their design was
again modern, though a bit more spacious and
with greater similarity to the original. The plans
went through the usual maze of planning commissions and bureaucratic procedures. One signature was yet needed: that of the Minister of the
Interior (a preview of the troubles we would
encounter years later with plans for our stadium –
see p. 119). He did not sign. He bowed to the
objections of Prime Minister Begin, who contended that only an exact replica of the original
Hurva could be acceptable.

Clore did not live to see the Hurva rebuilt. And
while he bequeathed vast moneys to charities,

many in Jerusalem, nothing was stipulated for the
Hurva, for no Hurva plan existed. But because of
Clore's passion for this project, his daughter
Vivien created the nearby square, an open space
vitally needed in this crowded quarter.

We saw no end to the Hurva quagmire and thus
decided on a temporary, symbolic solution: the
recreation of one of the four arches which supported the monumental dome of the original
Hurva. We had envisioned this as a temporary
solution, but, as the years pass, no plan seems as
appropriate as the single arch. And while I am
convinced that the Hurva will one day be rebuilt, I
bequeath this privilege – and the attendant trials
and tribulations – to my successors.

Just around the corner, on Lohame Harova
Betashah Street (literally, the 1948 Jewish Quarter
Fighters Street), there is a modest memorial to the
street's namesake and the residents of the quarter
who lived through the 150 days of a partial siege.
An arch from the eastern side of the Byzantine
Cardo is but a taste of what awaits us later.

While one would expect a proliferation of tourist shops, what has flourished in the Jewish
Quarter are study institutes and information
centres; signposts indicating one or the other are
prominent in storefronts and alleyways. A special
volume would be needed to guide you through
the maze of these institutions.

Jerusalem business is conducted not only on Jaffa Road, but also on New York's Fifth Avenue, London's St James's Place or Antwerp's Pelikaanstrasse. I was once a frequent traveller, long before the airlines usurped this title for their own complicated mileage plans, but my trips abroad have become far less frequent and far shorter. On one of my visits to New York, in 1975, I was approached by a friend of the Israel Museum who owns a photo laboratory service and had recently made prints of the work of a former photographer for *Life* magazine, John Phillips. He suggested that I meet Mr Phillips, as he had an inkling that what he had seen would interest me.

It did not interest me; it enthralled me. John Phillips had been a press photographer in Jerusalem during the siege of the Jewish Quarter. He had documented its fall and its surrender, though ultimately the photographs were never published since, by the time he was able to transmit the photographs to the magazine, the subject was no longer timely. The photographs remained in his archives and in his consciousness.

I sat with John and looked at the photographs again and again. And an idea slowly germinated: we would search out the people who appeared in the photographs and would have a 'then and now' exhibition at the Israel Museum. It would answer questions which John had posed to himself throughout the years: What had become of Tawil, the Haganah officer, who negotiated the surrender? Had the terrified girl running down the street ever caught up with her family? Had the young boy with the vacant look ever recovered from the shock of his mangled shoulder? What were all those prisoners lined up in Ashkenazi Square doing now? What did they look like, a quarter of a century later?

Rivka Weingarten was our primary source. She pored over the photographs and identified thirty of the people. But tracing them entailed intricate detective work, false leads and infinite patience. The eventual success we had was astounding as was the network of paths which these lives had taken. There was a bus driver, a butcher, a locksmith, two nurses, an interior designer, a cardiologist, an ambassador, two rabbis, a building contractor and a retired stationmaster.

John Phillips rephotographed his original subjects for the exhibition at the Israel Museum (and ultimately for a book, *A Will To Survive*). On the evening of the exhibition opening, we invited the entire cast of characters, the majority of whom had lost touch with one another, to a private gathering. I passed by a group milling about and overheard an argument of increasing decibels. The subject at hand: should they have surrendered or not? Yes, we had no choice, we would have all been killed. No, we should have fought to the bitter end...

THE BROAD WALL

Our walk continues past excavations of the square pillars which supported the arches and roof of the Cardo's eastern portico. If you follow along the railing to the right (past public restrooms), you will reach the Broad Wall.

One's eyes boggle at the blatant juxtaposition of the old and the new: Venetian-blinded contemporary apartments and the rectangular vestiges of buildings dating from the time of Hezekiah, 701 BC, abut the Broad Wall. In the Book of Nehemiah (3:8) there is mention of a broad wall: 'And they restored Jerusalem unto the broad wall'; 'And the other company of those who gave thanks went to meet them, and I after them, and half of the people upon the wall, above the tower of the furnaces to the broad wall' (12:38). But one cannot pinpoint the wall in this reference.

The discovery of this wall confirmed speculation that First Temple Jerusalem was larger than had been assumed, and there are archaeol-

Broad Wall in the Jewish Quarter.

Restored columns in the Cardo.

the signs' to the Israelite Tower, it is because of the assurance that it is far easier to do so than to follow a complex list of 'turn left and turn right' instructions which I can present.

The Israelite Tower is just that, a tower from the Israelite period, and can be visited for a pittance. For those for whom steps are burdensome, please note that it is forty-five steps down – and forty-five steps up. Just opposite is a permanent exhibition depicting the city in the First Temple period and it, too, is a chapter in 'Jerusalem Revealed'. (A joint ticket can be purchased for these two sites and the Burnt House.)

THE CARDO

We shall finally descend to the street of the Cardo, which was the Roman equivalent of Main Street. In Jerusalem, the Roman Cardo extended from Damascus Gate southward, but the Cardo which was excavated – is Byzantine.

You can enter the Cardo at the gate immediately opposite the square pillars or a bit further along. In any case, you might walk as far as the Arab market, turn around and begin your walk in a southerly direction.

Often in our restoration work we have given new content to ancient sites; in the Cardo, we merely resumed its original purpose. Today's modern shopping arcade was an open area until the Crusaders covered it. The Crusader shopper in the twelfth-century may not have had the same selection of goods we find today, but their shops were in the very same location. At the beginning of the arcade, the well-preserved façade of the Crusader shops can easily be discerned on the left.

The Hasmonean wall on the opposite side was found intact, probably because it had been rendered obsolete and thus there was no pressing need for any conquering army to destroy it. The columns of the Byzantine Cardo are visible atop the wall as is the Roman cistern built into the wall. Throughout the Cardo, there are covered shafts which allow a glimpse down into the past. These shafts invite use as wishing wells, as the collection of coins several millennia down attests.

We shall continue towards the covered portion of the Cardo beyond the shopping arcade. The columns are cemented to their original height; the wooden beams are copies of the original ones. We were able to determine the actual height of the columns not only from the proportions which allowed intelligent guesswork, but from our good fortune in finding a single column intact, which is now the second column on the left in the open Cardo.

In between the closed and open Cardos, we have placed a replica of the sixth-century Madaba map, which I have already mentioned, as reference material.

ogists who postulate that the end of the Broad Wall is in the Tower of David. To substantiate this point will take immense research, but, if correct, will entail redrawing the boundaries of ancient Jerusalem over a more extensive area than heretofore surmised.

Walls in Jerusalem were always kinetic, but the concept of walls, as defence, was resolute. Walls were built to ward off the next wave of conquerors, whoever they may be. The northern flank was the vulnerable one; thirty-seven of the thirty-nine times Jerusalem was conquered was from the north, following the biblical admonition: 'Out of the north the evil shall break forth upon all the inhabitants of the land' (Jeremiah 1:14).

Before I allude to a possible visit to the Israelite Tower, I might point out that the directions and explanations throughout the Jewish Quarter leave visitors, even those whose sense of direction cannot differentiate east from west, little chance to err. Thus, if I suggest that you 'follow

In the open Cardo, the fifth-century Byzantines quarried out the bedrock to make room for the shops, one of which can be readily distinguished. It is thought that the shopkeepers lived above the store, as was common with our grandparents.

Throughout the restoration of the Cardo, care was taken to allow easy differentiation between the old and the new. Where we added stones, they are conspicuously new stones; the new cement columns are easily distinguishable from the original columns and the restoration on the original columns can be clearly seen.

We re-emerge into the modern world at the corner of Beit El Road and walk a block until we reach an open square to our left, the Hurva Synagogue Square. In front of us is the Ramban Synagogue. In the thirteenth century, the Ramban came to Jerusalem and bought property on Mount Zion for a synagogue, establishing the Ramban congregation. A subsequent argument between the Jewish community and the Franciscans was settled equitably by the Moslems, who evicted both the Christians and the Jews. It is thought that the synagogue was then built in the Jewish Quarter for the local communities. In 1522, a visitor to Jerusalem, Rabbi Bassola, wrote: 'The community is mixed, with 15 Ashkenazi homeowners and a majority of Sephardim. There are three hundred homeowners in all.' On a pretext, the Ramban Synagogue was closed by the Turkish Governor in 1586 and this led to a split in the Jewish community.

THE BURNT HOUSE

For a visit to the Burnt House, again my recommendation is follow the signs (along Tiferet Israel Road to our left). An archway a block or so down is adjacent to the Burnt House, a luxurious home from the period of the Second Temple, which was burned at the time of the Temple's destruction in AD 70. When the archaeologists uncovered this find, I was brought a few of the charred bits; as I fingered them and the charcoal blackened my hands, the twenty centuries intervening were microscopically eclipsed.

WOHL ARCHAEOLOGICAL MUSEUM

Across the Hurva Synagogue Square is the Porat Yoseph *Yeshiva*, designed by Moshe Safdie, whose work we shall encounter in several corners of the city, and the Wohl Archaeological Museum, to which a visit is obligatory.

Here, too, we find another round in the past vs. the present competition. As required for all construction in the Jewish Quarter, the archaeologists preceded the contractors. The archaeologists excavated and excavated and the building was delayed further and further. When it became evident that this was not an undertaking of weeks, months or even years, a compromise solution was sought – and, surprisingly, attained.

The Madaba Map, a sixth-century AD mosaic map of Jerusalem showing the Cardo.

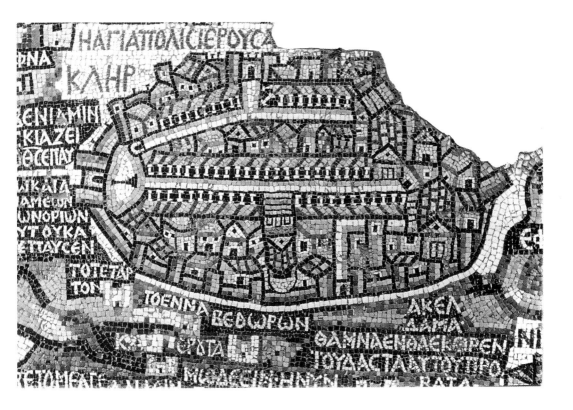

The building would be constructed on columned stilts so that it could proceed simultaneously with the search for the past.

The basements of six mansions from the Herodian period were revealed, mansions which were three or four storeys high. The rich stores of artefacts are on display and, together with the structures themselves, add a new volume to the anthology of Jerusalem's history.

These mansions evidently belonged to the Temple priests and nobility, the Jerusalem elite. Each of the mansions has remains of at least one *mikva*, a ritual bath. One house had five. We thus learn that while there were public *mikvas* in front of the Temple, the priests – who had to dip in the *mikva* each day before going to the Temple – did not bathe with the masses.

We pass from house to house. Each find is a clue in another chapter to a story: there are footbaths, frescoes, mosaics and the household which boasted four sets of dishes. Keeping up with the Cohens was not as simple as one might think.

CHURCH OF ST MARIA OF THE GERMANS

Leaving the museum, we find ourselves facing the vestiges of the twelfth-century Church of St Maria of the Germans and the adjacent hospice. When first uncovered, we knew it was a Crusader structure but little more than that, until Crusader historians finally succeeded in pinpointing the origin. It is assumed that the hospice was built because the Germans had no common language with their fellow Crusaders, the French order of St John the Hospitallers.

When these remains were uncovered, we were pressed by Jewish religious groups to obliterate what was found. There was opposition to having any indication of the existence of a church on one of the main routes to the Western Wall. But historical accuracy abrogated these objections and this picturesque corner bears witness to the German arm of the Crusades.

A walk down the steps brings us to the Western Wall, to the Mograhbi Gate and to Dung Gate.

5

THE MOUNT OF OLIVES

I can well imagine that those eager to start this walk might find the introductory pages rather cumbersome, but a brief overview of the history of the Christian communities in Jerusalem might enable a greater appreciation of the religious and historic sites. But as I shall not be looking over your shoulder, you need not hesitate skipping to page 59.

While the Christian community is the smallest in Jerusalem, about 15,000, its spiritual and physical presence is far weightier than evidenced by mere numbers. The history of the birth and growth of Christianity is tightly interwoven in the history of Jerusalem and almost forty Christian denominations have their holy places and churches, or parts of churches, throughout the city. One should thus not register great surprise to learn that more than half the tourists to Israel are Christians.

There are Churches ancient and venerable. There are Churches unknown in Western countries. There are Churches whose local adherents can be counted on the fingers of one's hands.

The Greek Church, established here under the Eastern Roman Empire in the fourth century, has had an uninterrupted presence until today. It surely qualifies as both ancient and venerable.

The Armenians and Ethiopians came here following the conversion of their respective kingdoms to Christianity in the fourth century, when the devout wanted to live in the city of Jesus. These Churches can likewise claim an uninterrupted presence over centuries.

The Armenian community in Jerusalem increased considerably after World War I with the influx of refugees following the massacre of Armenians in Turkey. The Armenian Patriarch, Yegishe Derderian (Elisha II), who has served in this post since the 1960s, originally came to Jerusalem as an orphan from the Lake Van region in eastern Turkey.

The Syriac Orthodox community traces its presence to the second century. In the Syriac Church of St Mark, mass is said in Aramaic – the everyday language of our region in the days of Jesus – and the community elders still speak Aramaic among themselves.

The Roman Catholics are relative newcomers,

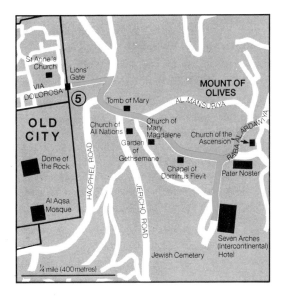

with a local history of about eight centuries. Following the arrival of the Dominicans and the Franciscans after the Crusades, the Franciscans were appointed as custodians of the Holy Land. The Custos Terra Sancta has its seat in Jerusalem and is in charge of the interests of the Catholic Church in the area which had been under Crusader rule. The Custos administers holy places, monasteries, parochial schools, health services and a printing press.

It was only 140 years ago that a Latin Patriarch was appointed in Jerusalem and thus by tradition the Father Custos remains the most influential Catholic dignitary in the city. The Apostolic Delegate, also ranking highly among Church dignitaries and enjoying diplomatic status, represents the Vatican State.

Anti-religious regimes also stand firmly by their rights in Jerusalem. Even before glasnost, Russian Church delegates came regularly to Jerusalem for holiday celebrations. This, however, is only a smattering compared to the mass pilgrimages from Russia before World War I. In the six months before the 'Guns of August', 26,000 Russian peasants reached Jerusalem, travelling by boat from Odessa to Jaffa. Tales are told of the handful of pilgrims who would traverse the entire distance from Jaffa to Jerusalem on their knees.

Even after severing diplomatic relations with Israel in 1967, the Russian Government continued its interest through its Church. It maintains a large ecclesiastical delegation here and Metropolitan Pimen, the head of the Church in Moscow, has visited here in recent years.

Of course, the official representatives of the Russian Church are regarded by the White Russians as KGB agents and pamphlets 'proving' this reach us on a regular basis; at the same time, the reverse claims suggest that the White Russians are undoubtedly in the pay of the CIA! Personally I do not doubt the religious devotion of either. The only meeting-place between the White and Red Russians is at the annual holiday reception which I host at City Hall – although not a word is exchanged between them.

A similar story repeats itself with Ethiopia, an absolutely anti-clerical government. On Easter, hundreds of Ethiopians come on pilgrimages to spend the holiday in Jerusalem. It is an outgrowth of the concern of the Ethiopian Government to safeguard its rights here.

The Greek Orthodox Church, unlike the Roman Catholic Church, does not have a single supreme authority like the Pope. Every country has its autocephalous church. At the Council of Chalcedon in 451, five ecumenical Patriarchates were created. The Patriarch of Constantinople became the *primus inter pares*, the first among equals. But in modern times, with the population exchange following World War I when the Greeks were defeated by Kemal Ataturk, the Patriarch's flock comprises but a few Greeks. Yet he does retain considerable moral influence.

When Pope Paul VI wanted to make a symbolic gesture of ecumenicism and meet with the Greek Orthodox Patriarch of Constantinople – the first such meeting since the Schism of 1056 – the Pope did so here in Jerusalem, during his historic visit in 1964.

The second Patriarchate was that of Antioch, an ancient city which had a million inhabitants, yet is today in ruins. The Patriarch of Antioch today sits in Damascus and oversees dioceses in Syria and Iraq.

The third Patriarchate, that of Alexandria, underwent a story similar to that of Constantinople. Alexandria had been a focus of Greek civilization; its rare library was ravaged by fire just before the Arab conquest in the seventh century. The present-day Patriarch of Alexandria, who visits Jerusalem on occasion, has few faithful in his domain and thus, while a very learned and cultured man, has limited influence.

The fourth Patriarchate, that of Rome, was the only one in the Western Roman Empire. Rome, the capital of the Empire until the fourth century and the site of the martyrdom of Peter and Paul, eventually emerged as the focus of temporal and spiritual power of the Catholic Church.

The fifth Patriarchate is that of Jerusalem. It has the Mother Church and the extensive properties of the Patriarchate, including holdings in the Church of the Holy Sepulchre and on the Mount of Olives, as well as extensive authority in the Church of the Nativity in Bethlehem. The late Patriarch Benedictos was the first to whom Pope Paul VI paid respects during his visit here.

The nature of the relationship was reflected during this visit. While not yet Mayor, I was involved on the Israeli side of the visit in my capacity as Director-General of the Prime Minister's Office.

The Basilica of the Nativity in Bethlehem, built over the manger, is a fourth-century structure of ancient beauty. The major part of this church, ninety per cent, is owned by the Greeks, with the remaining portions belonging to the Armenians, Syrians and Copts, all of whom have chapels and rights in the church. The Roman Catholic Church, in 1882, built the adjoining St Catherine's Church, from which the cave of the manger is also accessible, if less easily.

When the Pope decided to visit the Holy Land, his emissaries approached the Greek Patriarch Benedictos for permission to enter the manger from the ancient basilica. 'Please present an official petition,' was the Patriarch's bidding. The Vatican did so – and the request was denied. One day I asked the Patriarch why he had gone through the rigmarole of asking for the written entreaty if the reply was going to be a negative one. He explained that he made use of the opportunity to ensure that the Pope knew – in writing – who had the authority here.

A pilgrimage to Jerusalem follows very much in the footsteps of Jesus. There are, of course, the usual disputes and controversies among historians and archaeologists as to whether traditional sites are, in fact, historically or archaeologically authentic, but as this strife will undoubtedly last until the Apocalypse, we shall follow the accepted beliefs.

I personally believe that if a place has been revered for centuries, and if people have risked their lives to pay homage there, this is a more valid reason for reverence than archaeological exactitude which rarely can be proven.

The history of Christianity in Jerusalem is a story of layers, a saga of passing civilizations which recurs in each holy place. The earliest and thus lowest stratum is Judeo–Christian, taken over in the fourth century by the Byzantines; much of what was built by the Byzantines was destroyed by the Persians in the seventh century; what was destroyed by the Persians was rebuilt by the Byzantines, then destroyed by an Egyptian ruler in 1009, and rebuilt by the Crusaders in the twelfth century; what was rebuilt by the Cru-

THE MOUNT OF OLIVES

saders either remained, was destroyed or deteriorated in the Moslem and Ottoman periods. Many sites had several reincarnations, originating as churches, becoming mosques, reverting to churches, and then again to mosques and again to churches.

THE MOUNT OF OLIVES

The Christian sites atop the Mount of Olives are a logical point of departure for our visit, though a secular pause should be taken to enjoy the view from the observation point below the Seven Arches (once the Intercontinental) Hotel, where we shall begin our tour. One can reach here by bus, car, taxi or foot (a long walk from town). With the Old City in the foreground, dominated by the Dome of the Rock and the Al Aqsa Mosque, and the new city as the backdrop, the history of millennia is within arm's reach. While visitors tend to flock to watch the sunset from this point, it is at sunrise that the lacquered hues are nearly tangible, but this unfortunately takes place at a rather ungodly hour.

An aside for the courageous – and for those who believe that no photo-journalistic account of a visit to Jerusalem is complete without a camel ride: the opportunity awaits you here. The yelps of the neophytes, as the kneeling camel suddenly gains altitude, are continously audible.

The Jewish cemetery covers a good portion of the Mount of Olives. Legend promises that when the Messiah comes, the bodies of Jews everywhere will roll to the Temple Mount. Those who wanted to make the trip easier came to die in Jerusalem or asked to be brought to Jerusalem for burial. During the Jordanian period, the cemetery was wantonly desecrated. A road was built through it, destroying all the graves in its path. Tombstones were used as building blocks for latrines in legionnaire army camps. Hardly a grave remained intact. The vast repair work which was called for was not a simple task as it entailed research into decades-old ledgers of the city's burial societies.

The Mount of Olives has a wealth of significance for Christian pilgrims. It was here that Jesus stopped when coming from the Galilee, via Jericho and Bethany, for his Passover pilgrimage. And it was on the Mount of Olives that the Ascension took place. The hill itself and the Garden of Gethsemane below are literally dotted with churches.

PATER NOSTER

Walking around the bend from the hotel, the first church one encounters atop the Mount of Olives is that of Pater Noster, also called the Church of Eleona (Greek for 'olivet'). The original church was built by Constantine, the Roman Emperor, who was one of the prime factors in the spread of

The cloisters of Pater Noster.

the religion although he himself converted only before his death.

In AD 325 Constantine had called together the Council of Nicaea, where his mother Helena met Bishop Macarius, the delegate from Jerusalem (still known as Aelia Capitolina). Macarius reported to her on the precarious state of the sites 'hallowed by the steps of Jesus' and enlisted her help. Following Helena's visit in 326, Jerusalem took on renewed importance for the Christian world. Together with Macarius, she had located and identified the sites connected with Jesus's life by oral tradition and erected shrines to mark them.

The cave on this site is believed to be where Jesus 'revealed to his disciples inscrutable myster-

ies'. In 1870 it was discovered by the Princess de la Tour d'Auvergne, who built a cloister here. During World War I, Turkish soldiers used the cave as a kitchen, which caused the collapse of the cave's ceiling. What is left can be seen in the crypts.

In 1920, the Basilica of the Sacred Heart was begun by the French Eleona Society in collaboration with Pope Benedict XV and the existing cloister was destroyed so that the church could be built. But the church was never completed as the funds available were soon depleted; the idea had not found much favour with the Catholics.

Most distinctive about Pater Noster are the seventy translations of The Lord's Prayer, all set in beautiful Armenian tiles. One can read it in Swahili or Korean, Burmese or Portuguese. There is even a Braille edition.

The nuns at Pater Noster are of the Carmelite Order. While a few of the sisters are the mediators with the outside world, the majority are completely cloistered and kept secluded behind gates when there are visitors.

CHURCH OF THE ASCENSION

The next sanctuary along the main road is the Church of the Ascension, now in Moslem hands. It is revered as the site from which Jesus ascended to heaven. The original church was built in the fourth century by a pious Roman lady, Pomenia. The building was round, open to the sky and called Imbomon, which is Greek for 'on the hill'. It was abandoned during the Arab period, but rebuilt by the Crusaders on the Byzantine remains as the present octagonal structure. The Mamelukes were not inherently destructive so did not harm the church, but merely closed it.

Several Christian denominations have their designated altars in the church area. The rock inside carries an imprint which is said to be the footstep of Jesus.

It is not only archaeologists and historians who bicker over the actual location of the holy sites, but the Churches as well. Thus the Russian Orthodox Monastery and the Greek Orthodox Church in the nearby vicinity make their conflicting claims to the site of the Ascension.

Again we confront the seemingly unavoidable intertwining of politics and religion and the absurdities created. In 1948, Russia was the second country, following the United States, to recognize the State of Israel. The Israeli Government acknowledged the Moscow-based Russian Church (the 'Red Church') holdings throughout the country, in the Russian Compound and in the Ein Karem quarter of Jerusalem, in Capernaum on the Sea of Galilee, etc. And so this relationship continues, despite the severing of relations by the Soviet Union in 1967.

The Jordanians, on the other hand, did not have relations with the Soviet Union and accepted the authority of the Synod of the Russian Bishops in Exile (the 'White Russians'), headquartered in New York City.

I had occasion to visit the New York centre of the Russian Bishops.

Towards the end of the nineteenth century, the Russian Church had accumulated a significant collection of archaeology, comprised of antiquities uncovered during the construction of the Church buildings throughout the country. It was Professor Sukenik, the eminent archaeologist father of the eminent archaeologist Professor Yigael Yadin, who discovered the Uzziah Stone in a dusty corner of the church. Uzziah, the King of Judah, had not been buried in the royal graveyard of the House of David because he was a leper. The Uzziah stone marked the spot where his bones were reinterred after being removed from their initial resting-place. In clear Hebrew lettering the inscription reads: 'Hither were brought the bones of Uzziah King of Judah and do not open.'

We learned that the Uzziah Stone was up for sale in New York. In 1968, I called on the head of the Synod, Metropolitan Filaret, who bore a disconcerting resemblance to all depictions I had seen of Rasputin. He had reached the United States as a refugee after the Russian Revolution, but, half a century later, he had not yet acquired – or required – a word of English.

After protracted negotiations, the Israel Museum purchased the stone, the only original headstone of the tomb of a Jewish king. Beyond the labyrinthine negotiations with the Russians, there was internecine strife within the museum: though the cost was covered by special donations obtained for this purpose alone, there were objections to the outlay of $150,000 – then considered exorbitant – and loud murmurings about our purchasing a stolen antiquity.

I may not be as much of a purist as those who object to such purchases but merely imagining the Uzziah Stone turning up at auction in New York, or London, to be purchased as a backyard ornament, convinces me that there are times when purism can be deterimental to our heritage.

The last of the Russian nuns and monks who reached Jerusalem immediately after the Russian Revolution was Mother Tamara, the Abbess of the Russian Convent on the Mount of Olives, who was a blood Romanov. Shortly before her death at the age of ninety, she asked me for a personal favour: could I help her get a telephone installed? At that time, one waited years for a telephone and thus her request for my personal intervention. I was happy to help, although the question intrigued me: after all these years, whom did she want to call?

The Church of the Ascension.

GARDEN OF GETHSEMANE

The descent to the Garden of Gethsemane is a narrow passage across the road and back a little. As one walks into the Garden of Gethsemane, it takes little effort to abandon the anxieties and vexations of everyday life. Taking its name from the Hebrew, Gat Shemanim (Oil Press), the Garden of Gethsemane is replete with the olive trees its name implies. It is said that Jesus came here with his disciples following the Last Supper.

Because of the steep slope of the hill, the climb was prohibitive for the less-than-fit pilgrims. We thus helped build a narrow road which would enable pilgrims motorized access to Dominus Flevit and the Church of Mary Magdalene below it.

The black dome with the four tear-ampullae is the Chapel of Dominus Flevit, meaning the Lord Wept. It was here that Jesus wept and foresaw the destruction of Jerusalem. The present edifice was built in 1955 by the architect Antonio Barluzzi,

The Garden of Gethsemane.

atop the ruins of an ancient church, attested to by the Byzantine mosaic floor and other remains. The view of the Old City through the church windows makes a visitor rue having to leave.

One cannot mistake the origin of the onion-shaped, golden domes of the White Russian Church of Mary Magdalene, built in 1888 by Czar Alexander III in his mother's memory. It might have been trans-shipped from Kiev, although one night I drove an American family around the Old City walls, to see 'Jerusalem by night', and the comment from a seven-year-old in the back seat was: 'Look, it's Walt Disney's Fantasyland. . . .' The intermingling of the past and present is often of the most bizarre nature.

A sister of the last Czar of Russia, Elisabeth Feodorovna Romanov, founded the Imperial Orthodox Society of Palestine together with her husband, the Grand Duke Sergei. Although she had had a chance to escape Russia during the Revolution, she chose to stay and, as with much of the nobility, met a violent death at the hands of the Bolsheviks. She had often expessed her desire to be buried in Jerusalem and her sister Tamara carried out this wish, bringing her from Moscow to Jerusalem via China aboard a British warship, not exactly the most direct route.

Elisabeth's niece, Princess Alice of Greece – the mother of Prince Philip, Duke of Edinburgh – died in 1969 at the age of eighty-four. Her death-bed wish was to be buried beside her aunt, a seemingly uncomplicated request. But again not a simple story. The Princess had become a Greek Orthodox nun after the death of her husband, Prince Andrew of Greece, while St Mary Magdalene is Russian Orthodox. Nineteen years of negotiations ultimately brought about the fulfilment of this wish. In 1988, Princess Alice's body was reinterred at St Mary Magdalene. A Greek Orthodox memorial service at Viri Galilei, the nearby residence of the Greek Patriarch Diodoros I, was followed by a Russian Orthodox ceremony led by Archimandrite Alexis.

Beyond our natural desire to fulfil Princess Alice's dying wish, we had learned that during the Holocaust she had helped save the lives of many Greek Jews. It is perhaps an appropriate place to note that the Greek Orthodox Church was exceptional in its behaviour towards the Jews during the Holocaust wherever it had prominence in Europe.

Just a few steps away is the Church of All Nations, which acquired its name because twelve nations contributed towards its construction. Its distinctive façade bears a beautiful mosaic, which, sparkling as the day's light changes, depicts Jesus

A view of the Dome of the Rock and the Old City from the Dominus Flevit church.

The Mount of Olives, with the Church of all Nations in the foreground and the Mary Magdalene church and the Garden of Gethsemane behind.

assuming the pains of suffering of mankind. As elsewhere, there was a Byzantine church on this site, followed by a larger Crusader church. The present church, built in 1934 also by Antonio Barluzzi, follows the lines of its Byzantine ancestor.

A visitor to the church, also known as the Church of Gethsemane, would have no inkling as to the havoc it caused. When the Catholic Church proposed this building to Sir Ronald Storrs in 1919, he objected vehemently. He felt that the Garden of Gethsemane should be left untouched and, in fact, announced that this church would be built over his dead body. But he was unable to withstand the pressures of Rome – and the church was built. I can well commiserate with the battles he had to fight.

In the church courtyard, there were four olive trees proved scientifically to be over 2,000 years old. Three trees are healthy and still bear fruit. One tree, which had become diseased during the Jordanian period, was cut down, thus enabling experts to count its rings and attest to its venerable age. The tree also gave our meteorologists valuable insight into the climate over 2,000 years, affording comparisons of the wet seasons and the dry ones. It takes four men with outstretched hands to encircle one of these trees, which are the only witnesses of what transpired here.

One of the sweetest, most colourful personalities to roam the streets of Jerusalem was the Superior of this church, José Montalverne. Of mixed Portuguese and English blood, and a descendant of the Lancasters, he had begun his adult life as a nuclear physicist before becoming a priest. He served the church for fifty years before dying peacefully in his sleep in 1987. He was a weekly visitor to my office, coming regularly to report on new testimony to his conviction that Solomon's Temple did not stand where purported but, in fact, further north. He based himself on the Scriptures, on archaeological digs in Turkish times and on any bits of proof he could unearth.

He had such devotion not only to his church but to the people of Jerusalem that we resolved to confer on him the honour of Yakir Yerushalayim, Worthy of Jerusalem. He asked permision of his immediate superior, as is customary, but this was denied – on political grounds. He approached the Custos, the highest Franciscan official, but the Custos did not want to undermine the authority of Father Montalverne's immediate superior. Thus we had to content ourselves with a private ceremony in his honour rather than the public acclaim we had envisaged.

The adjacent Grotto of Gethsemane is by tradition the site on which Jesus was arrested, although for a period in the Middle Ages it was thought that it was the site of his agony. Within this grotto, one can easily traverse centuries: the water cistern is before the Christian era, the mosaics probably date from the fourth or fifth centuries, the wall paintings are Crusader.

The last site to complete the visit to Gethsemane is the Tomb of Mary, where it is believed that Mary, the mother of Jesus, was buried.

Not a great deal is known about the early Judeo–Christian community in Jerusalem; it is only in the Acts of the Apostles that there is a bare smattering of information. It is thought that after Jesus died, the Christian community was located on Mount Zion. The community moved beyond the Jordan before the Great Rebellion against the Romans, but some subsequently returned to

Palm Sunday procession of pilgrims entering the Lions' Gate.

Mount Zion. Mary is believed to have been staying with the Apostle John and her relatives on Mount Zion when she died around the middle of the first century. Christians, believing Mary was assumed into heaven, celebrate this event as the Feast of the Assumption. The Benedictine monks of the Dormition Abbey (see p. 44) on Mount Zion have a solemn celebration on 15 August, while the Greek Orthodox take part in an ancient processional rite to the Tomb of Mary thirteen days later (15 August in the Julian calendar). On 13 August there is an early morning procession of women, as the Tomb of Mary is venerated by women of all denominations, even Moslem.

Again we find Byzantine foundations while the structure itself is Crusader. Tradition has it that it is not only Mary who is buried here, but also her parents, Joachim and Anne, perhaps also her husband Joseph, as well as the Crusader Queen Melisanda.

The main custodians of the church are the Greek Orthodox, although the Armenians and the Copts have altars as well. The central area is used by all; the right side, leading to the tomb, also has a Moslem mihrab, and belongs to the Greeks; the prayer niche is Armenian, but they allow the Syrian Orthodox to use it; the Armenians have the rights on the left side, but they allow the Copts to pray here. It is all rather complex!

In years of normal or above-normal rainfall, the church was frequently in danger of being flooded to half its height. We thus installed modern drainage and it is now fully weather-proof. One can only wonder how it survived for so long.

The most compelling sight is the annual Palm Sunday procession of the Latins. Starting their descent from the Mount of Olives – although there are those who begin their pilgrimage in Bethany and ascend through Bethphage – tens of thousands of pilgrims, all bearing palm fronds, wind their way through the Garden of Gethsemane towards the Lions' Gate (St Stephen's Gate) and the court of St Anne's Church at Bethesda (see p. 67).

We shall follow in their footsteps. Leaving the Tomb of Mary, we turn right and follow the main road about 50 metres up the hill, crossing the road to the street leading to the Lions' Gate and the Via Dolorosa.

6
THE VIA DOLOROSA AND THE CHURCH OF THE HOLY SEPULCHRE

This walk can be a continuation of the previous one or a self-contained entity. In either case, we begin at the Lions' Gate. The figures of lions carved in the wall gave the gate its Hebrew name and one of its English names.

It was through this gate that Israeli soldiers entered the Old City following the Jordanian attack on West Jerusalem in 1967. We had given our soldiers an exacting task: to fight where they had to fight, to defend themselves where need be, but to take utmost care that no damage was incurred to the holy places. Similar imperatives guided the decision to fight hand-to-hand rather than to shell the Old City or bomb it from the air. It was not a decision taken lightly, since it exposed our soldiers to far greater dangers.

We lost many boys here, some of whose lives might have been saved had we used aerial bombardment or artillery. When the decision was taken to eschew such methods, we had a clear understanding of our responsibility to civilization and to our ties with other religions. Every decision we take is imbued with the sense of history, which is our watchdog.

I wonder whether this decision would be made so readily today. We had not anticipated the sight which awaited us when we entered the Haram al Sharif, the Temple Mount enclosure: hundreds of boxes of ammunition in the buildings adjacent to the mosques. What blatant disregard of the dangers and what callous use of a holy place.

The only damage to religious places was one bullet which hit a tile in the Dome of the Rock, some damage to St Anne's, and the lead roof of the Dormition Abbey, which had melted completely. The Municipality raised funds to pay for this damage, as well as to repair the 900 apartments in West Jerusalem damaged by Jordanian shelling. We had wanted to repair St Anne's but the French Government, which is the owner, insisted on providing the funds.

The heavy, wooden, metal-covered portals of Lions' Gate, knocked ajar by an Israel Defence Forces half-track during the 1967 break-in, were in a sorry state and the Jerusalem Foundation undertook their restoration, rebuilding them anew. Together with the Waqf, we planted a garden inside the gate adjoining the inner gate – Bab as

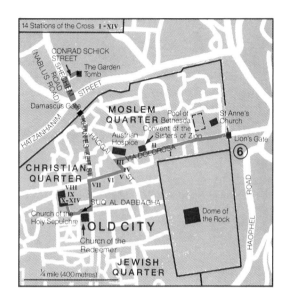

Asbat, Gate of the Tribes – which leads to the Temple Mount.

The Via Dolorosa which greeted us in 1967 was in a sorry state. Sewage flowed freely in the street and even the incense used in processions was not sufficient to mask the stench. It was one of the first projects we undertook, to ensure a respectful experience for the pilgrims who travelled vast distances to reach this site. Here, too, we uncovered Roman paving stones and we left these exposed in the new pavement we laid.

The first holy site we encounter inside the Lions' Gate is St Anne's Church. The saga is by now familiar. In the fifth century, the Empress Eudocia, expelled from Byzantium, came to Jerusalem and built the Church of St Stephen, remains of which have been found north of Damascus Gate. It is also thought that she built the original church of 'St Mary's at the Sheep's Pool' (Probatica or Bethesda). St Anne, the mother of Mary, is said to have lived here, and Mary may have been born on this site.

The building was destroyed by the Persians and eventually rebuilt by the Crusaders. The church we see today was built in 1140 and though simple and inornate, rare for a Roman Catholic church, it is a most striking example of Crusader architecture. Of course, it did not pass the eight centuries

since its construction uneventfully. In 1192, it was consecrated as a Moslem school by Saladin and was only returned to the Christian community in the nineteenth century, once again a gift to the French in gratitude for their participation in the Crimean War on the side of Moslem Turkey against Christian Russia.

The adjacent Pool of Bethesda is where Jesus is said to have healed the sick, and, for several centuries, Christians came to 'take the cure' in these waters.

St Anne's and the Pool of Bethesda are looked after by the White Fathers, an order established in the nineteenth century for the Christian missions in Africa and sent here to strengthen French influence in the Levant.

THE VIA DOLOROSA

The Via Dolorosa, the Way of the Cross, is for Christians a memorial to the passion of Jesus. Pilgrims speaking a Babel of languages follow the traditional path of Jesus along the Stations of the Cross. Every Friday, as they have done since the fourteenth century, the Franciscans lead a procession of pilgrims carrying a large wooden cross, over paving stones from the time of Jesus which we raised to the present street level.

Of the fourteen stations, most are in the bustling market-place, almost indistinguishable from the wholly secular streets and alleys of the Old City. I once walked on the Via Dolorosa behind two Christian tourists, one of whom was saying to the other with excitement and fervour: 'Tomorrow we will be going to the Via Dolorosa.' I did not have the heart to set them straight.

In order to enable pilgrims to identify the Stations more easily, we changed the pavement around many of them into a circular, brick-shaped pattern, although one still has to make a concerted effort to distinguish them.

Station I, where Jesus was brought before Pontius Pilate, is in the courtyard of the Omariyah Boys' School. There is more dissension than usual amongst scholars as to whether the Antonia Fortress, built here by Herod the Great and named in honour of Mark Antony, is indeed the Praetorium, where Jesus was tried before Pilate.

Station II, where Jesus took up the cross, is the Convent of the Flagellation and the Convent of the Sisters of Zion. The prominent arch overhead is the Ecce Homo Arch, where tradition has it that Pontius Pilate presented Jesus to the people, declaring 'Ecce Homo', 'Behold the Man'. There is a consensus by historians that this was actually a triumphal arch built by Hadrian when he ultimately vanquished the last Jewish Revolt of Bar

Kochba in AD 135. The continuation of this arch is behind the altar in the Convent of the Sisters of Zion, called the Basilica of Ecce Homo.

The convent is a treasure of archaeological/religious finds. The Lithostrotos is a Roman pavement originally postulated as the courtyard of the Praetorium. The Roman gaming boards, carved in the pavement, helped alleviate the ennui of soldiering. The pool, called the Struthion (Greek for sparrow), is Herodian, formed by its construction atop early Hasmonean canals, and is the farthest point of the Western Wall tunnel (see p. 21). When Warren discovered the access to the tunnel, the convent nuns realized this access could be two-directional and they constructed a protective wall.

We pass the Austrian Hospice, located at the corner of Haggai Street and the Via Dolorosa (a point at which the walker has to turn left for a quarter of a block and then continue right). Built by the Austrian Church in 1856 as a pilgrims' hostel – the Emperor Franz Joseph stayed here in 1869, when he came for the inauguration of the Suez Canal – the hospice was confiscated by the British in World War II as enemy property and turned into a hospital. The Jordanians continued to use it as such.

On several occasions, the Austrian Church had entreated the Jordanian Government to return the building. In 1966, the Jordanians informed the Austrians that the building would be returned upon the completion of a new hospital, but the Six Day War intervened. The use of the hospice as a hospital continued, even though the Austrian Church and succeeding Austrian Ambassadors have repeatedly appealed in this matter both to our Ministry of Health and to City Hall. We could not, however, sanction the return of the building as long as proper treatment of the indigent residents of the Old City, who used this hospital, was not assured.

There was extensive local opposition to the closing of the hospital, but the Ministry of Health finally did so on professional grounds. Equipment was outdated and the building was deteriorating and unsuited for use as a hospital. Even mass sums of money could not change this, since the owners objected to any major structural alterations. Facilities elsewhere were finally arranged, including medical care at the Sheikh Jarrah Health Centre and hospitalization at the city's other hospitals, both Jewish and Arab. A first-aid station will operate at the hospice building, but the rest of the structure has been returned to the Austrians.

Since we have taken a secular break in our walk, I might note two secular points of interest. While I have not been specifying either places to eat or places to shop, these two points have taken on the aura of Jerusalem's historic sites – though of recent vintage.

The beginning of the Via Dolorosa, spanned (in the foreground) by the Ecce Homo arch.

The first, before continuing up the Via Dolorosa, is Abu Shukery. While today it is a full-menu restaurant, it attained local fame for the best humus (chick-pea paste) in town. Indeed, the original eatery, at a near-by location, consisted of two tables and there was no printed menu, for the choice was between humus and humus. The entrance was crowded with lines of eager and hungry clients, often carrying bowls from home for 'take-out' portions, resembling Buddhist monks awaiting gifts of rice.

The second, opposite Stations V and VI, is Jerusalem Pottery, the Armenian tile makers, the Karakashian brothers, who practise an age-old craft of their community. Immediately after the city's reunification, we commissioned them to prepare street signs, in Hebrew, English and Arabic, for the Old City, but their true fame is for reasonably priced gifts and their gentility.

The left turn at the Austrian Hospice brings us to Station III, which marks where Jesus fell for the first time as shown on the relief. The chapel once belonged to the Polish Catholic Church. The site was purchased in the nineteenth century by the Armenian Catholic Church, a small denomination created, as were others, by proselytization between the various Churches, in this case the

Armenians and the Catholics. This had once served as the entrance to a Turkish bath in use until the eighteenth century.

Station IV, where Mary stood as Jesus passed, is next to the Armenian church, Our Lady of the Spasm. In the courtyard of the church, which is also the seat of the bishop, is a beautiful sixth-century mosaic of Roman sandals. Legend has it that they are the sandals of St Peter. Here again we walk for a short stretch on paving stones dating from 100 BC to AD 100, which are easily identifiable.

We now make a right turn to the fifth Station, where the Roman soldiers ordered Simon of Cyrene to help Jesus carry the cross.

At Station VI, marked by the Church of the Holy Face and Saint Veronica of the Greek Catholic Patriarchate, Veronica wiped Jesus's face with her handkerchief.

Station VII, a Franciscan chapel at the top of the street, marks the spot where Jesus fell for the second time.

We will now be turning left into Khan es-Zeit Street, but, beforehand, a few steps straight up will bring us to Station VIII. Here Jesus warned the daughters of Jerusalem of impending doom. The Station is marked by a Latin cross and an engraving in Greek, NIKA, which signifies 'Jesus Christ is Victorious'.

Walking along Khan es-Zeit Street, we reach a wide stone staircase on our right. At the very bot-

Easter pilgrims carry a large wooden cross along the Via Dolorosa, following the traditional path of Jesus.

tom is the Zalatimo sweet shop. Besides the very interesting sweet pancake it serves, the shop is known for having in the back room the remains of the original entrance to the Church of the Holy Sepulchre. And so, more often than is to the shop-keeper's liking, tourists tramp through to see these remains.

Walking up the steps to what is actually the roof of the Church of the Holy Sepulchre, we reach the Coptic Convent, the ninth Station, the last outside the church, where Jesus fell for the third time.

We walk back down the steps and continue a few steps until we see a sign in front of us, Suq al Attarim. We turn right on Suq al Dabbagha and pass the Russian Orthodox St Alexander's Chapel, which can be visited. Walking straight we also pass, on our left, the Lutheran Church of the Redeemer. Those who do not mind climbing the many steps can reach the bell tower at certain hours. This church also has beautiful concerts throughout the year.

CHURCH OF THE HOLY SEPULCHRE

Straight ahead, on our original path, is a narrow, inconsequential doorway. Yet it is through this that we reach the Church of the Holy Sepulchre, the last stop on our walk. Despite its magnitude, it is indeed almost hidden in the alleyways of the Old City.

Again we meet the familiar chronology of events. The first structure on this site was the Temple of Venus built by Hadrian; it is assumed that he chose this site so as to obliterate all associations with Jesus. The Emperor Constantine destroyed Hadrian's Temple in the fourth century to enable his mother Helena to build a church here, the Basilica of Anastasis, the Greek word for resurrection. There is a legend which tells that Helena found the cross and the torturing instruments with the help of Bishop Macarius and the city elders.

The Church was destroyed by the Persians in 614, but restored a few years later, in 628, by Abbot Modestus. The Omayyads, who conquered in 638, allowed it to remain standing, but it was again destroyed, in 1009, by Caliph al Hakim of Egypt (whose moniker was 'the Mad') – only to be rebuilt in 1048 by Emperor Constantine Monomachus during a brief period under Byzantine protection. In 1144, the Crusaders rebuilt the entire shrine, naming it the Church of the Holy Sepulchre. Godfrey of Bouillon, who led the first Crusade in 1099, was titled the Defender of the Holy Sepulchre. While the dome has been rebuilt several times, most recently in the nineteenth century, the main edifice remains from Crusader times.

When the city was conquered by Omar in 638, he did not pray in the church, for he did not want

Nuns at the Third Station of the Cross on the Via Dolorosa. This marks the place where Jesus fell for the first time.

to give his followers a pretext to convert it into a mosque. Apparently there was a Moslem prayer hall built near the original church entrance (at Zalatimo's sweet shop), but it was only later that a mosque was built nearby. It was several metres higher than the church as dictated by the Koran so as to prove, even physically, the superiority of Islam over all religions, including the monotheistic ones.

The last five Stations of the Cross are within the Holy Sepulchre compound. The name Golgotha, the site of the crucifixion, derives from the Aramaic word for skull, reflecting the skull-shape of the site.

Station X, a climb up a steep staircase, is where Jesus was stripped of his garments. The Stone of Golgotha (in Latin, Calvary) was encased in marble for centuries and thus hardly visible, but the glass encasement recently installed by the Greeks allows the pilgrim a more intimate encounter.

The domes of the Church of the Holy Sepulchre rising above the Christian Quarter of the Old City.

At Station XI, Jesus was nailed to the cross. Station XII, a Greek chapel, was the place of the crucifixion. Station XIII indicates where Jesus was removed from the cross. The fourteenth and last Station is the Holy Sepulchre in the centre of the church, an edicule containing a marble-covered tomb which extends unmarbled into the adjacent Coptic chapel.

One afternoon, shortly after the Six Day War, I had a call from the eminent economist/diplomat/author, John Kenneth Galbraith, whom I had met on several occasions both in Jerusalem and in the United States. He had just arrived – indeed, he was calling from the airport – had a few hours between planes and wanted very much to see the Old City. During our quick tour, using the last hours of sunlight, we stopped at the Church of the Holy Sepulchre. I took him to the crypt where a young man, bowing deeply over the sarcophagus, was immersed in devout prayer. The young man lifted his head just as Ken, who is very tall and could hardly stand erect in the crypt, entered. 'Jesus Christ, it's Professor Galbraith.' There could have been no more appropriate exclamation.

One can only do vast injustice by attempting to relate the story of the church in a few paragraphs. This brief outline can but give an inkling of its maze of chapels. It can give but a hint of the devastation wrought over the centuries by fire, by earthquake and by wanton human destruction. Even today, the Christian spirit is sometimes

tion work was finally completed. Of course, repairs to a building as old as this and as large can never entirely be completed and restoration in one corner or another is always under way.

The church is held by six denominations – the Greek Orthodox, Armenians and Catholics are the main shareholders, the Copts, Ethiopians and Syrians, the lesser ones. Each tile and each pillar is under carefully allotted ownership. Who cleans what door handle takes on crucial significance since cleaning represents ownership. Clerics have been killed in such disputes.

A few years ago, the *Wall Street Journal* wrote an updated report on the church, adding that the tenth commandment notwithstanding, 'there's a lot of coveting of thy neighbor's chunk of church'.

The most serious discord at present is between the Ethiopians and the Copts, a legacy of three centuries of dissension, though essentially the

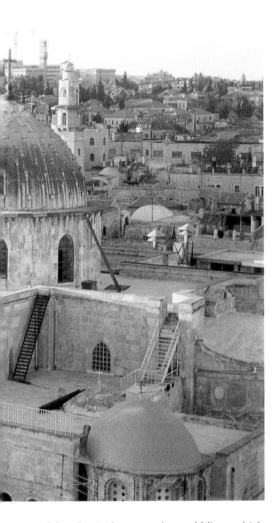

marred by the jealousy and squabbling which erupt from time to time. It is not only the past history of the church which tells of the frailties of human nature; a report of current events is equal witness to these foibles.

The church was severely damaged by an earthquake in 1927, but the church factions could not agree on the nature of the repairs. Architects representing the Greeks, the Armenians and the Catholics bickered interminably. The policy of the British and later the Jordanians was to divide-and-rule, which only served to exacerbate the situation. Thus in 1967, forty years after the earthquake, we found the scaffolding still in place with little progress made.

With infinite patience and, at the same time, concerted non-interference, we managed to encourage a relative consensus and the restora-

Celebrating Mass in the Church of the Holy Sepulchre.

two churches share the same dogma. There are two chapels which lead from the parvis (the entrance courtyard) to the roof, and both the Copts and the Ethiopians claim ownership of the chapels and the roof. The matter was brought to the British Mandate courts, which left it to be 'settled by King in Council', an indication that they could reach no judicial solution.

During the Jordanian period, King Hussein first decided for the Ethiopians but, following the intervention of President Nasser on behalf of the Egyptian Copts, then changed his mind. Thus when we arrived on the scene in 1967, the Copts were in possession. As we at the time had good relations with the Ethiopians and were nominally at war with the Egyptians, our tendency was to support the Ethiopians. During Easter 1970, while the Copts were at prayer, the Ethiopians sought a rather unorthodox solution and simply changed the locks, thereby gaining possession. The police were called in and the parties again had their day in court, this time an Israeli one. The conclusion after endless deliberations was along the lines of the British decision: it is impossible to decide this case on the law, only politically.

It was then given to a special sub-committee of the Israeli Government's Ministerial Committee for Jerusalem. The committee members tried to devise a compromise. They toured the area again and again. After each tour, they met to review the details of the case, again and again. In despair, they endeavoured to enlist the help of the Patriarchs of the three major Churches, but none would intervene. A retired judge has now been appointed to act as arbitrator. But, naturally, he has to review the case from the very beginning. Perhaps it is, indeed, a task for the Messiah.

Some years ago, the Armenians asked for the agreement of the other Churches to reopen a window which had been sealed for centuries in the Chapel of Saint Helena. Lo and behold, behind this opening there was a series of connecting rooms, which the Armenian Archbishop Kapikian cleared. The last room led to a quarry under the Armenian chapel, possibly the oldest quarry in Jerusalem. On one of the walls, one can see a drawing of a sailing ship, a Roman sea-going vessel of the second or third century, with the inscription '*Domine Ivimus*' ('We went, O Lord'), a memento of pilgrimage of early Christians. In fact, throughout the church, one can see crosses carved into the walls by pilgrims over centuries.

If relative peace is kept in the corridors, it is a result of the general acceptance of the 'Status Quo', fixed by the Ottoman Sultan, Abdul Mejid, in 1852. It set all the ownership rights in the church and the details of church ceremonies. Having been accepted at the time by the Churches and by all the European powers, it is still respected today.

It was true Solomonic wisdom which allotted the keys to the main door of the church to the care of Moslems. The Nusseibeh family, for generations, has faithfully fulfilled its task of guarding them impartially and, each day, opening and closing the church doors.

The unceasing competition among the Churches does complicate life for us. In 1967, just days after the Six Day War, Prime Minister Levi Eshkol, heading a National Unity Government, convened all the religious leaders in Jerusalem, Christian and Moslem alike, and reassured them that we would respect and preserve all their rights. We have kept this promise religiously, surely the correct term in this connection. We follow a policy of non-interference, treating the Christian community, all the churches, monasteries, convents and religious institutions as extraterritorial embassies.

What is lacking is a general agreement with the Churches, possibly similar to the concordat between the Vatican and Italy. But the Catholics regard themselves as the representatives of world Christianity with the backing of 800 million Catholics. The Greeks and the Armenians feel that seniority has more consequence than mere numbers and would never allow the Catholics to represent their interests. Thus the possibility of any unified representation is almost nil.

Another major hurdle preventing any agreement is the basic reluctance of the Churches to recognize Israel's rights in Jerusalem. It is particularly complicated when one is dealing with petty issues. For example, the Churches are exempt from paying the high customs levies on items imported from abroad. But as the law requires this payment – even hospitals pay customs duties – it is the Ministry of Religious Affairs which covers the payment for the Churches with an allocation received from the Treasury, a draconian bureaucratic procedure. But if the Treasury does not transfer the funds, the Ministry does not pay the duty and the customs does not release the items, which then sit and sit and sit (meanwhile accumulating port fees!). It is only one instance of the day-to-day problems we face, because even matters not under municipal jurisdiction are laid at our feet since we are easily accessible. The Church dignitaries know they have an open line to City Hall.

While it is often Church problems which reach my desk, I am also privileged to partake in the religious festivities throughout the year. There are traditions of centuries; there are solemn and joyful ceremonies.

The entrance to the shrine, or edicule, containing the Holy Sepulchre – the fourteenth Station of the Cross – lies at the centre of the church.

*Greek Orthodox Holy Week celebrations in the
courtyard of the Church of the Holy Sepulchre.*

The tradition of my attendance at the various
religious ceremonies began in 1967 and I probably
attend more Christian services than the most fervent Christian. I attend three Christmas Midnight Masses in Bethlehem according to the
Gregorian, Julian and Armenian calendars (the
Western on 25 December, the Orthodox on 6
January, and the Armenian on 18 January). I
represent the Government of Israel and the Municipality of Jerusalem, following a tradition
begun by the British and continued by the Jordanians. Mayor Freij of Bethlehem, who is Greek
Orthodox, also attends the masses of the Catholics and the Armenians in his official rather than
religious capacity.

I attend the Greek and Armenian feet-washing
and sometimes that of the Assyrians and the Ethiopians, and the Greek Holy Fire ceremony on
Easter Saturday. I also celebrate Easter at the Jerusalem headquarters of the Synod of Russian Bishops in Exile, a church unfortunately not open to
the public. Located near the Church of the Holy
Sepulchre, it has a rather unimposing exterior,
but a step inside and one encounters another

world in another era. There are numerous chapels
and prayer halls interlaced with Byzantine remnants and decorated with large portraits of the
czar and czarina. Old babushkas offer holiday
cakes and the clergy distributes hand-painted
Easter eggs, the forerunners of Fabergé. (Following a visit to Jerusalem by Malcolm Forbes, the
publisher of the well-known financial periodical
and the owner of the foremost collection of
Fabergé eggs, I began the practice of sending him
one of these original Easter eggs each year, but
none has as yet appeared in the collection.)

One of the most impressive ceremonies is the
feet-washing of the Greek Orthodox Church,
which takes place in the open square before the
Church of the Holy Sepulchre on Maundy Thursday, before Easter. As Jesus washed the feet of his
disciples, so does the venerable Patriarch bend on
his knees and wash the feet of twelve priests or
seminarians.

The Orthodox Churches in Greece, Romania,
Bulgaria and Russia have only Metropolitans, not
Patriarchs. Thus, the ceremony under the aegis of
the Greek Orthodox Patriarch of Jerusalem brings
adherents from these countries as well as countries as distant as Australia and the Americas.

The main influx of pilgrims for this ceremony
are the thousands from Cyprus and Greece. Many

are elderly – often resembling the black-garbed, keening women in *Zorba the Greek* – who their entire lives have saved their liras and drachmas to reach the Holy Land for this ceremony. They come on the decks of ships, carrying with them the food they will need for the few days of their stay. On the appointed day, they start filling the courtyard long before dawn, to ensure a place to stand, although there is no doubt that the number of pilgrims per square metre defies all laws of physics. I always have a feeling of guilt at the ease with which I arrive at 7.30 a.m. and sit comfortably on the terrace of a building overlooking the courtyard. But a Greek archbishop once explained to me that the devout are not interested in comfort but in the passion of the experience.

A Dominican professor at the Ecole Biblique in Jerusalem, Jerome Murphy-O'Connor, wrote in the spring of 1987 in *Eretz* magazine: 'For some an architectural monstrosity, for others a spiritual abomination, the Church of the Holy Sepulchre has always excited varied reactions. The scars of its chequered history are all too obvious. In the last analysis, however, they do not detract from its dignity. They are, rather, the wrinkles on a once beautiful face that has lived through interesting times. The Holy Sepulchre can be read as a stone book inscribed with the history of the Christian church in Jerusalem.

'But such an abstract approach misses the real point. For every mailed knight or supercilious tourist who visited, there were thousands of pilgrims who made their way to the church in simple piety at the risk of their lives. The Church of the Holy Sepulchre is a lodestone of courage and faith and few structures can claim as much.'

THE GARDEN TOMB
While the official tour ends at the Church of the Holy Sepulchre, some walkers might be interested in a detour to the Garden Tomb, also known as Gordon's Calvary, a site holy to Protestant denominations. It is about a ten-minute walk away, just across the main road outside Damascus Gate on Conrad Schick Street.

The Protestants in Jerusalem are the johnny-come-latelys. The first Protestant mission reached Jerusalem just 150 years ago, a joint Prussian –British mission under a bishop who was a converted Jew. The joint bishopric lasted from 1840 to 1887. Bishop Gobat led the community for thirty-three years, during which time he built a school for boys on Mount Zion. Until this very day, classes are taught there. A portion of the building is leased to an American biblical institute, which brings hundreds of young students to Jerusalem each year.

In Germany, Jerusalem was a focus of extensive scientific and archeological study. With this impetus, and under the leadership of King Friedrich Wilhelm IV of Prussia, various churches and church buildings were designed but were eventually built under Kaiser Wilhelm II, his grandson. These churches still dot the Jerusalem landscape, with Augusta Victoria on Mount Scopus, the Dormition Abbey on Mount Zion and the Church of the Redeemer in the Old City.

A British general, Charles Gordon, who ultimately met his death by beheading as a prisoner of the Mahdi in Khartoum, had been a pilgrim to Jerusalem. Like some, mostly Protestant, archaeologists, he had his doubts about the traditional site of the crucifixion. These sceptics were convinced that no crucifixion would have taken place within the city walls, and the contemporary city walls, as then conceived, encompass the church. He found a hillock outside Damascus Gate shaped like a skull and uncovered tombs presumed to date from the time of Jesus. A beautiful garden was created on that hill and is visited by tens of thousands of Protestants each year.

The postscript to the story is that our archaeologists studied these graves and date them from the fifth century BC, five centuries too early.

The serenity of this gentle garden is shattered by the racket of the Arab Central Bus Station at the foot of the hill. We built a subsidiary bus station some distance away to help alleviate this disturbance, but it is only partially successful. Elaborate plans exist to move the main depot and ensure the tranquillity of the Garden Tomb, a project which has particularly intrigued American evangelists, foremost among them Jimmy and Tammy Bakker. They had promised financial help, but, with their fall from grace (and from funds), the project has been put on hold.

THE MORMON CENTRE
The latest Church to reach Jerusalem is the Church of the Latter Day Saints, the Mormon Church, although in fact their roots in the city are also nearly 150 years old. In 1842, Orson Hyde, the first Mormon missionary, reached the Holy Land and, standing on the Mount of Olives, prophesied the return of the Jewish people to Jerusalem. His prayer became part of the Mormon liturgy.

In 1968, Mormon study groups began regular visits, locating their seminars at the Ramat Rachel kibbutz guest-house on the outskirts of the city. The success of their programme encouraged them to create a permanent branch of the Brigham Young University in Provo, Utah, and they purchased a plot of land on Mount Scopus. So began a saga whose ramifications far overran the borders of Jerusalem and even Israel.

The Mormons began their wanderings through the maze of Israeli bureaucracy. They had to obtain the recommendation of the Foreign Minister, since they were a foreign institution; they had to obtain the signature of the Minister of Education (a member of the National Religious Party), since they were an educational institution; they had to obtain the signature of the Minister of the Interior, who is in charge of overall planning (also of the National Religious Party); they needed my signature as Mayor of Jerusalem. Everyone signed. The Mormons had the reputation of being well disposed towards Israel and their university had an excellent reputation.

They then had to make their tedious way through the planning commissions. The Jerusalem City Council, convening as the town planning commission, gave its approval, which is done purely on architectural and planning considerations. The vote was unanimous, including the votes of the Orthodox and ultra-Orthodox councillors. The plan was then made public for three months to allow public objection. The single objection was that of the Council for a Beautiful Israel, protesting against the height of the building. The architect reworked the plans, the Council withdrew its dissent and the necessary stamp of approval was given.

Then all hell broke loose. The ultra-Orthodox parties, always looking for a peg on which to hang their coat of protectors of the faith, decided to make the Mormon Centre the peg. The outcry was deafening. This abomination has to be stopped. The Mormons are proselytizers and are going to convert the entire Jewish population, one by one. It is all Teddy Kollek's doing. Pickets took up position in front of my office each morning, leaving, however, by 1 p.m. (I envied them that they had only to work half-days.) Harangues appeared in their newspapers here and abroad, and threatening phone calls were received.

The fact is that this banner was also taken up by the middle-of-the-road Jewish community (not to mention some Christian communities abroad, whose attitude towards their Mormon compatriots was less than Christian). The anti-Mormon campaign was directed entirely towards me. The government ministers and city councillors who had given their assent side-stepped the fact that they had approved the plans and even joined the furore.

The fear of proselytization is not irrational. Our loss of six million Jews in the Holocaust makes us deeply conscious of the worth of each and every Jew. I was not inured to this fear and for this reason already in 1968 we had asked the Mormons, who indeed are a proselytizing faith, to undertake a formal agreement that in Israel they would not proselytize. They had been in Jerusalem for years before starting this new centre and had never broken their word.

My support of the Mormon right to build their centre derived from a deeply rooted belief in freedom of worship, for everyone, everywhere. If we were to bar the Mormons from building in Jerusalem, what right would we have to object when similar constraints were placed on Jews in Russia, Argentina or even in Utah? Incidentally, the rabbi in Salt Lake City informed me that every year several Mormons convert to Judaism, rather than the other way round.

Despite continual threats of arson, the building was built – one of the city's most attractive modern buildings, I might add. Known as the Jerusalem Centre for Near Eastern Studies, it is easily visible from the north-east corner of the Ramparts Walk (see p. 38) as well as on the route of the 99 bus (see p. 139).

7
THE CULTURAL MILE

There are sites in Jerusalem which can be viewed in terms of 'before' and 'after', but none more so than those along the Cultural Mile. The 'before' for this area has discernible historical layers: two millennia ago, three centuries ago, two decades ago. The 'after' is often only just nearing completion.

Even before the reunification of the city, we found ourselves confronted with the challenge of how to preserve ancient and historic buildings. I was convinced that the best way to assure their demise was to chain the doors and place appropriate plaques on them, indicating their historical importance: King Solomon slept here. I felt that the only way to preserve these buildings was to give them new content. And it was with this principle that we set out on our way.

We had barely taken our very first steps – the restoration of the Khan Theatre and of the Yemin Moshe Quarter – when the Six Day War created an entirely new reality. Sites which had lain in no-man's-land for nineteen years, rapidly deteriorating, were suddenly prime properties in the centre of the city. Each structure demanded individual attention.

And while we approached each project on an individual basis, we ultimately found that we had, indeed, created a 'Cultural Mile'. The hubbub of a flourishing city took over where desolation had reigned in divided Jerusalem.

THE CITADEL

This Cultural Mile starts out at the Citadel, the Tower of David, which commands the entrance to Jaffa Gate. The 'before' of the Citadel is an archaeologist's paradise. Its earliest remains date from Hasmonean times in the second century BC, although there are indications that the Broad Wall of Hezekiah, even four centuries earlier, ended in the dry moat of the Citadel (see p. 54). The moat never did have water, but it nevertheless rendered an additional obstacle to any conquering army. The Citadel, as we know it today, was built by Herod and added to by the Crusaders, the Mamelukes and, finally, by the Ottoman Turks.

Through the nineteen years of the city's division, the Citadel was merely 200 metres beyond the border. One had only to glance upward from Mamilla Road to catch a glimpse of the Arab

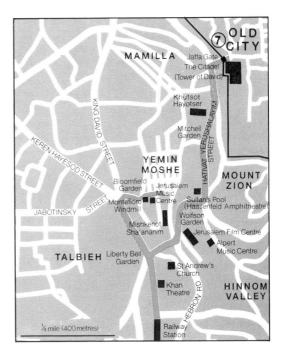

legionnaires atop the walls. It was not the first taste of a military encampment for this fortress, which indeed had served similar purposes all through its history.

It was perhaps the recollection of the machine-gun emplacements atop the Citadel – and our belief that they should never return – that was the catalyst for our decision to ensure the structure's use for peaceful purposes. During the late 1960s, we began the first archaeological excavations.

The overwhelming emotional and physical power of the Citadel, reminiscent of the Forum in Rome and the Acropolis in Athens, inspired the creation of a Sound and Light programme in several languages. King Herod's call to his wife Mariamne can be distinctly heard in the courtyard echoes. The trumpets of the Crusaders herald the arrival of their conquering forces.

Each step we undertook led naturally to the next. The throngs of visitors converging on the Citadel every evening to walk with us through history reinforced the idea of creating a museum of the city of Jerusalem on this site. The massive towers, the transcendent views from the para-

ABOVE *No-man's-land opposite Jaffa Gate and the Citadel during the period of Jordanian occupation.*

pets, the hidden nooks and crannies, the walkways, the newly excavated central open area, stirred the imagination of what could be done here. The dream began to take on form.

A Mayor can be neither profligate nor impractical. The first stage of any dream is a meeting with the City Treasurer. I harboured the hope (well, the fantasy) that he would tell me that this was indeed viable, that he could find an empty line in the budget even for an undertaking of such magnitude. He reported what I well knew: our budget, with its narrow tax base, was so overburdened that we already had to struggle to prevent the paring of allocations for the transportation of handicapped children or for the care of the indigent elderly.

Again, a friend from abroad, through the Jerusalem Foundation, became our saviour. The Jerusalem Foundation today touches every aspect of life in every corner of our city. From the restoration of Damascus Gate and the Ramparts Walk to the creation of the Sheikh Jarrah Arab Health Clinic, from libraries to swimming-pools, from

LEFT *Sound and Light display at the Citadel.*

supplementary tutoring for the young to heating for the aged, from art centres to music centres to film centres, the friends of Jerusalem, through the Foundation, have indeed changed the fabric of life in our city.

The Jerusalem City Museum in the Citadel opened to much fanfare in April 1989, the culmination of years of intensive work. No account could be more descriptive than that of the opening speech by the museum's donor, Vivien Clore-Duffield, who was a fully fledged partner in the nitty-gritty of this project: 'Inevitably, there have been terrible problems, awful arguments and prolonged discussions. I suppose one should have expected that the development of a place where the Hasmoneans, the Romans and the Crusaders, the Mamelukes and the Ottomans, the British, the Jordanians and the Israelis have ruled, strutted, worshipped, feasted, built, fortified and fought would not be easy, and it wasn't. Architects collapsed, archaeologists departed, gardeners despaired and all the experts argued. Every move was scrutinized and criticized by religious experts of each faith.' Yet the result is stupendous.

The entrance is from Omar ibn al Khattab Square inside Jaffa Gate, crossing a dry moat which now boasts an archaeological garden and passing by an open-air mosque. The entrance is a modern gate in an ancient gateway, possibly Crusader or Mameluke. An orientation area clearly outlines the five possible routes: the exhibition route, the observation points route, the archaeological route, the short route and the route for the handicapped. An introductory film ensures that few questions remain unanswered.

The museum is one of dioramas, paintings, models, holograms and videos, laid out chronologically from the bread-and-wine reception accorded the patriarch Abraham by Melchizedek, King of Shalem, as recounted in the Book of Genesis (ch. 14).

The first step is a view of the Citadel and the hexagonal structure built by the British. And then history takes over: the Canaanites, the First Temple portrayed hologramically, the Return to Zion, Hellenism, the Hasmoneans, the death of Herod and the destruction of the Second Temple. We continue with the Romans, the establishment of Aelia Capitolina and the Byzantines. The Omayyads are vanquished by the Crusaders, who meet their fate at the hands of Saladin. The Mamelukes bring us to the Ottoman period and Suleiman, whose legacy is the Old City wall. Then the arrival of the great powers in the nineteenth century, the

defeat of the Turks by the British, the early Jewish settlers, the divided city and its dividing walls, which crumbled as did the walls of Jericho. A multi-media presentation portrays the vision of Jerusalem. And a shop and cafeteria cater to more earthly pursuits.

A highlight of the museum is a detailed nineteenth-century model of the city. The tale of its discovery is one of which mystery novels are made. The story had a simple start: the cafeteria of the Hebrew University in Jerusalem. A young Swiss student, while not meaning to eavesdrop, overheard fragments of a conversation by another student, who had been following the trail of a model of Jerusalem. This model had been created for the 1870 Vienna International Exhibition by a Hungarian Catholic, Stephan Illes, who had lived in Jerusalem from 1860 to 1872. References to the model were found in several documents, but the model had vanished.

The student had found an article indicating that Stephan Illes had travelled around Europe, with the model in tow, and that his last known stop was Geneva. The Swiss student was on her way home to Geneva for the university holidays and offered to try and help with a bit of sleuth work. She knew she could easily ignite the enthusiasm of her historian father.

A nineteenth-century model of Jerusalem in the City Museum at the Citadel.

Her father eagerly took on the case and succeeded in tracing the model to the storehouse of the Maison de la Reformation, where it lay in utter neglect, practically forgotten. The Geneva burghers had acquired it in the 1870s and had exhibited it for some time before relegating it to storage and obscurity. Once it was located, cables and phone calls flew back and forth between Geneva and Jerusalem. This detailed model of Jerusalem in the nineteenth century was a treasure trove of information. Unanswered questions found long sought-after answers.

Our next challenge was to bring the model from Geneva to Jerusalem. With the help of the Maison de la Reformation, which arranged the loan of the model to Jerusalem, with the help of the restorer of the Israel Museum, who had to repair the damage of a century's neglect, with the help of a friend in Geneva, who helped finance this undertaking (as a group of Genevans had helped finance the exhibition of the model over a century ago), this model found its natural home in the Jerusalem City Museum.

There is no question that after a visit to this museum, neither Israeli schoolchildren nor foreign tourists will confuse the Byzantines and the Crusaders, the Omayyads and the Mamelukes.

KHUTSOT HAYOTSER

We leave the Citadel, cross the road and walk downhill, reaching Khutsot Hayotser (in Arabic Jorat el Einab, the Valley of the Grape). This had originally been a neighbourhood of Sephardi Jews living in small, simple houses, yet with a fine synagogue, but by the turn of the century the founding families had moved on to better housing, with only the poorest families remaining. Khutsot Hayotser was then rebuilt in the 1920s and 1930s as a market and workshop complex of mainly Arab artisans.

In 1948, this site became part of the neutral no-man's-land, dangerous, deserted and deteriorating. It seemed an almost impossible task of renovation when the barbed wire was removed in 1967. And yet today it seems as if the art galleries, artisan studios and restaurants have been permanent fixtures at least since the time of King David.

It takes one trip down the steps of Khutsot Hayotser (or, probably more convincing, one trip back up the steps) to realize that one is entering a very defined valley. This is the historic Gei Ben Hinnom, Valley of the Son of Hinnom. Its notoriety dates from the seventh-century BC reign of King Manasseh, whose barbaric practice of child sacrifices took place here. Gei Ben Hinnom led to the Hebrew word Gehennom, then reflected by the New Testament Gehenna, hell. Here again we felt that devising a peaceful purpose would help obliterate its past and we created the Mitchell and Wolfson Gardens in the valley below.

We continue downhill on the main road. On the slope to our left is Mount Zion (see p. 42) and the vast open space in the valley to our right is an open-air concert area.

SULTAN'S POOL

In 1978, a legion of national committees gathered to discuss ways to celebrate Israel's thirtieth Independence Day. There were as many suggestions as there were committee members. My thoughts were already well crystallized. I felt that the era of military parades, as had been the tradition for earlier anniversaries, was no longer appropriate. It was time we celebrated in ways other than with tanks and half-tracks.

With the help of two of Israel's most dedicated friends, Isaac Stern and Zubin Mehta, a novel notion evolved: an outdoor concert in the Sultan's Pool (a reservoir built by the Mameluke Sultan Barkuk in the fourteenth century, then restored by Suleiman but empty for more than a century). Isaac would play, Zubin would conduct. The persuasive powers of these two men filled in the roster: Mstislav Rostropovich, Leontyne Price, Jean-Pierre Rampal, the Israel Philharmonic. Of course, nothing goes entirely smoothly: Rostropovich did not have a visa, Isaac forgot his violin, Rampal's plane was grounded by fog in Europe.

A rickety stage was erected, but there were no frills – like dressing-rooms. We, therefore, commandeered the house of friends in nearby Yemin Moshe, who can tell their grandchildren of the great artists who changed clothes in their bedroom.

Despite the rarity of terrorist acts in the city, just a week before the concert a bazooka rocket had been fired, landing in a residential quarter not far from the Sultan's Pool. The security experts had untold qualms about this Independence Day concert, particularly as this makeshift concert area did not allow for proper security arrangements. As the concert was about to begin, the concern increased. The one practical proposal was that I be somewhere on the stage to have access to a microphone if need be. Zubin swiftly devised a solution: I would emcee the evening. My contention that I did not even know the programme did not dissuade him; he scribbled the works on little slips of paper. Few people noticed. I was not happy about the reason for my new job, but I enjoyed it, particularly as its primary purpose proved unnecessary.

Twelve thousand people filled the pool area, displaying a decorum rarely seen in our part of the world. Perhaps it was in the air: the knowledge that this was to be a memorable evening.

An evening like this would be incomplete without the '1812 Overture'. We had informed the residents of the Old City of the impending cannon shots so that there would be no unnecessary fear.

And while the fireworks atop the Old City wall may not have been historically accurate, the trumpets and cannons surely were. As the concert ended, with these eminent stars of the world of music standing together to sing and play the 'Hatikvah', our national anthem, there was not a single dry eye in the audience or on the stage. The sin of pride did not allow for any humility: it was a historic night for Jerusalem.

(A piquant epilogue. The following day I was called by a hysterical clerk at our Mishkenot Sha'ananim guest-house. Rostropovich was missing. Missing? Gone. Had left earlier in the day and said he would return soon. Had not returned and had not been heard from. We sent out search parties in every possible direction. One began to conceive even the most irrational fears. This was the pre-glasnost era. Perhaps the Russians had kidnapped him. We directed one of the search parties to the Russian Church, where we succeeded, finally, in finding our missing cellist. He had gone to visit the church and, ensconced in reminiscences with the priests there, had not quite noticed the passage of many, many hours.)

This concert fathered the concept of a permanent outdoor amphitheatre. And again my hand was out. Where Jerusalem's needs are concerned, one cannot be shy. It took a few years. Acoustic experts and lighting experts and security experts and landscape experts met and re-met, planned and re-planned. For the dedication of the Hassenfeld Amphitheatre in the Sultan's Pool, it was our friend Leonard Bernstein who led the celebration, conducting the Israel Philharmonic before a sardine-packed audience. No one was going to be caught missing this concert.

At the bottom of the hill, we turn right, continuing on the bridge-like portion of the road. The decorated stone structure on our right is a sabil, a camel drinking fountain, which we restored some years ago but only for its architectural value since the demand for camel drinking fountains has drastically decreased.

JERUSALEM FILM CENTRE

Just a short climb away (although, in honesty, I drive it more frequently than I climb it), under the pedestrian bridge, is the stairway leading down to the Jerusalem Film Centre, another example of an old building given new content. The centre perches on the side of the valley to our immediate left, immediately opposite the imposing slopes of Mount Zion and overlooking the more distant view of the Judean Desert, with its sedate pink and purple hues.

Until 1968, for both ideological and practical reasons, the State of Israel had no television. Ben-

The 1978 Independence Day concert in the Sultan's Pool.

Gurion was convinced that it would be the ruination of our youth. I was sure that he would relent, as the rest of the world became more and more enmeshed in the television age, but he stood fast. What did emerge from that television-less period was a love of films. Research studies of that period time and time again adjudged Israel first in films-per-capita consumption records worldwide.

Times, of course, have changed. Israel has a television station as well as access to Jordanian and Lebanese transmissions in both English and Arabic. Almost every Israeli home has a television (except the ultra-Orthodox Jews, who eschew television – and radio and films) and a majority have video cassette recorders. (The story is told of a Japanese company which, receiving an order for VCRs for Israel, was convinced it was the order for all of Europe.) And this is not to mention illegal cable stations as well as the proliferation of satellite dishes which give Jerusalemites a choice of the *Today* show on the American Armed Forces Network or Communist situation comedies from the Soviet Union. But despite this new-fangled technology, Israelis remained dedicated, and knowledgeable, movie-goers, and I was well aware of this, even though I had long before given up hope of finding time in my daily schedule for movie-going.

The Jerusalem Film Centre-Cinémathèque was the dream of a woman who lived originally in Haifa. Lia Van Leer envisaged a facility which would make available the best of the world of film, which would house a major film archive and which would give courses in all aspects of the art of the film.

We searched for a location almost as assiduously as do film-makers. The easiest solution was, of course, to choose an empty plot of land and build a building. But once the possibility cropped up of using the present building, with its nineteenth-century grandeur, all practical notions of what would be easiest became non-considerations. Many friends in the film industry were intrigued, and the centre became an international group effort. Help came from Los Angeles, New York, Washington, London, Paris and Holland.

The scope of programmes and activities at the centre is vast, including an international film festival which almost paralyses life in our city for a week each summer. (When a member of my staff took a week's vacation to see ten films a day, I almost began to regret the enthusiasm with which I had helped further this project.)

But I am guilty of favouritism. The programme which most excites me is that of the joint film classes for Arab and Jewish youth. Political differences, social differences, economic differences are all inconsequential when Ingrid Bergman takes leave of Humphrey Bogart in the last scene of *Casablanca*. What better circumstances for encouraging our young people to learn to live together and be respectful of one another.

For Jerusalemites, there is one feature of the Film Centre building which attained instant fame: the architectural anomaly of the steps descending to the building. These steps do, indeed, defy all rules of basic engineering as the visitor will discover. (A common joke in Jerusalem: What is worse than nuclear warfare? The steps of the Cinémathèque.)

The Hinnom Valley, below the Film Centre, is far deeper than at its northern end. But, in fact, it never seemed as deep as when the tightrope walker, Philippe Petit, crossed it on a piece of wire, another instance of the derring-do of the Israel Festival directors. The starting-point was just above the Film Centre, where a cable crossing the valley had existed since 1948. During the War of Independence, when the Old City was under siege and completely cut off from the rest of the city, this small cable car was the lifeline to the military forces on Mount Zion. The Zion Gate, nearest to the Jewish Quarter, was mostly closed and defended by the Arab Legion.

Philippe Petit did not, however, use this cable, but brought his own wire and prepared for his walk with an amazing equanimity. Having one day sat and talked with this most pleasurable young man, I was consumed by remorse at my involvement in this foolhardy undertaking. I did watch as he took his first step, but my usually stalwart nervous system gave way by the second. My eyes remained sealed until the roar of the tens of thousands of courageous viewers announced the successful completion of his mission. And I thought being Mayor was a hard way to make a living . . .

The fact is that I often feel as if I am walking a tightrope, trying to keep a balance so crucial in this city. This past year I used the photograph of Philippe Petit's feat on my New Year's card – and I keep the photograph on my desk – to encourage me when one of the balancing steps seems particularly precarious.

The large building one sees just across the valley is the Alpert Music Centre for Youth, a music project undertaken by Herb Alpert of Tijuana Brass fame. Here, too, Arab and Jewish youth share an interest which transcends politics and even language: a love of music. The Jewish children quickly become accustomed to the unusual sound of Eastern music; the Arab children become equally accustomed to the less familiar sound of the West.

The Jerusalem Film Centre overlooking the Hinnom Valley, with the St Andrew's Church behind.

The Film Centre and the Alpert Music Centre had belonged to a turn-of-the-century Jewish neighbourhood, the Shama'a Quarter, also called Sha'arei Zion, the Gates of Zion, whose residents had been living in veritable hovels. In winter, water seeped into their houses; in summer, the houses were stifling. We relocated the inhabitants to proper housing, saving the two buildings which had renovation potential.

ST ANDREW'S CHURCH

Across the Hebron Road from the Film Centre (now, more accurately and safely, across a bridge to save the lives of our film-lovers, who had dodged trucks and buses to reach their goal) is St Andrew's Church and the Scottish Hospice, built after World War I, in honour of the British victory and the role of the Scottish soldiers.

Philippe Petit crossing the Hinnom Valley on a tightrope at the start of the 1987 Israel Festival.

St Andrew, one of the twelve disciples of Jesus, is the patron saint of Scotland and the flag atop the building depicts St Andrew's cross (he was thought to have been crucified in Greece on an X-shaped cross), the devoluted Scottish third of the Union Jack, with St George representing England and St David, Wales. An inscription honouring the fourteenth-century King Robert the Bruce, who had wanted his heart buried in Jerusalem, is only one symbol of the centuries-old ties with our city.

There were assorted proposals submitted over the years to utilize the area just below St Andrew's. One plan included a building which would have blocked the church's view of the Old City. The Warden of St Andrew's asked that we undertake a commitment that any structure on this site would not obscure their view. The World Centre of the B'nai B'rith charity organization, to be built here, will adhere to our obligation.

One of the city by-laws requires that construction work anywhere in the city first pass the mus-

ter of our archaeologists. The expectations here were dim, with archaeologists predicting a barren area. But after finding Turkish rifles from World War I, the archaeologist digging here began his search downwards. He discovered a Byzantine church floor mosaic and an area of First Temple burial caves. Over the centuries, these caves had all been picked clean. Grave robbers were a fixture of every generation. But in one of the burial chambers, there was evidence that a ceiling had collapsed. With the chance that this collapse could have occurred before the arrival of grave robbers, the archaeologists took shovel in hand.

People use the expression 'wildest dreams' loosely, but nothing could be more apt here. One thousand items were discovered in the cave: pottery, jewellery and perfume bottles, indicating persons of means. Important lessons were learned: if there was Jewish burial following the destruction of the First Temple and before the return from Babylon, perhaps the destruction of the city had not been complete.

The finds of this excavation, called Ketef Hinnom (the Shoulder of Hinnom, referring to its location on the slope of the Hinnom Valley), included Egyptian and Persian jewellery and early Greek coins. But the exceptional finds were two small silver amulets, tightly rolled. Again the laboratories of the Israel Museum tackled what seemed impossible: unrolling these brittle items. Each step was painstaking and intricate.

When the scrolls were finally unrolled, one could detect very faint markings, barely visible. A draughtswoman, whose task it was to copy the lines, discerned the outlines of ancient Hebrew letters. Further study brought about the unravelling of this riddle: it was the Priestly Blessing – 'May the L-rd bless thee and keep thee, may the L-rd cause His face to shine upon thee and be gracious to thee, may the L-rd lift up His countenance to thee and give thee peace.' This blessing, in these very words, is today recited in daily prayers and is the prayer with which fathers bless their children. These silver amulets predate by 400 years the oldest known biblical documents, the Dead Sea Scrolls. A truly monumental find had been made.

Following years of laboratory work and research, these amulets were put on display at the Israel Museum. Interest in this rare taste of our history has not ebbed, perhaps because it is such a tangible tie between our forefathers and our generation.

KHAN THEATRE

Just beyond St Andrew's, to the left, is the Khan Theatre. This building began its career in the nineteenth century (perhaps even the eighteenth) as a Turkish inn, a caravanserai, with a well-defined area for parking one's camel. With the coming of the automotive age, its popularity as a wayside station suffered a rapid decline. It underwent subsequent transformations, first as a German beer hall and ultimately as a carpentry shop specializing in ice boxes! A step into the low-slung stucture quickly reveals a theatre (with Jerusalem's only repertory company), a nightclub and a restaurant.

One of the most memorable occasions at the Khan Theatre took place in the summer of 1973 with a visit of the cellist Pablo Casals, then ninety-six years old. The Jerusalem Music Centre was not yet completed and so the Master Class which Casals conducted every day for an entire month took place at the Khan. Casals, assisted by two strong men in walking to the hall, gave the impression of severe frailty. But the very instant he took his baton in hand, conducting a youth orchestra which the musician Sasha Schneider had prepared for him, one witnessed a vitality and virility of a man a fraction of his age. His voice took on renewed strength, keeping time, and his arms swung as if he could thus impart his talent to these young people. When the music ended, he resumed the frailty of a nonagenarian.

The Jerusalem Railway Station opposite has nearly reached a state of oblivion similar to the camel stop. Our country unfortunately chose to imitate the Americans in building mass highway systems rather than following the Europeans in creating a first-class railway system. Thus there is one passenger train a day from Jerusalem to Tel Aviv. Because none of the infrastructure has been improved in decades, the ride takes two hours, twice the time by bus or car. The train is used mainly by nostalgics or romantics, since its route traverses the deep ravines of the hills of Judea.

Before the founding of the state, I was a frequent passenger on the railway's Jerusalem –Cairo line, since the headquarters of British intelligence, with which we co-operated closely during and after World War II, was located in Cairo. The trip to Cairo was an overnight journey, leaving the Jerusalem Railway Station in the afternoon, crossing the Sinai to reach Kantara. There the train was put on a ferry for the crossing of the Suez Canal, arriving in Cairo the next morning. The train had very elegant sleepers and an excellent buffet, and even one's shoes were shined. A veritable Orient non-Express.

Before reaching the Liberty Bell Garden, we pass a 1989 addition to the cityscape: *The Lions Fountain* by the German sculptor Gernot Rumpf, a gift of the German Government and Chancellor Helmut Kohl. The art critics have yet to render judgement, but Jerusalem's children, far more dependable, have.

We cross to the Sonol petrol station. The funny beeps one hears at this traffic light enable the blind to cross safely to a nearby garden and clubhouse with special accoutrements, an idea we stole from the city of Vienna. Located on a seam between Arab and Jewish neighbourhoods, this facility serves both communities.

We reach what is undoubtedly the most popular train in Jerusalem albeit a stationary one: the Train Theatre, an old railway carriage used for daily puppet shows.

LIBERTY BELL GARDEN

The Liberty Bell Garden is our city's outdoor community centre and, together with the nearby Bloomfield Garden, creates a recreational and cultural centre for the city. Young and old, rich and poor, religious and secular, Jew and Arab, share the gardens matter-of-factly. The Jerusalem Foundation subsidizes cultural programmes to ensure equal opportunity, at least here, for our residents. There are concerts and roller skating; there are picnic areas and an open-air library.

In 1976, as the United States prepared to celebrate its bicentennial, we sought a way to honour our close ties and to say thank you. A replica of the Liberty Bell, a gift of a long-ago Philadelphia delegation, was rusting in a neglected corner. We dusted it off, shined it up and placed it at the centre of this garden, with pergolas radiating from the bell as their hub. While today the pergolas greet the visitor in green profusion, they were the source of untold anguish. We planted ivies and flowers and waited for them to grow. And we waited. And we even prayed a little. And nothing happened, except the deluge of newspaper caricatures about our folly. But eventually our prayers were answered.

The replica of the Liberty Bell carries the quotation from the Book of Leviticus: 'Proclaim liberty throughout all the land unto all the inhabitants thereof.' What better proof of the long ties between the Land of the Bible and the United States?

One of our purposes in creating these gardens was to ensure that the vista towards the Old City would remain unmarred. This land was owned by the Greek Orthodox Patriarchate, one of the earliest dabblers in Jerusalem real estate. There were unceasing pressures on the Church leaders from entrepreneurs who envisioned high-rise buildings in this area. It would, of course, have been far more profitable for the Church to lease to these commercial interests (the Church may not sell land, but leases it for 100 or even 150 years), but the Patriarch, sharing our concern for Jerusalem's future, agreed to our offer. A 140-year lease ensures these open vistas if not in perpetuity, at least until the year 2110.

There is a single high-rise to the left, built before we were sensitive to the preservation of open vistas. The area had been called Omariyah and the single tower is known by that name. The original plan called for seven high-rises, including the Laromme Hotel. The plan was scrapped and the hotel, built on that site, is a low-slung building at the end of the garden.

We shall be leaving the garden at the crossroads of Jabotinsky Street (the Laromme Hotel), Keren Hayesod Street (the Moriah Hotel) and King David Street (the King Solomon Hotel, the King David Hotel and the YMCA). We cross the main road to our right, towards the Bloomfield Garden across the way.

YEMIN MOSHE

Walking straight on to the side road, we are welcomed to the Yemin Moshe neighbourhood by the Yemin Moshe windmill, a true aberration in our city landscape, though it was one of the first structures outside the Old City wall. In 1860, Sir Moses Montefiore travelled to the Holy Land from England. His visit to the severely crowded Jewish Quarter of the Old City led to a paternal concern and he built a long, low house called Mishkenot Sha'ananim (Tranquil Dwellings) to

The Yemin Moshe windmill, one of the first structures to be built outside the Old City wall, now a small museum.

relieve the overcrowding he had witnessed. Its twenty-four apartments were to be equally divided between Sephardi and Ashkenazi Jews. Building the house was a relatively manageable undertaking; convincing the Jews to leave the security of the Old City walls to live in this unprotected area – who would ward off the bandits and marauders? – was the major challenge. Sir Moses finally achieved partial success: the Jews would live in Mishkenot, but only during daylight hours.

A portion of the funds for Mishkenot came from a New Orleans Jew, Judah Touro, who had bequeathed $50,000 (a very considerable sum in the nineteenth century) to Sir Moses to use for an almshouse in Jerusalem. Sir Moses had planned to use this to build a hospital in the Old City, but, as the Rothschilds had already built the Misgav Ladach Hospital, the Mishkenot housing project became his priority.

Sir Moses's equal concern was for the livelihood of the people and hence the windmill. He was convinced that this would be the beginnings of a major flour industry in the area. Unfortunately, the technology failed and his windmill quickly became an aesthetic landmark. Its arms stationary, it today serves as a small Montefiore museum.

The Yemin Moshe neighbourhood, named for Sir Moses Montefiore who was 100 years old when he last visited here, and the Mishkenot Sha'ananim building were a focus of our reno-

vation plans. Situated on the border during the years of the divided city, open to occasional sniping and shelling, much of Yemin Moshe had become a slum. Whoever could move to safer quarters did so; the empty homes were quickly taken over by squatters.

Squatters in Jerusalem were not the young, drug culture hippies one thinks of when picturing squatters in London or Amsterdam. They were immigrants, in fact refugees, who came with the mass immigration in the 1950s and yearned to live in Jerusalem. As this quarter was part of our restoration programme, even before 1967, we obtained alternative housing for the squatters so that we could renew the quarter and create an artists' colony here.

The Mishkenot Sha'ananim complex in Yemin Moshe has become a guest-house for creative visitors to Jerusalem. The list of tenants would be a chapter in itself: Saul Bellow, Simone de Beauvoir, Isaiah Berlin, Milan Kundera, V. S. Naipaul, Artur Rubinstein, Isaac Stern, the late Gina Bachauer, Yehudi Menuhin, Rostropovich, Marc Chagall, Robert Rauschenberg and Jim Dine.

Adjoining Mishkenot is the Jerusalem Music Centre, again an old building given new content. The centre was a result of the concern of violinist Isaac Stern that there was no facility to promote contact between the world's great musicians and the finest of our country's young musicians. Israel, rich in native talent, was far from world centres. With the creation of the centre, eminent world musicians could give Master Classes and expand the musical horizons of these young people. The joyous opening of the Music Centre, as Pablo Casals, Sasha Schneider, Leonard Rose and Eugene Istomin joined Isaac Stern, was a royal festival of music as befits the city of King David.

I attended the centre's first Master Class. It was in the midst of a harried day, as all days seem to be, but I felt it was well advised that I stop by. I had pencilled in a fifteen-minute stay in my diary, which seemed adequate for a quick impression, but I had not anticipated the enchantment of watching a sixteen-year-old Jerusalemite being taught by the master. An hour later, I was still seated in the visitors' gallery.

BLOOMFIELD GARDEN

The official conclusion to our tour should surely be a walk through the adjacent Bloomfield Garden, a possible picnic when the sun is shining. During the spring and summer months, this area is covered with a blanket of tulips, daffodils and

Mishkenot Sha'ananim, the guesthouse in Yemin Moshe for creative visitors to Jerusalem, originally built in 1860 by Sir Moses Montefiore to relieve overcrowding in the Old City.

hyacinths, an annual gift of the flower-growers of Holland.

In 1980, when Prime Minister Begin promulgated the Jerusalem Law stating that Jerusalem was, indeed, the capital of Israel, a fact which I felt needed no parliamentary reconfirmation, many countries moved their embassies from Jerusalem to Tel Aviv. The Dutch flower-growers, in a show of solidarity with Jerusalem, sent us a gift of 100,000 flowers. When publicly expressing my thanks, I noted that if I had to choose between an embassy and 100,000 flowers for the city (not even anticipating that this would become an annual gift as it has), my choice would undoubtedly be the flowers. This statement, of course, caused mass frenzy at our Foreign Office.

PERFORMING ARTS COMPLEX

A postscript to the Cultural Mile walk is a night-time visit to our performing arts complex, on the corner of Chopin and Marcus Streets in the Talbieh Quarter (see p. 102). The first stage of this centre was the Sherover Theatre, a 1,000-seat theatre opened in 1971. As had been the case with

the Israel Museum a few years earlier, the thundering cries of 'white elephant' greeted this project from all directions. Who needs a theatre of this size? The city's population was then 335,000, 253,000 Jews and 82,000 Arabs. But the majority of this population, both Jew and Arab, had no tradition of theatre or concerts. Our goal was to change this percentage through a programme of art and culture for schoolchildren. We wanted to ensure that every schoolchild, each year, saw at least one concert and one play, and made one visit to the Israel Museum. Sixteen years later, we already see the success of this programme.

What we learned over the years was that, indeed, our judgement had been incorrect: the theatre proved inadequate to fill the growing demand. We began our usual planning (and scheming and plotting) and this time had the ear of Lester Crown, a friend in Chicago, who wanted very much to honour his parents. This particularly touched me, since I had met Lester's father Henry, a prominent American businessman, on my very first trip to the States. For a nervous young Israeli neophyte, confronting the vastness of the United States, Henry's warmth was the best antidote to a serious case of stage fright. I owe him an unpayable debt.

In 1986, we opened the Henry Crown Symphony Hall, in which the Jerusalem Symphony Orchestra is housed, and the Rebecca Crown Auditorium. There are evenings when all three halls are filled: a concert at 'Henry', a dance performance at 'Rebecca' and a play at the Sherover Theatre – which creates horrific parking problems.

I long ago determined that the true burden of the life of a Mayor, any Mayor, is that there is no real differentiation between on-duty and off-duty. If en route to a private dinner-party one passes a broken water main or a burned-out street light, one cannot sit down to eat without first making the necessary calls. An evening at the theatre entails worry about available parking, about the overflowing garbage bins and the pothole at the corner.

Of course, there are also the Jerusalem residents who feel that a *public* official is always at the *public*'s disposal. The tales are endless.

A resident once called my home at 11.30 p.m. and reached my wife Tamar, who often bears the burden in what has become a City Hall annexe. The tone of the caller bordered on hysteria. 'I just finished listening to the radio broadcast of the Israel Philharmonic anniversary concert. Why was it only played in Tel Aviv? Why not Jerusalem? I must talk to Teddy about this.' Tamar explained that I had not yet returned home (I was undoubtedly out soliciting for one project or another) and 'couldn't this have waited until tomorrow morning? Don't you think it was a bit inappropriate to call our home at this time of night?' 'This is an urgent matter; you don't understand,' was the reply. The caller left her name and number. I returned home around midnight and Tamar relayed this 'urgent' message. I worked for some time on various papers, letters and articles. It was almost 2 a.m. when I was ready to call it a day, but I still had one urgent matter to complete. I phoned the concerned citizen and explained why the concert had not been played in Jerusalem. . . .

8
MAMILLA AND THE GERMAN COLONY

In some ways I feel like Hillel, the sage of yore, who was asked by a heathen to teach him the entire Bible while standing on one foot. While I allow you to stand on two feet, I am nevertheless placing you on a street corner and then proceeding with a brief history lesson, giving the green light for the walk only on page 96.

We begin at the edge of the 'Mamilla area', though, while taking a backward glance, we shall not be walking through it. It is in such a state of flux, both in stone and on paper, that a definitive walk would be replete with uncertainties while a description of present-day Mamilla will be obsolete five years hence. But its salience in Jerusalem's

past and its expected resurgence in Jerusalem's future are such that it requires a lengthy discourse despite the blemish it is at present. In contrast with the historic sites of Jerusalem, Mamilla will be built up rather than dug down.

Linking old and new Jerusalem, the Mamilla area conjures up a medley of sentiments. During the pre-state years, it was a bustling commercial district – called the New Commercial Centre – with an interweaving of Jewish, Arab and Armenian merchants. It was thus commonplace to find a Polish Hassid speaking passable Arabic and an Arab speaking a heavily accented Yiddish.

With increasing tensions in the period preceding the conclusion of the British Mandate, Arab pogroms took place in Mamilla with increasing inter-communal clashes. Mamilla's centrality in Jerusalem life came to an abrupt halt with the War of Independence. The ceasefire lines assigned Mamilla frontier status. The bustle to which one had become accustomed was reduced to the spectral silence of a danger zone. Whoever could leave, left. Whoever needed a place to live and had no other, came. Squatters took over the living quarters and car mechanics took over the abandoned shops. Where once elegant shoes had been custom-made (with customers from as far away as Cairo), carburettors were now overhauled.

The wide main street of Mamilla was a favourite target for potshots from the ramparts of the Old City wall and, therefore, massive anti-sniper walls were placed across the street. There was a narrow opening for pedestrians and a space for a single car to pass, though few actually did. Mamilla had become a dead-end, leading to nowhere. While the garages flourished during the nineteen years of the divided city – Jerusalem was rapidly entering the motorized age – Mamilla itself became a symbol of urban neglect. It was an inhabited no-man's-land.

Mere days after the reunification of the city, we bulldozed the anti-sniper walls and reopened the Mamilla expanse. Architects ran to their planning boards. The challenge of recreating Mamilla was prodigious.

It did not take long, as is wont in Jerusalem, for Mamilla to become a source of controversy and

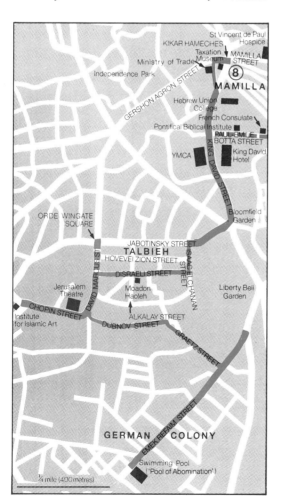

argument. Should the old structures, many of them crumbling, be destroyed or reconstructed? Should the area be residential or commercial, or a combination of both? There were 700 residents, businesses and institutions which had to be relocated.

Miraculously there was consensus among the planners on one point: the garages had to go. But it was a consensus not shared by the garage owners. They rejected our proposal to build a proper garage complex at the southern end of the city, contending that they would lose their clients. Our counter-claim was that if all the garages were moved, the car owners would have no alternative but to follow. Eventually our logic triumphed.

We thought we had won the most difficult battle; we had, in fact, won the easiest. Families had to be relocated, also a complicated (and expensive) procedure. Having lived alongside a border for almost two decades, the residents had created a tightly knit communal fabric, even though living conditions were often sub-standard.

The Fast Hotel, now a huge crater (the 'Fast Hole') at the north-west edge of Mamilla opposite City Hall, had been built in 1890–92, well-known lodgings for pilgrims and tourists and the favourite watering-hole of the Australian soldiers in World War I. An advertisement in May 1925 assured the public: 'Here you shall find all you want: Comfort and rest. Plenty of water. Running hot and cold water in every room. Rooms with private bathrooms. Airy halls and sitting rooms. Electric light. European cooking and service. Garden terrace arranged for afternoon tea.' But this 'elegant' hotel had become a forfeiture of the divided city, visitors unwilling to risk the dangers of the nearby border.

Elias Mizrachi, one of our municipal employees, had lived in the Fast Hotel, his entire family having come as squatters to this abandoned building in the early 1950s. I wondered what it had been like to grow up there. Was it disquieting for a child to glance out of his bedroom window into the gunsights of the legionnaires? Elias's memories attest to an incongruous actuality. While there were occasional 'incidents' – a nervous or trigger-happy Jordanian soldier – the border was a natural part of their childhood. The children, for whom Arabic was often their native tongue, would banter with the soldiers. 'Hey, please turn up your radio?' was a common request from children whose families often could not afford one. A commonplace game entailed sneaking through holes in the fence and touching the city wall (and returning safely). The water supply was a well in the nearby Sultan's Pool (see p. 83). That it was located in no-man's-land was no barrier for the resolute.

In 1967, the Fast Hotel housed seventy families, mainly immigrants from Moslem countries. We wanted to relocate them, but the Fast Hotel was their home and, though the building was almost crumbling, they did not want to move. They, indeed, had been an unknighted civilian border patrol for nineteen years.

In 1969 a small bomb went off in a paintshop in the building. Fortunately there were no casualties, but some damage had been caused and I accompanied the police to examine it. On my return to the office, I was greeted by an unnatural fidgeting amongst my staff. The silence was broken by one brave soul, who assumed the role of group spokesman and, hesitatingly, asked whether perhaps, by chance, I had had something to do with the bomb. After all, what better way to convince an intractable group to acquiesce to an unwanted move? Not everyone seemed convinced by my disclaimer.

The initial plans for Mamilla were prepared in 1967 by Moshe Safdie. The plan was grandiose and overly ambitious, perhaps inspired by the euphoria of the city's reunification. It called for high-rise hotels, exclusive shops and vast underground parking, and soon became a target of attack by local civil groups.

We brought the Mamilla plan to the plenary of the Jerusalem Committee, an international advisory committee we had created soon after the city's reunification. Faced with overwhelming tasks of physical and social planning, of preserving the heritage of the past while providing for the needs of a modern city, and with the eyes of the international microscope on Jerusalem, we decided to enlist the assistance of that very community. With the inspiration of Dr Franklin Murphy, then Chairman of the Board of the *Times Mirror* in Los Angeles, and with the drafting talents of Sir Isaiah Berlin, the renowned philosopher at Oxford, the basic tenets of the committee were set.

We enlisted members of international repute: architects and artists, theologians and historians, town-planners and sociologists. Louis Kahn, Buckminster Fuller and Philip Johnson agreed to join, as did Henry Moore, Jacques Lipchitz, Jorge Luis Borges, Heinrich Böll, Reverend Theodore Hesburgh and Dr Ursula Niebuhr. The roster was an honour roll of brilliant minds and unequalled expertise. Only Jerusalem could have drafted such talent.

We convened the first plenary session in 1969. Barely a year had passed since the city had been reunited, and Jerusalemites were taking their first wobbly steps towards co-existence. Committee members gathered from all corners of the world impelled by the uniqueness of the challenge and motivated by their love for Jerusalem. They had taken three days off from their busy schedules, travelled a long way, and we could not even offer them the most meagre honorarium. These $1-a-year advisers never even got their $1. We did pay their flights – tourist class, of course.

But they came. We met. We toured. We talked. We put forth our ideas. Some were accepted readily; others rejected outright; and others bandied about, until a middle-of-the-road compromise was reached. During these early years the physical planning of Jerusalem was paramount, because these decisions would engulf the social and even political planning for the city.

We were given the luxury of learning not only from our own mistakes, but from the mistakes of others. Major highways planned for sensitive areas were scrapped as were massive urban renewal projects similar to those which had gutted the hearts of Western cities. The wisdom of restoring old neighbourhoods rather than razing them was imparted by those whose own city fathers had taken another course and were now beating their breasts in repentance.

The Jerusalem Committee over the years opted for a modest renewal plan, a compromise, for Mamilla: restore what can be saved; remove what cannot, or should not, be preserved. Mamilla was planned and re-planned and re-planned again. Finally – and I say finally with a sense of both exhaustion and enthusiasm – a new plan by Safdie was approved, more modest and more appropriate.

The site comprises 28.5 acres. To ensure its vitality and integrity, the plan encompasses a variety of land uses. There will be a boulevard and park in the valley; a commercial district with a pedestrian mall along Mamilla Street, a retail arcade and a parking facility at Jaffa Gate; a residential quarter along the southern slopes of the site; and a hotel area. The façades and several complete buildings on the northern side of Mamilla Street will be preserved and restored; the major part of the southern side of the street will be rebuilt.

Since the rule of thumb is that nothing can ever go smoothly, there is still one building which is a source of dissension. It was said that Theodor Herzl, who came to Jerusalem in 1898 to meet Kaiser Wilhelm and ask for his help in creating a Zionist homeland, had stayed in one of the houses slated for the wrecking ball. The owners, who made a small museum of Herzl's Room, are fighting this decision. But having grown up in Vienna a few streets away from where Herzl had lived (and having been named for him), I contend that he would have been the first to agree that places where he had slept are anything but holy. But in spite of my convictions, indeed certitude, the Herzl Room will probably remain intact.

When ruminating on projects like Mamilla, I am often of a divided mind. I am by nature an impatient man. I like to see decisions made and implemented. Yet at times it is the slow and deliberate path which should be taken. Had we renewed Mamilla post-haste twenty years ago, we would have made grave mistakes. Moreover, since the project then on the planning boards was far beyond any realistic financing, public or private, whatever we started might have remained unfinished.

KING DAVID STREET

We begin the walk at the intersection of Mamilla and King David Streets with Mamilla Street to the east. The resplendent building on the north side of the street, towering above all others, is the St Vincent de Paul Hospice, an orphanage built in the late nineteenth century by the Sisters of Charity, a worldwide order headquartered in Paris, with over 30,000 nuns. This charitable order does outstanding work in the care of the handicapped, in particular brain-damaged children.

One cannot speak of the St Vincent de Paul Hospice and twentieth-century Jerusalem without telling the story of Mère Bernes. The tales of this true Sister of Charity have become part of Jerusalem's lore.

In the early years of our state, Independence Day celebrations comprised mass folk-dancing in the city streets, all-night campfires and a military parade. The 1968 parade was the first to be held in the reunified city. Shortly past midnight, I drove out to inspect the parade route and saw a familiar figure walking by the side of the road. It was Mère Bernes, scattering sacred pictures of the Holy Virgin along the route, to protect the soldiers who were to march the following day from any possible harm.

I do work long, hard hours, under unceasing pressures, but I never feel that my work falls into the realm of what I call 'God's work', irrespective of any religious connotation, as 'God's work' is carried out by atheists and agnostics as often as by people of the cloth.

Mère Bernes, and the love and care she invested in the St Vincent de Paul home for retarded children of every religion, was in that realm. Honoured in 1988 by 'Elwyn', a leading American organization which deals with handicapped and retarded children and has now taken on similar work in Jerusalem, she truly could not understand why she was deserving of this honour. The decision that she take on her work had been made on high; she was merely carrying it out.

Soft-spoken, with an all-pervasive French accent which spiced every language she spoke, she was eighty-five when the Order felt that she should take life easier and transferred her to Alexandria. At a farewell gathering in my office, she talked of her years in Jerusalem, of the children she had cared for who had become her children, and of her sorrow at taking leave of her friends.

Theodor Herzl (extreme right) with a local Jewish family in Mamilla during a visit to Jerusalem in 1898.

She left us all with a feeling of inadequacy, with a feeling that no matter how much we do, there is so much more we should be doing.

We shall start walking at the south-west corner of this intersection. (A compass is not an essential piece of equipment for these walks; Jerusalem's sun can be counted on for directional assistance throughout most of the year.)

The intersection is named 'Kikar Hameches', 'Customs Square'. For anyone who has lived even a short time in Israel, the role which the customs authority plays, even with the arrival of a package of used T-shirts, is a prominent (rarely pleasant) one. The building to our left is the customs authority and there is even a museum of taxes which can be visited. Among the stated aims of this museum are to be 'a show window to the public: instilling tax-consciousness and imparting tax know-how' and to be 'a source of inspiration to the employees and imparting a sense of self-identification with the administration'.

Reaching the corner of this short block, we face the grandeur of a bygone era. Presently housing the Ministry of Trade and Industry, this building was once the Palace Hotel and is still known by

that name to veteran Jerusalemites. It was built in the late 1920s by Haj Amin al Husseini, the notorious Mufti of Jerusalem, and by the Moslem Waqf. The Arabic quote from the Koran still adorns the building.

The land for this hotel was part of a Moslem graveyard dating from the twelfth century, which, it is said, gave the area its name, Mamilla being derived from 'Ma-Min-Allah', 'that which comes from Allah'. (Other theories postulate an ancient church named St Mamilla.)

In Islam, it is permissible to move cemeteries after a certain number of years. Thus Haj Amin al Husseini had no compunctions about building on this plot and closed the cemetery to new burials in 1927; in the early 1950s, we followed his steps and moved an additional part of the cemetery, which was in Independence Park, just across the road. This was done with the permission of the Qadi in Jaffa, the supreme Moslem authority in Israel.

A Jewish contractor, Baruch Katinka, who also built the nearby YMCA, coveted the bid for this hotel, but was convinced that it would not be given to a Jew. Thus, a well-known saga in other countries, Katinka took on an Arab partner and created the firm of Katinka, Donya and Awad. In a book he wrote years later, Katinka had only praise for Haj Amin al Husseini, who is remembered mainly for his staunch pro-Nazi stance and

*The King David Hotel (centre) and the YMCA
(bottom right), with the Dormition Abbey behind.*

his ardent support of Hitler, whom he actually
visited.

With 400 Arab and Jewish workers, this building was completed in thirteen months. The hotel
was opened in 1930, only to fold in 1933. In the
mid-1930s, it was converted into an office building for the Mandate and the Israeli Government
subsequently took it over.

Turning left at the corner, we walk up the short
back street which returns us to King David Street.
Crossing at the cross-walk (a wise precaution) and
backtracking a few steps, we reach the Jerusalem
branch of the Hebrew Union College, the Rabbinical School of Reform Jewry in the United States.

The campus was designed by Moshe Safdie and is
that rarity of modern architecture, a building as
functional as it is beautiful.

While the campus is a creation of the 1980s, the
main building was erected in 1963, the dream of
an archaeologist/educator Nelson Glueck, then
President of the Hebrew Union College. He had
spent several of his war years mixing archaeology
and intelligence for the American army, a latter-
day Lawrence of Arabia. He wanted to build a
school of archaeology in Jerusalem as the Hebrew
University facility had remained inaccessible on
Mount Scopus when the city was divided.

He came to the Prime Minister's Office, in the
years that I was its Director under Ben-Gurion,
lobbying for a plot of land. We were convinced
that an American-sponsored school of archaeology would become a landmark for the city and

suggest a ten-minute detour to our left, though it will entail ultimately retracing our steps. It is also not an easy walk to manœuvre since you will be sharing the minuscule pavement with parked cars.

The Pontifical Biblical Institute on the left is the only Jesuit institution in the city. Future clergy, mainly from African and Asian countries, spend a year at the Institute, which has close ties with the Hebrew University. Its museum library, open to the public a few days a week, is replete with archaeological relics, though none as popular as its mummy, not as familiar a sight in Jerusalem as in Cairo.

The Institute's neighbour is the French Consulate, which is not hospitable to the passer-by, but a peek through the gates gives a glimpse of the creation of the French architect M. Favier, who was brought to Jerusalem to design the Consulate. It justifiably claims the finest view of any foreign mission.

At the end of the block, down to the right, is the Zionist Confederation House, an old building beautifully restored and given new content, which has concerts, lectures (often in English) and an excellent spinach quiche.

Backtracking to resume our course, we pass on our left, near a small parking lot, a set of geometric figures, *Four Cubes Cut into Halves*, a sculpture by the renowned Swiss artist Max Bill. We now find ourselves returning to King David Street, with a chance for a backyard view of the King David Hotel, whose entrance is to our left.

KING DAVID HOTEL

To give data about the King David – how many rooms it has or how much a night's lodging costs – would be to miss the essence of the hotel. Designed by the Swiss architect Emil Vogt, for an Egyptian Jewish family in 1930, the King David Hotel ranks with the handful of hotels which have achieved world eminence. It has housed kings and sheikhs, presidents and prime ministers, authors and actors. Winston Churchill and King Abdullah stayed there as did Elizabeth Taylor and Kirk Douglas. Even before Egyptian President Anwar Sadat's arrival there, traffic in front of the hotel was snarled as Israelis gaped in disbelief at the Egyptian flag flying from the hotel mast. The laundry bags hanging on the bathroom doors once listed (with only a few mis-spellings) the world-renowned personalities who had signed the hotel register. But the litany of complaints they elicited – why is A included and not B? – caused more trouble than the originality of the idea was worth.

On occasion I have tried to convince the Government to house official visitors, especially those involving motorcades and heavy security, at one of the hotels at the city entrance, near the

thus proposed the site on King David Street. But we made the land allocation conditional. We felt it was not sufficient to give lip service to the centrality of Jerusalem in the life of the Jewish people and we asked that every HUC rabbinical student be required to spend a year of study in Jerusalem. While today this approach is accepted, even common, this idea then was innovative, even maverick. The uproar of Israel's religious establishment at the suggestion that Reform Judaism have a foothold in the Holy City began even before the draughtsman's tools were laid on the drawing-table, and this for an institution a fraction of the size of today's campus.

Continuing up King David Street, in our original direction, we pass a modern apartment house on the corner of Paul-Emile Botta Street. While officially our route is straight on, I cannot help but

Prime Minister's Office and the Parliament, thus becoming less of a disruption for the city, but others are far less troubled by municipal considerations.

The notoriety of the King David Hotel dates from July 1946, when its southern wing was blown up by the Irgun, the underground movement led by Menachem Begin. No other act, except the murder of Lord Moyne on 6 November 1944 in Cairo, brought as serious a setback in Anglo–Israeli ties. However one evaluates Churchill's disposition towards Zionism, these two events closed all paths of access, even for Chaim Weizmann.

I was in London on a political mission on the day of this bombing. The author Arthur Koestler, whom I had met a decade earlier when he visited Palestine – he dedicated his book *Thieves in the Night* to three couples including 'Tamar and Teddy of Ein Gev' – had helped set up a meeting for me in the House of Commons with an expected attendance of fifteen or twenty Members of Parliament. The meeting was scheduled for 2 p.m.; the midday news carried the report of the bombing and 150 Members of Parliament appeared to confront – and garrotte? – this Haganah officer. I still squirm.

YMCA

Opposite the King David Hotel is the YMCA (pronounced locally as 'Yimka'). Designed by Arthur Louis Harmon, the architect of the Empire State Building in New York, the YMCA was considered the most beautiful of the YMCA world network. It probably is still so today.

The Jerusalem Young Men's Christian Association was established as long ago as 1878 and occupied numerous homes in succeeding years. The present building was the inspiration of Dr Archibald Harte, a native of Mobile, Alabama, who served as Director-General of the Y in Palestine from 1920 to 1930. It is told that on Christmas Eve 1925, he was given a gift of $1 million to create a YMCA which would serve 'as a memorial and a pious offering to the One Lord, God of Christian, Jew and Moslem, alike'.

But Harte had a falling out with his building committee and in 1930, with the building half-completed, he resigned. He ultimately built himself a retreat in Peniel on the Sea of Galilee. The story is told that whenever he reached Jerusalem, he would pass the Y but always with his face averted. It was only on its completion that he was willing to look at the building, and the bench in front of the Y, where he is said to have sat to contemplate what had been achieved, is still called Harte's Bench. Another story told is that he never set foot in the building until the 1940s and, when he did, his first act was to rearrange the furnishings. A postscript to his life is that he bequeathed

his house in Peniel to the Y, which rents out its rooms. Even though a well-guarded secret of its *cognoscenti*, the hostel is fully booked throughout most of the year.

The formal dedication of the YMCA took place on Easter Sunday 1933. The main address was given by Field-Marshal Edmund Lord Allenby, the very same Allenby who had accepted the Turkish surrender in 1917. He told of a project 'intended and calculated to promote a better understanding of each other; in the city which is Holy to all three faiths. . . . Under its shadow, jarring sectarians may cease from wrangling; fierce passions be tamed; and men's minds be drawn to loftier ideals. . . . Here is a spot whose atmosphere is peace; where political and religious jealousies can be forgotten, and international unity be fostered and developed.'

He concluded: 'Surely, the sentiment which has inspired the designers and builders of this monumental edifice should move the Nations to agree that now is the time and Jerusalem the place for ending their differences. Let us, then, hope; or, rather, let us confidently believe; that here, at last, we are witnessing the inception of an accord – liberal and without reserve – destined to extend, unceasingly and illimitably, its power; until it brings together, in perpetual amity, all the peoples on earth.'

The four-directional view from the belfry tower encompasses the city and its abrupt entry into the Judean Desert. While the tower was closed for some time after a suicide attempt, it is again open to the pubic during daylight hours. There are concerts of the YMCA *carillon*, whose resonance is sure to stop pedestrian traffic, and occasionally even motorists pull over for a musical interlude.

For decades, until the opening of the Crown Symphony Hall in February 1986, the Jerusalem Symphony had its home in the YMCA concert hall. I stopped there one afternoon to watch Danny Kaye rehearse the orchestra for a concert he was to conduct on our Independence Day. A musician was irritating him and he finally countered with: 'Why don't you go excavate a hill or something?'

As we reach the traffic lights, we pass the King David Gardens on the left, the city's most luxurious apartment building. While its amenities – a swimming-pool, a garage – are commonplace in other parts of the world, in Jerusalem they merited being 'the talk of the town'. And, indeed, a good number of the residents are foreigners.

The tall white building across the road is the King Solomon Hotel; a bit further down the side street is the Moriah Hotel. The Bloomfield Garden on the left is a temptation for the visitor to abandon the walk and find a comfortable bench or spot on the grass and merely people watch.

We pass the windmill on our left (see p. 90) and,

crossing the main road to the Laromme Hotel, we reach Jabotinsky Street. At the first corner, we turn left. The street is named Isaac Elchanan Street after a Talmudic sage, but it would be useless to ask for directions as no one beyond the actual residents has an inkling as to the street's name. The first right is Hovevei Zion Street, but we will turn up the second right, Disraeli Street. You might, however, glance at Hovevei Zion Street 24, the Greek Consulate, a first taste of the architectural treats in the Talbieh neighbourhood.

TALBIEH

As we walk along Disraeli Street, we feel a sense of contentment with the old Arab buildings we pass and an impatience with the modern buildings as our footsteps hasten by them. This area was always that of the gentry and never had to undergo the gentrification which we shall see later in the German Colony.

Talbieh was built in the earlier part of this century by Christian Arabs from Bethlehem and Beit Jalla. Having made money in the early Mandate period, through construction work and food supply for the British army, they invested their profits in the Talbieh area and built houses which they rented to British government officials and army officers. The rooms were large and spacious, to cater for the British style. Most of the building work was completed between 1924 and 1936, although building did continue until 1948.

At the foot of Disraeli Street, we pass the Talbieh Psychiatric Hospital in buildings on both the left and right. It often seems an anomaly to find a psychiatric hospital of this size on the city's choicest land. Note also no. 13, on your right, which is the Israel Institute of Psychoanalysis, founded by Professor Max Eitingen, a student of Freud.

On the next corner, Alkalay Street, is a building used for the immigrants' associations, Mo'adon Haoleh. (It has an excellent *ulpan* – an intensive Hebrew language course – should you decide that a one-week or two-week visit is not sufficient and you find yourself toying with the thought of a longer stay.) On the green gate you pass are the initials A.J. Annis Jamal was an Arab doctor, one of three brothers who built three houses here. He was married to a beautiful Russian duchess and was a romantic figure on Jerusalem's streets.

Diagonally-across from the Mo'adon Haoleh (on the far right corner), no. 17, is one of the architectural triumphs of the neighbourhood, incorporating all the elements of the Arabian Nights. Called Beit Jalad, it belonged to an Arab contractor, whose family lived in the entire house. In general, in this neighbourhood as well as in the nearby Katamon area, homes were built by an Arab clan, the '*hamula*', with the family often living in one part of the house and renting out the

The fine doorway of a house in the Talbieh Quarter, a wealthy area built in the early part of the twentieth century by Christian Arabs.

other. This building then served as an orphanage, the Motza Institution, which had relocated here when the Jerusalem suburb of Motza came under Jordanian attack in the War of Independence. It now houses AMIT, a religious women's service organization. This building had been offered to Ben-Gurion as his official residence, but he declined. He had personal compunctions about living in abandoned Arab property.

At the end of Disraeli Street, we reach Marcus Street, named for the American colonel, Mickey Marcus, who fell in the War of Independence. A West Point graduate, Mickey was a prime force behind the establishment of our infant army, a legendary figure in the history of our nation.

Mickey had fought with the Allied forces in World War II and, following his return home, had envisioned settling down to a quiet life with his wife Emma. His planning had not taken into account the persistence of a yet unborn state and he was 'drafted' into service at the outbreak of the War of Independence.

He was killed soon after. The natural assumption was that he had been killed in action, but the true account of what took place was soon common knowledge. Mickey, having forgotten the unfamiliar Hebrew password, was shot by a Jewish sentry who had mistaken him for the enemy.

I was in New York at the time, raising funds, arms and sundry goods (ranging from dishes to brassières to 'flying fortresses'), for the new state. Having been partially responsible for the pressure on Mickey to fight in this faraway war and to train an army of amateurs, I felt it was my responsibility to tell Emma of his death. I rode out to the school where she taught, remembering little of the taxi ride there. In the principal's office, I carried out a task for which no amount of preparation could ever be adequate. Emma was stalwart and courageous, but her heart was broken. As they had had no children, her comfort was Mickey's contribution to Israel's morale and fighting capacity.

In 1973, as we prepared to celebrate the twenty-fifth anniversary of the state, my thoughts frequently reverted to Mickey and to Emma, with whom I had kept in touch over the years and who by then was nearly blind. I could never rid myself of a feeling of guilt and decided that Emma should be with us, in Jerusalem, for this celebration. I hustled funds from a few friends and brought her as an official guest of the state, with a young woman army officer as her escort throughout her stay. But our debt will always remain unpaid.

Many of Jerusalem's streets have names universally recognized – King David Street, Herzl Boulevard, King George Street (the Balfour Declaration was issued during his reign), Bethlehem Road, Harry Truman Square, Chopin Street and even George Eliot Street (a modest alley alongside the American Consulate). Yet the visitor will again and again encounter streets with veiled or obscure references – Wedgewood Street or Hamem Gimmel ('the 43'). Helga Dudman, a local journalist, wrote a book called *Street People*, and, while those with an acutely developed business sense, unlike me, would baulk at the idea of one author recommending the book of another, this is a handy guide for those with a more than passing interest in Jerusalem's street names.

The city has a street-naming committee (on which fortunately I do not serve) comprised of scholarly members, who have the Herculean task of choosing names for a handful of new streets from an endless list of requests, for the desire to immortalize in Jerusalem a loved one, a colleague or a hero seems to be a ubiquitous one.

While our route is left on Marcus Street, down the hill, I would again suggest a five-minute detour to the right. The newly renovated building as one approaches the circle houses the CRB Foundation, founded by Charles Bronfman of Montreal. It is worth a glance if only to see how a house can be restored without impinging on its original architecture.

The building across the circle, easily identifiable by its Belgian flag, houses the Belgian Consulate. This building, Beit Salameh, was built by a wealthy Arab construction contractor, Constantin Salameh. Smitten by the magnificence of the French Consulate, he commissioned Favier to build his home. He had dreams of a unique house, unlike any other, and his dream was realized. In 1947, Salameh went abroad and leased the house to the Belgians. Thus, unlike most of the Arab homes, this building never became 'abandoned property'. Until 1986, rent was paid through the Foreign Office to Mr Salameh, living in Baden Baden in Germany. Salameh again and again refused offers of reparations, but ultimately his children, living in Greece, persuaded him to settle with the Israeli Government, which now owns the building.

While this expanse is officially named Wingate Square, honouring Orde Wingate ('The Friend', as he was known by the Haganah, who later won fame in World War II in the Ethiopian and Burmese campaigns), there are still old-timers who call it Salameh Square.

Resuming our way down Marcus Street, we reach no. 18, built by a contractor named Bisharah and called Villa Harun al Rashid, noted in tiles on the top floor of the house. A wholly unsubstantiated, but widespread, tale relates that when Golda Meir was Minister of Housing and lived on the top floor, a UN official was scheduled to visit her. She had the tiles chipped away as she did not want it known that an Israeli minister was living in an Arab house. Considering that the architecture itself is a dead giveaway, I tend to discredit the story.

A right U-turn, past the Sherover and Crown Theatres, brings us to the L. A. Mayer Memorial Institute for Islamic Art. It was built by an Englishwoman, Mrs Bryce Solomons, in honour of Professor Mayer of the Hebrew University, an eminent scholar of Islam.

I met with Mrs Solomons in my guise as Director of the Prime Minister's Office. We offered her $1\frac{1}{4}$ acres of land near the site of the Israel Museum, feeling that each institution would enhance the other. At the next meeting, Mrs Solomons brought a British expert with her – Sir Anthony Blunt, who was later to achieve far greater fame as a spy. Under his guidance, she decided that the

Islamic Museum should be separate and she chose the site on Palmach Street. She proved somewhat clairvoyant, since the neighbourhood has now become the home of several other cultural and public institutions.

Adjacent to the museum – a strange juxtaposition – she built a home for elderly academicians, ensuring that Professor Mayer would have a proper place to live out his life.

The museum has a superb collection of Islamic artefacts from every Islamic country and every Islamic period and is well worth a visit. It was once renowned for its collection of watches, but the finest of these were stolen one Friday night and have never been recovered, although recently new old watches are replacing the former occupants of the showcases. It was only fortunate that a catalogue of the collection had been completed shortly before so that at least a record remains for posterity, if not the watches themselves.

We retrace our steps to Marcus Street and resume our original direction, turning left on Dubnov Street. The massive abandoned-looking structure before us is a leper hospital, which was built in the nineteenth century as part of the humanitarian involvement of the German Christian community (be it Lutheran, Templer or Catholic). They built hospitals and orphanages, catering mainly to the Arab population. Their work, on the whole, was more humanitarian than missionary.

A mosque lamp in the Islamic Art Museum.

They knew that they had little chance of converting the Moslems, although a few Arab women did become nuns.

Lepers in Jerusalem, as almost everywhere, had an ever harder lot than that which fate had decreed on them. In the mid-nineteenth century, they were forced outside the city walls and lived in shacks on Mount Zion. The first leper hospital (now a Dominican house, Beit Isaiah) was built in 1860 on the upgrade of Mamilla Street (now Agron Street), but the demand soon outpaced the available space and a new hospital for lepers, which we are now passing, was completed in 1887. There are still about a dozen elderly people living there and, while their disease is not contagious, they have known no other life and have nowhere else to go. We have in mind one day transferring the patients to a proper hospital setting and utilizing the building for a cultural purpose in the context of the Cultural Mile (ch. 7). It is a vast space, though the building has fallen into such a state of disrepair that the renovation needed would be extensive (and expensive).

As we walk along Dubnov Street, we pass private homes on our left. On the right is an empty lot, which will one day become either a green area or residential housing, depending on whether City Hall or the Land Authority wins this tug-of-war.

On the left, at the corner, is the back entrance to yet another rose garden, although we must give proper obeisance since this was the first garden to bear this name and serve this function. It was here that official receptions were held by the British and by all former Mayors, as did I until the reunification of the city.

As we reach the intersection with Graetz Street, we once again confront one of the secret ingredients of Jerusalem's enchantment: the amazing views which unfurl when least expected. At this corner, the fascinating facet of the view is the grave distortion of perspective, with the Church of the Ascension on the Mount of Olives in the background seeming but a short distance from the Dormition Abbey on Mount Zion, when in actuality the entire Old City and Gethsemane separate the two. The flag flying to your right is, of course, St Andrew's.

THE GERMAN COLONY

Turning right, we descend Graetz Street and reach Emek Refaim Street and the Germany Colony. The Germans were, in fact, the only community which actually built its own settlement in contrast to the American Colony, which rented existing buildings.

While our walk will be to the right, it might be worthwhile walking the half-block to our left to begin at the beginning. This colony was built in 1873 by German Templers from Württemberg, a sect of the Protestant Pietists which had separated from the Lutherans. Their motto was 'Emigrate from Babylon to settle in Palestine'. The Templers were, in fact, early 'Zionists', inspired by their religious beliefs and fulfilling their desire to settle in the Holy Land. They created a handful of settlements throughout the country, tilling the land and prospering. The Jews in Palestine admired the Templers, respecting their work ethic, their efficiency and their tenacity. This admiration is expressed in the writings of the period.

Despite the heavy traffic of Emek Refaim Street, the walk will skip from one side of the street to the other. The first building across Emek Refaim Street was the Gemeindehaus, the Templer Community Centre, which is now an Armenian church though hardly used. The next two buildings, now the Israel Fibre Institute, were a lyceum where students – including a few Jewish students – studied for the German matriculation. The clock which signalled the students to class is still on the lyceum building.

Germans from the six other settlements throughout the Holy Land sent their children to this school and they lived down the block at the Pension Nikolai Schmidt. (Nikolai Schmidt could be considered my predecessor, since he called himself 'Herr Bürgermeister'.)

A doorway in the German Colony.

The community was built along the lines of German town planning, called *Strassendorf* (a street village). There was a main street with smaller side streets, all on a straight grid pattern, so very different from the rest of Jerusalem with its circular and abstruse layout.

The buildings copied typical German architecture, though in the local stone rather than in wood, with occasional additions of Eastern elements. The layout was similar to the Arab layout: a central room with two rooms on each side. There was also a German-style attic as well as a wine cellar. The first house, built in 1873 by Mattheus Franck, a grinder, even had a steam-driven mill to run the grinding machine.

On no. 9, one can see the head of a lion (the head somewhat resembles Einstein), the only house with a figure of this kind. The house was built by Theodor Zandel, the architect of the old Shaarei Zedek Hospital on Jaffa Road. The family had owned a pharmacy in Bavaria, the Loewe (lion) Apotheke, and the lion commemorated the shingle of the pharmacy.

Crossing the street, we pass no. 12a, the International Cultural Centre for Youth, which indeed serves that purpose. The ICCY has an illustrious Hollywood lineage. Spyros Skouras, the Hollywood film mogul in the 1940s and 1950s, had a managing director named Murray Silverstone. One was Greek, the other was Jewish, but both shared a love for Jerusalem. They raised money throughout the film industry to establish this centre, which serves as an institution 'to teach young people how to live together in peace and harmony' through the arts. The ICCY garden is dedicated to Skouras's daughter, Dionysia, who had died at a very young age.

Gothic inscriptions, as on no. 16, are from the Old Testament witnessing the scriptural ties of the Templers to Jerusalem.

At no. 39 is the Templerfriedhof, the Templer cemetery since 1878. It may seem as if the cemetery had been located in the middle of the colony, but, in fact, it was on the outskirts. While present-day terminology identifies the entire length of Emek Refaim Street as the German Colony, it was true of only a portion of the area. On no. 25, you can already recognize Moslem architecture, with inlaid Armenian tiles.

Until 1878, the Templers had buried their dead in the Protestant cemetery on Mount Zion (see p. 43). But a fight between the Protestants and the Templers on religious matters led to the refusal of the Protestants to allow the Templers to use their cemetery, leaving the Templers no alternative but to acquire land for their own cemetery. Even today an Arab gardener, hired by the Templers in Germany, ensures that it is well cared for. Ironically, there is a Protestant cemetery next door, still in use.

The Natural Science Museum in the German Colony.

What was the fate of the Templers? With the rise of the Nazis, relations between the Templers and the Jews declined. There is even stationery indicating the existence of a branch of the Nazi Party in the German Colony in 1933. Subsequently, with the deterioration in relations between Britain and Germany, a parallel deterioration took place in relations between the British and the Germans in Mandate Palestine. In 1938, Orde Wingate, then a captain in the British army, was invited to an official dinner. When the German Consul walked in, Captain Wingate turned to his wife and said: 'Lorna, come, let us go. We have nothing to do here.'

In the autumn of 1938, I was sent to London to assist the Habonim youth movement. The boats plying the route were Italian, leaving Haifa port and reaching Trieste. Our boat had barely skirted the territorial waters of the British Mandate when a group of Templers donned their Nazi paraphernalia. They were en route to Germany to volunteer their services to their Führer.

Shortly after my arrival in London, the world witnessed *Kristallnacht*, the wanton Nazi destruction of thousands of synagogues and Jewish stores throughout Germany and Austria. My mis-

sion abruptly took on a new countenance: the rescue of young people from Nazi oppression in those countries.

This rescue was spearheaded in England by two remarkable people, Rebecca (Becky) Sieff, a scion of the Marks and Spencer family, and Michael Foot. A succession of ideas was proposed, analysed and discarded until a strategy was devised to obtain entry permits for young people as agricultural workers. While there was widespread unemployment in urban areas, there was a dearth of farm workers. With the approval of the two agricultural unions, the Home Office agreed to issue entry permits for 3,000 youngsters. A single condition was imposed before the permits were issued: that we show proof of placement for these youngsters. We combed the countryside. We cajoled and wheedled and coaxed. Our wanderings brought us to the Cotswolds, to a farm under the stewardship of German monks. When they learned that I had come from the Galilee, they asked: 'Brother, do you come from Nazareth?' My geographic origins brought us fifty more permits.

In 1939, the British deported the Templers to Australia, where they formed the basis of a very prosperous community. Members of this community continue to make a biennial pilgrimage to Jerusalem, joining groups of Templers from Germany in paying their respects at the graves of their ancestors. One of those most active in organizing these visits is Waldemar Fast, grandson of the builder of the Fast Hotel (see p. 95). Waldemar had been sent with his father to Australia in 1939 and then moved to Germany, where he founded a travel agency which organizes the Templer visits.

The German houses in 1939 were taken over by the British as enemy property and inhabited by British officers and clerks. It should be noted that in 1952, in the reparations agreement between the Israeli and German Governments, the Templers asked the German Government for reparations for their properties in the Holy Land and were awarded fifty-two million marks. After the departure of the British, the abandoned homes were taken over in the influx of the mass Jewish immigration and the story here, as elsewhere, is one of deterioration, repurchase, renovation and gentrification.

The German Colony in the 1950s, as in similar nearby quarters like Bakaa and Katamon, was a source of grave social problems. The squatters who had taken over the homes were often newly arrived immigrants from Moslem countries, from Morocco, Algeria, Libya, Tunis, Iraq and Yemen. Israel in the early 1950s was a poor country, food was rationed, and yet it was suddenly faced with the assimilation of hundreds of thousands of immigrants. They arrived faster than even rudimentary housing could be built and so their first homes were often tent cities and asbestos transit camps.

But they swarmed to Jerusalem. For generations they had prayed for a return to Zion. Zion was Jerusalem and the reality of the modern State of Israel was not yet understood. They had borne the trials and tribulations of their arduous journey with the hope of reaching Jerusalem. Their first disappointment was that the Western Wall was beyond their reach, that they could not touch its stones or weep in its shadows. The 1949 Armistice Agreement had, in fact, stipulated that the Western Wall would be accessible, but this condition was never met.

Nevertheless, an empty room in Jerusalem was enough for the fulfilment of these yearnings and they filled the abandoned buildings. A house in which a wealthy family had once lived in elegance was now home to half-a-dozen families in less than elegance. Families were large and sleeping quarters were often mattresses laid end-to-end in the main room.

These families also faced serious social problems, a story familiar to students of immigrant societies whether they be Italians in the United States or Pakistanis in Great Britain. The parents could not speak the local language and thus entered the mainstream of life far more slowly than their children. They had difficulty finding work and the structure of the family moved rapidly towards disintegration.

And we made mistakes. There was such eagerness for a single unified society – Jews from four corners of the world becoming one nation, speaking one language – that the fabric of the multicoloured heritage was not darned but rather discarded. These immigrants were given a Westernized ideal to achieve. They could not achieve it and yet they lost pride in what was theirs. They did not want to eat gefilte fish, but felt shame in their addiction to kubeh (an oriental stuffed meat dish).

The resurgence of ethnicity began in Jerusalem long before it became internationally fashionable, for it was soon clear that the melting-pot being fashioned was at the expense of a rich and varied heritage. It was then that we devised the concept of a mosaic, encouraging each community to maintain its identity while coalescing as a unified creation. In the interim, however, the scene was not rosy. Social problems were colossal and many of the neighbourhood areas, owing to the severe overcrowding and the lack of means, became instant slums.

Gentrification – a notion of modern society – began in the late 1960s. The beauty of these old Arab buildings, with their variegated tiled floors, arched entries and high ceilings, was an attraction to a new generation. But it was a gentrification with a distinct Jerusalem twist to it. While some of the families were eager to sell and move to new, modern apartments, others resisted these offers, however tempting they were. They stayed in their homes and, as time passed and they too prospered, they were able to gentrify their own homes. Thus the indigenous population has merged with the newcomers and given these areas a polychrome character.

The tour ends at the swimming-pool of the German Colony, built in the early 1960s, where tourists can buy a one-time entrance ticket. As the first public pool in the Holy City, it was a source of contention with the ultra-Orthodox community, which demonstrated violently against the 'Pool of Abomination'. The abomination was that men and women were to swim together.

Jerusalemites had heretofore been the butt of derision from their out-of-town peers since Jerusalemites, who reached a beach perhaps once a year, were known as those who could not swim. We have since built several swimming-pools and the dry-docked Jerusalemite belongs to the legends of yesteryear. Jerusalem youngsters have even become gold medallists.

I have been considerate in ending the tour here because it leaves the visitor in the centre of a conglomeration of international fast foods: hamburgers, pizza, croissants and falafel.

9

THE ISRAEL MUSEUM
AND THE KNESSET

My almost daily visits to the Israel Museum, I should confess, are not wholly culturally inspired. As a legacy of the museum's frenetic early days when, as chairman (and overseer), I spent the majority of my waking hours, and many of my sleeping hours, there, I still have an office at the museum. It basically serves as the English-language branch of my municipal activities. In the age of the facsimile machine, it is not that awkward an arrangement; in less technologically advanced eras, it was a set-up which befuddled every efficiency expert. This hideaway office is particularly convenient for late-night meetings when City Hall is closed – and also serves as an occasional refuge when my notorious temper brings me to storm out of my city office . . .

But even when merely passing by, I look with pride at what has become the most eminent cultural institution in our country.

Today it seems rather far-fetched to imagine that in the early 1960s the very notion of a museum was viewed by most as pure folly. Our state had barely reached puberty. The planned museum site lay two miles from a border: the fortifications, barbed wire, tank traps and anti-sniper walls dividing Jerusalem between Israel and Jordan. The tent cities and asbestos huts erected overnight to house the hundreds of thousands of immigrants, Holocaust survivors and refugees from Moslem countries, had barely been dismantled. Our country, with minimal means available, faced overwhelming demands for security, for housing, for education and for medical care. And I tried to speak of museums.

The roots of this fantasy lay a decade earlier. In the early 1950s, I had served as Minister in our Embassy in Washington. During this period, two major Jewish art collectors whom I knew gave their collections to the Metropolitan Museum in New York and to the Fogg Museum at Harvard. I became convinced that had we had an appropriate facility, major works, if not entire collections, might reach Israel. I felt an urgency to this matter: if we were to wait, we would miss our chance.

In my Viennese upbringing, culture had been as vital a form of sustenance as the roof over one's head and the food on one's plate. This was so even in circumstances where the roof and the

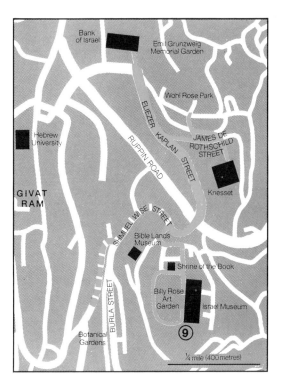

food were not so readily available. Thus my single-mindedness as to the crucial consequence of fostering the arts in our fledgling state may trace its roots to my childhood.

My fantasy was soon given a modicum of pragmatic backing. Baron Edmond de Rothschild of Paris made an offer we could not refuse, the stupendous eighteenth-century French period room which had been in his family's possession for generations. The offer bore but a single condition: that a fitting location be found.

The seeds were thus sown, but it was not a simple mission. While a few stalwart colleagues joined these efforts, the general reaction was a raised eyebrow at best, though more often outright scoffing. A museum? How many families could be housed in its galleries? How many schoolrooms could fit in its pavilions?

Even among those who accepted the principle, there was no lack of controversy as to the nature of this museum. What should be its scope? Ancient art? Jewish art? Modern art? Israeli art?

While guidelines were to allow for evolutionary development, basic precepts had to be set. We had to create a museum which would entertain, enlighten and educate the one-time foreign tourist while playing an entirely different role for the frequent local visitor.

And who would fund this? It was rather evident that it would be years, even decades, before a museum would find a notch in the government budget. We began a search – for money and for art – covering every continent. We badgered anyone who would listen and even some who wouldn't. We convinced a few and they helped convince others. We used tactics ranging from gentle persuasion to gentle coercion.

Even the United States Government played a significant role in our quest. The Government had available what were called counterpart funds for disbursement in Israel. Bernard Katzen, a New York lawyer, was appointed by President Eisenhower and sent to Israel to determine these allocations. Before his feet touched the ground, the number of requests had already approached deluge proportions. But we had the good fortune that the idea of a museum intrigued him. He agreed to help and we took a giant step forward.

Amidst the rabid discord on the nature of this new museum, there was one consensus: that it was to be a home for the archaeology of the Land of Israel. Until 1948, archaeological finds had been housed in the majestic Rockefeller Museum (see p. 38) building opposite the north-east corner of the Old City wall. But with the division of the city, this building and its contents were no longer accessible. Archaeological finds after 1948 were stored in makeshift premises throughout the city. There was no dissent on the need to find them a proper home.

One other point of consensus was that the museum would house the Dead Sea Scrolls, one of the fundamental relics of our ancient heritage. In 1947, these scrolls, 2,000-year-old remnants of a monastic Jewish sect, had been discovered purely by accident, when a young Bedouin shepherd followed a stray goat into a cave at Qumran, near the Dead Sea. While he could not grasp the enormity of his discovery, he did realize that they had some value and sold them in Bethlehem. These scrolls were identified by Professor Sukenik, who succeeded in purchasing three of them in 1948 at a bargain rate, surreptitiously meeting the Bethlehem dealer under difficult and dangerous circumstances as fighting had already started.

On 1 June 1954, an ad appeared in the *Wall Street Journal*, in a 'Miscellaneous for Sale' column under an ad for Kalamazoo Stove and Furnaces.

Bird's-eye view of the Israel Museum, including the Shrine of the Book and the Billy Rose Art Garden.

'The Four Dead Sea Scrolls', read the title. 'Biblical Manuscripts dating back at least 200 BC are for sale. This would be an ideal gift to an educational or religious institution by an individual group. Box F206, The Wall Street Journal.' A bishop of the Syrian Orthodox Church had acquired the scrolls from the same dealer who had sold scrolls to Professor Sukenik.

The purchase of the scrolls entailed John Le Carré intrigue, involving political intricacies (the scrolls theoretically belonged to Jordan where the Qumran caves were situated) and hurried financing, but the deal was eventually consummated.

These scrolls now required a proper setting, befitting their unparalleled significance for the Judeo–Christian tradition. In seeking the necessary help, we called forth the wisdom of our Talmudic sages. The Talmud admonishes one 'who begins a Mitzvah, a good deed, to finish it'. Years earlier, during our frantic search for funding for the purchase of the scrolls, a friend in New York, Samuel Gottesman, had come to our rescue. We now approached him to sponsor the building to house the scrolls, invoking this Talmudic precept.

The Shrine of the Book, the first of the museum buildings, is one of the most distinctive architectural structures in our city. Designed by Armand Bartos and Fredrick Kiesler, the white dome mirrors the contours of the lid of the jar in which the scrolls were found. Adjoining the white dome is a black granite wall and together they symbolize, in

The distinctive interior of the Shrine of the Book, showing the cabinet built to house the Isaiah Scroll.

modern expressionism, the 'War of the Sons of Light Against the Sons of Darkness', one of the scrolls housed within.

Amidst the museum's founding fathers – and mothers – there was also consensus concerning the inclusion of Judaica and Jewish ethnography. A core collection had been established and housed in the small Bezalel Museum, created by Mordechai Narkiss and Boris Schatz early in this century. This was the nucleus of the present collection, which has since become one of the foremost in the world.

With all our planning and re-planning, at times serendipity dictated our decisions. We surely had not thought of an outdoor sculpture garden as a *sine qua non* for this museum, if we had thought of one at all. But my wanderings brought me the good fortune of a meeting with the renowned showman, Billy Rose, who happened to be the owner of a superb sculpture collection. He was fascinated by our idea (and by our *chutzpah*) and, while I was hoping to walk out with one or two major pieces under my arms, he offered his entire collection. When later asked by Ben-Gurion whether he did not have qualms about having his art works within spitting distance of a frontier, Billy Rose's rejoinder was swift: 'Mr Prime Minister, if you have a war, take my bronzes and melt them down for bullets.'

Perhaps it was the touch of lunacy which helped us inspire others. The Japanese–American sculptor Isamu Noguchi, already an internationally known figure in the art world, agreed to design the Art Garden. And so was born one of the most volatile collaborations ever known: Billy Rose and Isamu Noguchi. Their daily squabbles often became fully fledged battles and the scenario became a familiar one: every morning Billy Rose fired Noguchi; every afternoon, Noguchi quit. Such is the work of geniuses. Having finished the sixteenth version of the plan for the garden, Noguchi was asked why he had taken this on. 'Jerusalem', he said, 'is an emotion.'

Walking through the garden today – sometimes to see a new sculpture – I often reflect on the vicissitudes of life. I think of the grandeur of Billy Rose's achievements in his lifetime. And I think that, today, hardly a soul of the younger generation in New York has an inkling of who Billy Rose was. But the Billy Rose Art Garden, with its sculptures by Rodin, Moore, Picasso and Maillol, will bear everlasting witness to this formidable personality. What he and Noguchi created, together, has few equals anywhere in the world.

There was still one more wing to be planned: our youth wing. Israel is justifiably known as the most child-oriented society in the world, but then our children are our greatest natural resource. Even the small Bezalel Museum had classes for children in a cramped attic. Israel's most

The Greek Orthodox Monastery of the Cross, rebuilt in the eleventh century after the original sixth-century building was destroyed by the Persians.

eminent artists tell of their earliest dabblings in this room.

The Ruth Youth Wing in the Israel Museum is a sparkling jewel in the crown. Beyond the special exhibitions, which attract as many adults as children, and beyond an esoteric array of courses available, the noteworthy achievement of the youth wing is that it gives our children a familiarity with museums, an ease which our generation never felt. We were always taken to museums as if they were morgues. One could barely breathe aloud, let alone make anything which resembled noise.

It was also decided that the Israel Museum would be an art museum as well, though this led to the most serious point of dissension in the planning process among the museum's founders: the inclusion or exclusion of Israeli art. There were those who deemed this a priority. There were others who, like me, felt that in principle this should be incorporated, but at a later stage. Our primary fear was that the museum would become provincial. We thus felt that we should first estab-

lish its scope, ensure the highest international quality, and then we could confidently include our local art.

Through the years we frequently mounted temporary exhibitions of Israeli artists, but it was only in 1986, with the creation of the Ayala Zacks Abramov Pavilion for Israeli Art, that we fulfilled this debt.

The design of the museum building was decided by an international competition, won by two local architects, Professor Mansfeld and Dora Gad. The complex they designed is reminiscent of a Mediterranean village, gently climbing the slope of the hill, evolving naturally.

From this hill, the view encompasses the Monastery of the Cross, a massive fortress-like structure built in the sixth century, destroyed by the Persians in the seventh century and rebuilt in the eleventh century, in which a few Greek Orthodox monks live; the Knesset (the Parliament) building; and the Hebrew University campus on Givat Ram.

The museum opened in May 1965 with great fanfare. The sceptics had remained so and we were accused endlessly of creating a white elephant. But the people's vote overrode media cynicism. Our fantasy was an annual attendance of 250,000. Today there are almost a million visitors.

The museum has trebled in size: galleries were added for ethnic arts, Impressionism, French, English and Venetian period rooms, Old Masters, temporary exhibitions, Far Eastern art and the archaeology of neighbouring cultures, design, ancient glass and ancient script. The present construction of the Nathan Cummings Wing for twentieth-century art will complete the museum master plan.

What I deem unique about the museum is the meld of the inanimate art works and that special touch of humanity unique to our city. Walking through the ethnography wing, one encounters a group of Kurdish old-timers who have spontaneously burst into their native dance, inspired by the exhibition of items from the 'old country'. Walking through a photography exhibition, one encounters a soldier wearing a sign, 'Back injury: please be careful.' Walking through the archaeology galleries, one encounters a seven year old clutching her grandfather's hand to show him 'her most, most favourite piece'.

We had thought, originally, that once the museum existed, we could rest on our laurels. Little did we consider that the laurels were barely seedlings. We had now to ensure the first-class quality of the collections and the exhibitions. It was not always easy: we were often confronted by package deals. We could get a first-class Renoir, but it would be encumbered by three major works of the donor's nephew. The decisions were not always easy for a young institution.

The man who did the most to imbue us with the continued quest for excellence was a sixty-seven-year-old Dutchman, Willem Sandberg, the founder of the Stedelijk Museum in Amsterdam and a world expert on modern art. His willingness to come and live in Jerusalem, and serve as the first art adviser to the infant Israel Museum, was a notable coup in the art world of the 1960s.

His modesty was legendary and when we wanted to confer on him a special honour, he agreed reluctantly. In his acceptance speech, he told the following story: 'I had been in the Dutch underground during World War II. Walking along the street one day, I learned that the five others in my group had been arrested by the Gestapo that morning and that I had to go into hiding. For the next six months, I slept in a different bed or field each night. At one point, the Gestapo came to harass my wife, in their attempt to learn where I was hiding. "Don't you realize", they told her, "we are talking of the Gestapo's Enemy Number One?"' Sandberg paused and added: 'That was the last great honour I ever accepted.'

Despite the possible danger to works of art, within the museum's first two years, we showed the internationally acclaimed Joseph Hazen collection and the Marcus Mizne collection. These international shows opened up new worlds at a time when trips abroad were exceedingly rare and Israel was very isolated.

During the first two years of the museum's existence, the overall security question often arose. We were concerned with all aspects of security and detailed contingency plans existed. Even the Shrine of the Book was built so that the main Isaiah scroll could be lowered beneath ground level, like a periscope, if need be.

When the Six Day War broke out after a three-week period of threats and tension, we had had time to take precautionary steps. We felt it essential to keep the museum doors open, if only to help boost the morale of the women and children left guarding the home front. But we did take valuable works down to the storerooms, replacing them with less important works. We taped the windows to prevent shattering. (The children of our Youth Wing classes subsequently painted in the squares of the taped windows so that they looked less ominous.)

With all able-bodied men called up for reserve duty, the women staff members bore the yoke of the burden of these preparations. One day they were called on to fill sandbags, which would be used to cover the outdoor sculptures. They filled sandbags for eight hours under a blazing sun. With the work completed and with every muscle sore, they sat back admiring their handiwork. It was only then that they learned that they had used the wrong sand. The pile which they had used was intended for the Picasso sculpture and the sand contained bits of gravel which could cause bullets to ricochet. And so the next day they spent emptying sandbags and refilling them – with the proper sand.

On the morning of 5 June, additional objects were removed to the cellars. The Jordanians began shelling at 11 a.m. and, around noon, a shell hit the museum, removing a corner of the building. Every window shattered, but no one was hurt and no objects were damaged.

As night fell on that first day of fighting, with a complete blackout in the city, the darkness was suddenly broken by a bright burst of light as the artistic illuminations of the museum building, set by an automatic timer, lit up the museum and the nearby Valley of the Cross. The Valley was filled with soldiers, with artillery and with anti-aircraft guns. It took a soldier only seconds to solve the problem: a few well-placed shots and the Valley was again shrouded in total darkness.

In 1966, some months after the opening, our dreams took a giant leap forward. Mrs James de Rothschild of London, sharing our concern for quality, wanted to ensure that the highest standards were set and thus the Yad Hanadiv Foundation presented the museum with five major Impressionist works – two Van Goghs, two Gauguins and a Cezanne. It was with awe, almost disbelief, that we unpacked the crates. (In 1988, twenty-two years later, our Gauguin was on loan to the National Gallery in Washington, the focus of a definitive Gauguin retrospective there.)

Other friends followed suit. The Duke of Devonshire visited Jerusalem in 1976 and, a few weeks after his visit, wrote, in typical English understatement: 'In case they might interest you, I enclose a guide book to my house and also a catalogue of an exhibition, shown in America, of Old Master Drawings from Chatsworth. I do not know whether you would be interested in mounting an exhibition of such Drawings in your Museum, but if the idea did appeal to you, I would naturally give it the most sympathetic consideration.' The excitement on the Jerusalem side was typically Israeli and the shouting was undoubtedly heard as far away as Chatsworth.

An exhibition of Armand Hammer's paintings brought 300,000 visitors in a three-month period. Not everyone standing on line had been brought up in homes with a tradition of museum-going. Seeing these crowds afforded such pleasure that I foreswore grumbling about the intricate weaving manœuvres needed, through cars and people, to reach my museum office.

Perhaps the true 'coming-of age' of the museum was not through an exhibition shown in Jerusalem but through an exhibition we sent abroad: 'Treasures of the Holy Land: Ancient Art at the Israel Museum', which was shown at the Metropolitan Museum in New York, at the County Museum in Los Angeles, at the Museum of Fine Arts in Houston and at the Royal Ontario Museum in Toronto.

Of course, as with everything which touches our lives, this too was fraught with political convolutions. The Metropolitan Museum had originally wanted to exhibit the show, but a number of their artistic demands emanated from political concerns. The core of the subsequent brouhaha was the Met decision to omit all objects from the Rockefeller Museum in East Jerusalem. People incorrectly surmised that the objects on display there had been excavated in the occupied territories. We explained time and time again that the division of objects between the Rockefeller Museum and the Israel Museum was merely chronological: what had been excavated before 1948 – anywhere in the country – was housed in the former; what was discovered after 1948 – anywhere in the country – was housed in the latter. We also explained that the only reason that the Rockefeller Museum was under Israeli jurisdiction was that the Jordanians, in 1964, had illegally nationalized it. Otherwise it would have remained a private institution endowed by the Rockefellers.

The show was then undertaken by the Smithsonian in Washington, although it did not take long for political machinations to reach there as well. The exhibition then returned to the Met (almost a fully fledged shuttle commuter), which agreed to make decisions only on artistic merit. Naturally each step of this process was accompanied by headlines in the *New York Times* and the *Washington Post*.

TOUR OF THE ISRAEL MUSEUM

It is surely time for our visit to begin. I hesitate setting out a route since a museum visit is such a personal experience. But I cannot resist including a sample of what awaits you.

The walk up to the main entrance is an effective introduction to the museum, with the Shrine of the Book and the Billy Rose Art Garden, on the right, already beckoning the visitor. The modernistic building on the left is a 1988 addition: the Weisbord Pavilion for Temporary Exhibitions.

I must admit that for over two decades, the walk up to the main entrance was a source of dismay. While for the young or the hearty it seems a mere sprint, for others the incline and the steps dissuaded visitors – or exhausted them before they even entered the building. Today a minibus (named Doris) plies the route throughout the day and for a nominal fee will bring the visitor to the museum's front door.

The large staircase in the entrance (twenty-eight steps) will bring you down to the main museum level; there is also an elevator, which the guard will point out.

You reach the museum's shop, although I would suggest leaving the shopping spree until the end so that you need not be encumbered by packages throughout your visit. (There is also a shop at the museum's entrance pavilion.)

You are now at a cross-roads: the road taken will depend very much on your interests and the time at your disposal. Even a half-day visit is cursory – if you want to see it all. (After 1991, with the completion of the wing for twentieth-century art, there may be a few changes in the route.)

We will walk straight ahead to the galleries for Jewish ceremonial art, one of the finest displays, if not the finest, in the world. In renewing these galleries in 1988, we decided that a comprehensive overview of this subject was lacking, not only for our non-Jewish visitors but also for those Jews who have scant education in their heritage. The audio-visual presentation, in Hebrew and English alternately, provides this overview.

We walk through galleries for the Sabbath, for the Torah (the Bible), for the holidays. We can visit an eighteenth-century wooden German synagogue (in the large gallery, on the right) from a town called Horb, one of the few such synagogues not destroyed because it had been dismantled and stored in a basement. It is on permanent loan from the city of Bamberg.

The contrast of a visit to the eighteenth-century

The Italian Synagogue exhibit in the Israel Museum dates from 1702.

Italian synagogue (at the far corner of the gallery, on the right, down the steps) is the best introduction to the vast influence which each country had on its Jewish community. The Italian synagogue could have existed nowhere but Italy.

We pass from Jewish ceremonial art to the Ethnography Pavilion. It is not always easy to find the dividing line between these two areas. Why is a circumcision knife in the Ethnography Gallery rather than in Judaica?

The left wall of the main gallery is that of the life cycle, from birth to death; there are even Jewish tombstones on display. The right-hand wall displays two salons, one of a typical Moroccan Jewish home and one of a typical German Jewish home.

Before reaching the last gallery of the Ethnography Pavilion – costumes and jewellery which can in themselves take half a day – we pass a corner dedicated to artists who perished in the Holocaust. This corner was given by a couple, both refugees from the Holocaust, who felt the importance of a constant reminder of the talent and creativity which died alongside the six million Jews.

We reach the Impressionist Gallery. When this

gallery was being planned, we faced the quandary of how to light it. Our curators wanted natural light, but they sought light of Northern Europe rather than of the Mediterranean (which was what was available). We presented the problem to the Technion University in Haifa, whose engineers devised a ceiling which created the muted light we sought. It is worth an upward glance.

At the far end of the gallery, we exit into another world. On the left is the eighteenth-century French Room and immediately in front of us is the eighteenth-century Venetian Room. A walk down the flight of steps (which you will have to climb back up) brings you to our Old Masters galleries and an eighteenth-century English dining-room.

Retracing one's steps through the Impressionist Gallery (always a treat), one reaches the pavilion for ethnic arts: a taste of New Guinea and the American Indian, a peek at the African world and a chance for a visit to pre-Columbian cultures. The Far Eastern Gallery on the left leads to the Israeli art galleries and our design pavilion. If you walk straight on, you reach the Numismatics Gallery and the entrance to the museum auditorium (for night-time concerts, lectures, films).

The visitor who walks straight on will come to our original cross-roads, but this time we will turn towards the archaeology pavilions. The visitor who walked through the Israeli art galleries will have to descend the staircase once again.

The archaeology galleries are in order of chronology, beginning with prehistoric times and concluding with the Islamic era. I cannot resist pointing out my favourite: the gallery for ancient glass. Beyond the superb beauty of each piece, I find myself in awe of the aesthetics of the past, two millennia ago.

I had inherited the collector's fever from my father, an inveterate collector of anything collectable, and often scoured antiquities shops and antiquarians when the prices for museum-quality objects were usually very reasonable and often very cheap: ancient pottery, ancient coins, ancient glass, items of Judaica, rare maps and early views of Jerusalem. Our museum curators often took advantage of the free hand I gave them in my collection. But the gift which gave me the most satisfaction was that of a handful of European glass pieces which were practically the only objects with which my parents had escaped from the impending Holocaust.

Leaving the glass pavilion, we reach the gallery of the Roman period, where the famous bust of Hadrian is on display. This bronze bust was actually discovered in the Galilee by an American tourist walking about with a mine detector. It took several years of laboratory work to clean and stabilize the bust and, throughout that time, the tourist would bring family and friends to see his find.

Several weeks after this bust was uncovered, I was travelling to New York for a fund-raising din-

The second-century AD sculpture of the Roman Emperor Hadrian in the Israel Museum.

ner for the American Friends of the Israel Museum. I thought it would be a major coup if we could display the Hadrian bust on that occasion and I approached the head of our government Department of Antiquities with my request, explaining that I would hand-carry the bust in the aeroplane cabin. The reply was simple, if a bit disconcerting: 'What if the plane crashes?' It takes an archaeologist to put things in proper perspective.

Passing a superb collection of oil lamps, we descend another wide staircase into the world of neighbouring cultures. We then pass through the wooden doors – into the world of our young people. This is the main exhibition gallery of the Youth Wing. Whatever the exhibition, the focus is didactic, whether an exhibition of ancient Egypt or paper-making or colours or self-portraits or historical India or even comics. The downstairs area is additional exhibition space, classrooms, an auditorium, a library, a 'recycling room', and hundreds and hundreds of babbling children of all ages.

There is also an exit, which brings you almost to our starting-point, although you are surely far more exhausted – and exhilarated – than when you started out.

The Israel Museum will be the core of a complex of new museums to be completed in the vicinity. Across the road is the Bible Lands Museum, which will house the unique artefacts of a single collector: Dr Elie Borowski of Toronto. His collection in the field of biblical archaeology is singular and an untold number of museums throughout the world wooed him in order to acquire the collection. But his and his wife Batya's love was Jerusalem and, as he wanted to keep the collection as a single entity, the Bible Lands Museum was created.

The other new museums will be located near the Givat Ram campus of the Hebrew University on the next ridge: the Bloomfield Science Museum, the Jerusalem miniature equivalent of the San Francisco Exploratorium, and a new natural history museum. We often create facilities which we claim are for our children but they equally besot the child in us. What Israel has learned is that museums are not a luxury, that it is as important to feed the soul and the intellect as the body.

Food for the soul is aplenty in this neighbourhood with its cluster of parks and gardens, within a walk of minutes. The Botanical Garden of the Hebrew University below the museum was also a dream which took years to realize, independent of growing time. It is a wonder of nature in that its various continental divisions – the American sector, the European sector, the Asian sector, the Australian sector – prove what can be achieved in Jerusalem soil with, or despite, Jerusalem weather conditions. It is a wonderland for amateur botanists – and for the professionals.

The greenhouse in the Botanical Garden on the Hebrew University's Givat Ram campus.

GIVAT RAM CAMPUS
OF THE HEBREW UNIVERSITY

The Botanical Garden is an integral part of the Givat Ram campus of the Hebrew University. Following the War of Independence, the Armistice Agreement stipulated open access for Israelis to the Hebrew University campus on Mount Scopus. Although the access agreement was not kept, Mount Scopus nevertheless remained in Israeli hands throughout the period of division, a bizarre concoction entailing an Israeli enclave surrounded on all sides by Jordanian territory. The only 'students' who reached the Mount Scopus campus were soldiers brought to guard the area, escorted across the border in a fortnightly United Nations convoy from the Mandelbaum Gate.

Thus the Hebrew University became, almost overnight, a ghost university. Initially, to continue quasi-functioning, its classrooms were scattered in apartments and sheds throughout the new city, hardly an ideal learning climate. When the reality was ultimately confronted, that the campus on Mount Scopus was no longer a viable entity, a new campus was built in West Jerusalem on Givat Ram.

The reunification of the city in 1967 brought Mount Scopus back into the everyday world. Once again the number 9 bus, which decades earlier had carried students to Mount Scopus – in the nineteen years of the city's division, no new bus route was assigned the number 9 – was again ply-ing its route. One of my vivid memories of the Six Day War was a busload of soldiers driving towards Mount Scopus with a hastily affixed number 9 on the bus window.

Step by step, department by department, the university on Mount Scopus was reborn. What remained behind on the Givat Ram campus were the natural sciences faculties as well as the beautiful Henry Moore sculpture, which had been the meeting-point for young couples courting. The white domed campus synagogue on Givat Ram is more often than not confused with the somewhat similar shape of the museum's Shrine of the Book.

The Givat Ram campus also houses the Jewish National and University Library, the finest repository of books and valuable manuscripts in our country. I added to its collection, passing on a gift given to me by Igor Stravinsky: the original manuscript of *The Sacrifice of Isaac*, a piece he had written to a Hebrew text for the Israel Festival when he came here in 1964. My memories of his visit are always tinged with embarrassment: I had been given the privilege of driving him to Caesarea for the première of his work, and my car broke down en route!

We now cross Ruppin Road and go up Eliezer Kaplan Street, where the main government office buildings are. A right turn on to James A. de Rothschild Road brings us to the Knesset, the Israeli Parliament.

THE KNESSET

With the creation of the state in 1948, it had been obvious to all that there could be but one capital: Jerusalem. Enactment of this decision had at first to be delayed, since Jerusalem was severed from the rest of the country. Jerusalemites were the last to sense that a state had been declared. Under constant bombardment, with food and water severely rationed, they were busy defending their future capital. Rejoicing would have to be postponed.

Tel Aviv served as the functional capital for several months. Major businesses, like banks and insurance companies, transferred their headquarters there, ultimately remaining there, and thus today Tel Aviv is Israel's financial metropolis.

As soon as Jerusalem was accessible, Ben-Gurion took his Bible, his notebook and his pen, and with these three items in hand moved his office to Jerusalem. He established the Prime Minister's Office in a building belonging to the Jewish Agency. The Knesset was housed in temporary quarters in an office building on King George Street, the Froumine Building. These 'temporary' quarters lasted eighteen years (see p. 134)!

In the early years one could disregard the accoutrements of nationhood. But as the state grew out of infancy, the less than dignified premises of the Knesset could no longer be ignored. James de Rothschild of London, sensitive to this need, wrote a letter to be delivered posthumously to Ben-Gurion, requesting that the Rothschilds be allowed to build a proper Parliament building. Permission, of course, was readily granted and a site chosen in what was to become the government compound.

The rabid arguments concerning the architectural design were precursors to those which would become daily fare in this legislature, but eventually a decision was made and an imposing building was built. The Menorah sculpted by Benno Elkan, which had been a gift of British Jewry and had graced the park adjoining the old Knesset, also moved to this new home.

The dedication of the Knesset building was a bitter-sweet occasion. Speakers of legislatures throughout the world – including the Speaker of the House of Commons, a personal honour for

The Knesset, Israel's Parliament.

the Rothschilds – converged on Jerusalem amidst much fuss and ado. But for me the ceremony was tainted. Ben-Gurion had been on the blacklist of his former Labour Party colleagues and thus was not invited to speak. They could not rise above political in-fighting to acknowledge the founding-father of the state and of the democratic tenets of the Parliament and, practically speaking, the recipient of the gift which had enabled the creation of this new building. A petty lot, they were.

One memory which crops up again and again when I visit the Knesset is that of Ben-Gurion's death in 1973 and his lying-in-state in the expanse at the Knesset entrance. For me, he was more than a mentor. He was a man of vision and yet a man of deeds; he almost always knew when to be flexible and when to be obstinate; his understanding of people and of history enabled him to make decisions which were effective both in the short run and in the long run.

At about 3 a.m., there were still endless lines of people who had come to pay their last respects. Despite the throngs, there was an overwhelming silence. I stood on the sidelines, transfixed by the scene before me, for indeed everyone had come. Despite the late hour, little children were held in hand by their parents, who had brought them to

The Wohl Rose Park opposite the Knesset.

honour this unique man. The elderly stood waiting in line with infinite patience, some speaking Yiddish, others speaking Moroccan. We all shared the knowledge that we were witnessing the end of an era.

The public can visit the Knesset on Sunday and Thursday mornings (passport in hand). The beautiful tapestries by Marc Chagall, commissioned by the Rothschilds, are in themselves worth the stop. On a long-ago visit to Paris, I called on Chagall, who took me to see the work-in-progress on the tapestries. Early one morning we walked from his home on Ile Saint Louis to the Palais de Gobelins. I accompanied Chagall into the workroom expanse, where dozens of young ladies, wih maquettes at their side, were creating these gobelins. I found the scene intriguing. While I knew that such handiwork was used to make carpets in Iran, I had not anticipated seeing it in an industrialized nation. The workers were accustomed to Chagall's almost daily visits and his arrival did not cause a stir. While he did not use a jeweller's glass, his check of the threads was as microscopic. When a shade of the dye did not entirely satisfy his expert eye, parts of the tapestry were summarily unravelled.

The tapestries depict the history of the Jewish people, from the creation of the world to modern days, from Moses's first arrival at the borders of the country to the return to Zion.

Across from the Knesset is Demonstration Hill. What is most notable in the area of the Knesset and the government buildings is that one can always encounter one form of demonstration or another: doctors or farmers, teachers or television engineers, left-wing and/or right-wing activists.

Not long ago even I staged a one-man demonstration in front of the Prime Minister's Office – protesting the Prime Minister's dilly-dallying in giving his approval for the city's soccer stadium. One fact of life has become evident: nothing in Jerusalem is uncomplicated.

Soccer is Israel's acknowledged national pastime and the city desperately needed a proper stadium. But as the games are held on the Sabbath, as they have been since time immemorial (or, more exactly, since soccer began here in the 1920s), and as the religious parties are continuously in need of political fodder, the stadium had become a political issue.

We had started work on a site in the late 1970s, but, after entreaties by Prime Minister Begin, we chose another site. Plans were submitted and approved by the endless commissions which exist, as befits a bureaucratic society. We were one step away from our goal (pun unintended), a mere formality, the signature of the acting Minister of the Interior, Prime Minister Shamir. Weighing political considerations rather than the needs of Jerusalem, and confident that he would not lose the votes of loyal football fans, he delayed signing.

In frustration, I finally decided that there was no recourse but to demonstrate in front of his office. But as the reality of a Mayor's life does not allow for the leisure of a day spent quietly holding a placard, I moved my entire office to the demonstration: desk, secretaries, telephones and all. Unfortunately to no avail. The Prime Minister chose non-action, forcing us to bring the matter to court. His attempt to have his cake and eat it left Jerusalem's soccer fans scrambling for crumbs. (The 1989 postscript: the court decision was in our favour and work is well under way.)

WOHL ROSE PARK

At least one can quickly if not easily forget the political problems of the Government simply by crossing the street and entering the Wohl Rose Park. In contrast to the Israel Museum's Billy Rose Garden, where roses are incidental, this is truly a magnificent celebration of roses. The beauty of this garden is not merely food for the soul but a veritable feast. There are 650 varieties of roses, including the Lili Marlene, the Maria Callas – and the Peace Rose.

This park was chosen by the Government as the official spot to welcome and bid farewell to visiting dignitaries: the Presidents of Costa Rica and El Salvador, French Prime Minister Jacques Chirac, British Prime Minister Margaret Thatcher, American Vice-President George Bush. The only downside is the twenty-one gun salute, which often gives nearby picnickers a rude awakening.

Perhaps it is a universal truth that there is no joy without sorrow, though it seems a truth all too prevalent in our city. Thus, when one leaves the sanctuary of the Wohl Rose Park, one encounters the Emil Grunzweig Memorial Garden. This garden bears the tragic story of a young member of the Peace Now movement, who was killed as he led a demonstration on this site against the war in Lebanon. The grenade was thrown by an Israeli follower of the infamous Rabbi Meir Kahane, who objected to Grunzweig's political views.

When we had the dedication of the garden, Prime Minister Begin attended, although he also had no sympathy for Grunzweig's political views. The time, however, had come for him to dissociate himself from the increasing violence of his followers. The enormity of Grunzweig's death sent such tremors throughout the country that the waves of violence subsided measurably.

The last building on this route – an upside-down topless pyramid – is the Bank of Israel, where crucial decisions affect what we earn (little), what we can afford to buy (little) and what we save (little).

10
FROM THE TICHO HOUSE
TO MEA SHEARIM

While the Ticho House (Beit Ticho), Harav Kook Street 7–9, where we start our walk, does not have the myriad archaeological layers characteristic of Jerusalem's more ancient sites, it does have a series of modern permutations. The house was built in the late nineteenth century by Hajj Rashid, a prominent Arab, who then sold it to Wilhelm Moses Shapira, a Jew who had converted to Christianity. Shapira sold antiquities, many newly manufactured. His duplicity earned him widespread notoriety and he subsequently committed suicide.

The Tichos purchased the house in 1924. Theirs was a story of which novels are written and films are made.

Dr Avraham Albert Ticho, born in Boskowitz, Moravia, in 1883, studied medicine in Vienna and became an eminent eye doctor. As eye disease was rampant in this part of the world, his services were desperately sought and he was brought to Jerusalem in 1912. Within a year of his arrival, he had instituted preventative measures in the Jerusalem schools to constrain the spread of trachoma.

It was not uncommon among Jewish families at the time for first cousins to marry. Thus no eyebrows were raised when Dr Ticho married his first cousin Anna, born in Brünn, Moravia, sharing

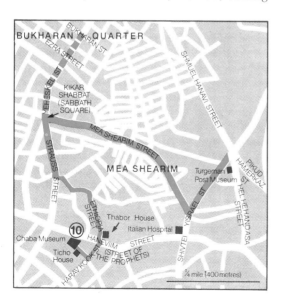

with him the same birthday but eleven years his junior. Barely eighteen, she had already studied art in Vienna, where her talent was acknowledged. But, upon her arrival in Jerusalem, the impact of the stark landscape was such that she stopped painting.

The newlyweds were soon packing their bags again, this time en route to Damascus, where Dr Ticho was stationed as the Austrian army chief ophthamologist. It was in Damascus that Anna resumed her painting.

In 1918, they returned to Jerusalem, where Dr Ticho headed the ophthamology department at the Rothschild (later the Hadassah) Hospital. And he opened his private clinic, which attained fame as the finest in the Middle East. He treated pashas and rabbis, effendis and the indigent, even Abdullah, the Emir of Transjordan. When Dr Ticho was stabbed during the Arab riots of 1929,

The Ticho House museum, Harav Kook Street.

get-well wishes arrived from England, Antwerp and Rabat, letters which are on display on the second floor of the house. There is a thank you on behalf of Emir Abdullah sent in 1941.

One document both intrigues and saddens me: a notice promulgated by the Chief Rabbinate beseeching all of Israel to pray for the recovery of Dr Ticho following the wanton attack. What saddens me is the knowledge that today a notice such as this would never be affixed in the streets of Jerusalem were the victim a non-observant Jew.

While helping her husband run the clinic, Anna painted, capturing the landscape and the people. This diminutive figure – less than five feet tall – could often be found on remote hillocks, sketchbook in hand.

Following her husband's death in 1960, she leased the first floor of the house, where the clinic had been, to the Israel Radio. The second floor became her home and her studio and was accessible via the flight of steps one first encounters, on the side of the building. I often expressed concern, when she reached her eighties, that the stairs might be too burdensome, but her love for her home dispelled any notion of moving elsewhere.

Anna's plans were to bequeath her home to the people of Jerusalem, and we often discussed how it would be restored and for what purposes it would be used.

She became ill a few weeks before her death in 1980. While in the hospital, having lost her ability to speak, she wrote a note to the woman sitting by her bedside, Elisheva Cohen, Chief Curator of the Israel Museum and Anna's closest friend. 'Please be sure', she wrote in German, her mother tongue, 'that I have a respectable funeral. And please be sure that good care is taken of the house.'

Anna died on a day of one of Jerusalem's rare snowstorms, when life in the city was seriously disrupted. I called the Burial Society to ensure that all was in order for her funeral, offering to supply any heavy equipment that was needed. As roads were still hard to drive on (only emergency vehicles have snow tyres), a mere handful of Anna's friends succeeded in reaching the funeral parlour, which, though covered, is an outdoor structure. The cold was blistery. We waited and waited. I became livid when I learned that the delay was because the road to the cemetery was impassable, despite the Burial Society's earlier assurances. A short service finally took place, but I felt heavily burdened that we had not fulfilled one of her death-bed wishes.

Thus I became even more determined to fulfil the other, ensuring that the restoration work on the house be impeccable. Anna's paintings are beautifully displayed as is Dr Ticho's collection of Judaica, mainly Chanukah lamps. The library on the first floor has its serenity broken each week by a story-telling hour for children. The second-floor space is a popular venue for chamber concerts and for lectures. The indoor/outdoor café, with a tasty strudel, rarely has an empty seat, and the tree-shaded garden below is a welcome respite not only for visitors walking the streets of Jerusalem with guidebook in hand but for the local populace walking the streets with shopping bags in hand.

It was only when I stood at the dedication of Ticho House that my conscience was assuaged with the completion of a debt to Anna Ticho.

Leaving the Ticho House, one can stop at two additional 'museums', both open to the pubic during morning hours. Following the path just past the outside steps to the Ticho House and following the signs and arrows (ducking the barriers of low-hanging laundry on sunny days), one reaches the Chaba Museum of Jewish Micrographic Art, the art of miniature writing. I have sometimes wondered if the geographical juxtaposition of this museum and Dr Ticho's eye clinic was purely coincidental.

Just past the main entrance and exit to the Ticho House complex is the house of Rabbi Kook, the first Ashkenazi Chief Rabbi of Palestine. Visitors are welcome.

We leave the Ticho House and, turning left on to Harav Kook Street, we reach Haneviim Street. While few streets in Jerusalem are known by the English translation of their name – one would never call Hatayassim Street, The Pilots' Street, or Mechalkei Hamayim Street, the Water Carriers' Street – Haneviim Street is often called Street of the Prophets, perhaps because of the conglomeration of pubic and once-public buildings located here, many of which were once, or still are, Christian institutions.

Turning left on to Haneviim Street, after the parking lot, a glance to the left brings an old railway carriage into view. This serves as provisional offices for a voluntary organization called Yad Sarah, which supplies medical equipment (crutches, wheelchairs, respirators) on loan for home care. When the railway carriage was first placed there, against every conceivable municipal ordinance, we were torn between municipal considerations – have it removed immediately! – and reverence for the works of mercy undertaken by these dedicated volunteers. We ultimately agreed to allow it to remain in place, until proper facilities for the organization are available.

A continuation on Haneviim Street to our left would bring us to the Bikur Cholim Hospital, one building of which had been a nineteenth-century German hospital designed by Conrad Schick, to the St Joseph Convent School at no. 66 and to the Jerusalem residence of the nineteenth-century English painter William Holman Hunt at no. 64. But we are going to cross Haneviim Street at the parking lot and stop at no. 58, the Thabor House, built and lived in by Conrad Schick, a name already familiar as the architect of numerous prominent buildings scattered throughout the city (and throughout these walks). The present owner is the Swedish Theological Institute, which is a fine guardian for a fine property.

Conrad Schick was a southern German Protestant dispatched as a missionary to the Holy Land in 1851. The funds sent to support him were not even subsistence level, so he called on the folks back home to send him a consignment of cuckoo clocks for which he thought there might be a market. He underestimated the success of these clocks with the effendis and he was soon master of a prosperous venture. In fact, too prosperous for his liking. Fearing that it was making him more of a businessman than a Christian, leaving him little time for missionary work, he took the extraordinary step of closing it down.

He was the ultimate Renaissance man, with multi-faceted talents. He was a self-taught architect, as most architects of the period were, and he had extensive knowledge in geology and archaeology. He designed the Leper Hospital (see p. 103), the Talithakumi Orphanage and the German Hospital at the end of his block. He was deeply respected abroad and was awarded several honorary degrees from German universities. At the same time, he was very much accepted and admired by the local Jewish community and, in fact, was commissioned to design Mea Shearim (see p. 125).

Conrad Schick's house is a miniature of a German castle, with a private chapel on the right. The coat of arms lists CSFD, Conrad Schick and his wife Frederika Dobler, who are buried in the Protestant cemetery on Mount Zion (see p. 43).

His love of archaeology is evident from the artefacts embedded in the building façade. On the top left, you can see an example of these. This treatment of ancient artefacts would be deemed sacrilegious by present-day archaeologists, but it portrays a human and intimate approach to these objects.

We turn up Ethiopia Street (right of Thabor House), which derives its name from the Ethiopian Cathedral dominating the right side of the street. (You will see that 'street' is an exaggeration for this narrow road, which includes parked cars along the left and traffic, coming from behind, along the right. But, somehow, as is the way of miracles, there is room for all.) Logic has it that amidst the picturesque dwellings of Ethiopia Street one can find the Ethiopian Church, which still houses a handful of monks, even though the prayer centre for this community is in the Old City.

The close ties between Israel and Ethiopia during the reign of Haile Selassie have long since disintegrated, but an item of proof remains to this day in our city's land registry as Haile Selassie owned a house on this street and it is still so registered. At one time a bombastic plan for the construction of a pilgrims' hostel and an amphitheatre was proposed for this site – to be funded partially by Jews who had business dealings in Ethiopia – but with the change of government there, this proposal achieved instant obsolescence.

The end of this street serves as an unmarked border, sadly at times a frontier, with the Mea Shearim neighbourhood. While in recent years the ultra-Orthodox neighbourhoods have spread far beyond the borders of Mea Shearim, this remains the most traditional example and, in some ways, the most extreme community.

We continue to Strauss Street, passing on our left the former B'nai B'rith Library dating to 1903. It was the original building housing the National University Library and its newest tenant is the Rabbinical Council of America.

Turning right on Strauss Street, at the second traffic lights we reach a teeming intersection. Seemingly innocuous, it was once the site of weekly Sabbath demonstrations, thus acquiring the informal name 'Kikar Shabbat', 'Sabbath Square'. Orthodox Jews do not travel on the Sabbath, and the cars which once passed here were made to understand this in no uncertain terms. Cries in Yiddish of *'Shabbos! Shabbos!'*, with an occasional missile to make the point even clearer, were a weekly fact of life. Following the reunification of the city, alternative routes became available, enabling vehicular traffic to bypass this intersection. Together with neighbouring Mea Shearim, the road is closed to traffic on the Sabbath.

BUKHARAN QUARTER

While we shall eventually enter Mea Shearim by making a right turn at 'Sabbath Square' on to Mea Shearim Street, the shopping mecca of Geula, a 'suburb' of Mea Shearim, I would like to suggest a detour to the Bukharan Quarter for those who have the time and inclination. To reach the Bukharan Quarter, continue straight on Yeheskel Street until Ezra Street, where we turn left.

The Bukharan Quarter, built at the end of the nineteenth century, differed fundamentally from the other Jewish residential areas, where generally the communal institutions built housing quarters and then rented space to the community members. The Bukharan Quarter was built by wealthy Jews from Bukhara and Tashkent, in today's Soviet Republic of Uzbekistan. These were their summer homes.

There was no strong communal life and no central synagogue. Almost each clan had a synagogue in its home; the families themselves were large enough for the traditional *minyan*, the quota

of ten men needed for public prayers. It was similar to the private chapels in Christian mansions.

While the homes were regal and spacious, there was none like that at Ezra Street 19. Built in 1904–5, Beit Yehudayoff was called 'The Palace'. People gazed in wonder, speculating why anyone would build a thirty-room house for use every second summer. It was said that Yehudayoff's intention was to ensure a fitting abode for the Messiah on his arrival.

The homes often have the six-pointed Jewish star engraved or affixed to their gates, doors or walls. The Bukharans missed no opportunity to proclaim their Jewish identification, which could not be expressed as openly in their Bukharan homeland. Not all the Bukharans were well-to-do, and on the corner of Yeheskel Street and Bukharan Street is a building which served to house those less fortunate.

The Russian Revolution stopped the flow of Bukharan visitors and few Bukharans remain in this area. The houses are often the property of dozens of heirs scattered in dozens of countries and, sadly, the Quarter has a neglected air about it. The influx of the ultra-religious 'haredi' community has changed its character, with their traditional black garb replacing the multi-coloured garments of the Bukharans.

MEA SHEARIM

Retracing our steps on Yeheskel Street, we again reach 'Sabbath Square', but, as we are coming from the opposite direction, access to Mea Shearim is now with a left turn. The road narrows and one enters a self-contained community. The original plan for Mea Shearim was a row of houses around an inner courtyard for synagogues, houses of learning and water cisterns. But as the neighbourhood quickly became overcrowded, dwellings filled the open spaces and few of these inner courtyards remain.

The only way to experience Mea Shearim is to meander through its alleyways. For visitors who come from cities with similar communities – New York, London, Antwerp – the sight is a familiar one. For others it may be less so: the black-garbed men with their curled sidelocks, the women wearing long-sleeved dresses, black stockings (even during the heat of the summer), and their heads covered either with a black scarf or a 'sheitl', a wig. A host of little children pull at the skirt of their mother who is certainly already carrying the newest addition to the family. The language spoken is often Yiddish, not Hebrew. There is no radio and no television, no cinemas or secular newspapers, and time is spent in religious study. It is a step

Facade of 'The Palace', or Beit Yehudayoff, in the Bukharan Quarter.

backward in time, into the villages of nineteenth-century Poland, a real-life version of *Fiddler on the Roof*'s Anatevka.

The population of the official Mea Shearim neighbourhood is just over 5,000, all ultra-Orthodox Jews, though of a variety of hues. And while inter-communal relations are not always placid, the intra-communal relations are almost commune-like. The needs of an individual become a communal undertaking. If money is needed for a daughter's wedding, it is provided; food is supplied to families in want; health needs are covered from an amazing array of funds. The community has its own 'health minister', who ensures that proper treatment is obtained and the costs covered.

In Mea Shearim the Jewish holidays are all-pervasive and any of the festive seasons warrants a special visit. Indeed, these visits should be

The Mea Shearim district showing the booths, erected against each house during the Festival of Succoth.

A Hassidic Jew in a Mea Shearim study house.

while in most religious homes this is done with coins, the people of Mea Shearim adhere to the age-old ritual of using a live chicken in this ceremony.

Succoth follows (October) and the traditional lulav branch and citrus ethrog have to be purchased. Each item demands perfection, without a single blemish, and the decision often takes hours: a jeweller's eyepiece is not an uncommon sight.

Jewish law – *Halacha* – dictates living seven days in makeshift tabernacles (*succoth*) to remember the forty years during which the ancient Israelites wandered in the desert. Ritual entails starting *succah* construction just after breaking the fast of the Day of Atonement and the night is filled with incessant hammering. The Mea Shearim apartments are small and the balconies often minuscule, but there is not a single balcony which does not boast a *succah*. While many observe the law to the extent of eating every meal of that week in the *succah*, the ultra-Orthodox keep this law to the letter and sleep there as well.

The Chanukah holiday (December) dictates having the Chanukah lamp visible to the passer-by. Most consider the dictate fulfilled by placing the lamp in a window; in Mea Shearim the lamps hang outside the homes.

Purim (March) is a fancy-dress holiday and the streets are filled with little Queen Esthers and little Mordechais (the heroine and hero of the holiday) as well as little Hamans (the villain) – not to mention assorted cowboys and supermen. The holiday also prescribes getting so drunk that you cannot differentiate between Mordechai and Haman. As with every precept, this is also fulfilled very literally in Mea Shearim. One can only be thankful that the neighbourhood is a few blocks long and the distance from synagogue to home can be covered by foot. Drunken pedestrians cause less damage than drunken drivers, at most knocking over a garbage can or two.

Passover (April) brings the holiday of the unleavened bread, the matza, and every corner of Mea Shearim miraculously boasts a two-man matza factory. One learns that there is matza and there is matza. There is the machine-made matza we are accustomed to buying in our supermarkets. There is machine-made matza for which the flour has been supervised from the very wheat fields. And there is the hand-made matza made from special flour, which is considered the paragon of matza. The diameter of this matza can reach a metre and its taste is a cross between cardboard and plaster. You will see these matzas being carried gingerly through the streets since even a small break in the matza makes it invalid for ritual purposes.

Shavuoth (Pentecost), the last of the three biblical pilgrimages to Jerusalem, is the harvest holiday. Children are adorned with wreaths

undertaken during the pre-holiday period as the entire neighbourhood becomes engrossed in the specific rituals of preparation for the specific holiday.

Before the High Holy Days (September), one can sense the tension as supplicants prepare to give their annual accounting for the Book of Judgement. Everyone is busy, making one final visit to the ritual bath, the *mikvah*, or one final purchase. Throughout the entire month before the Jewish New Year, Rosh Hashanah, the ram's horn is blown during the early morning service and, because there are prayer halls in every nook and cranny, the area reverberates with the sound of this trumpeting.

The eve of the Day of Atonement entails a complicated ritual of transmuting one's sins and,

symbolizing the first fruits; the holiday food is cheese cake, cheese blintzes and cheese kreplach (European dough arrangements); and it is the custom to sit and study the Torah the entire night. Thus, if you walk through Mea Shearim in the wee hours of this holiday, it will seem as if it is midday.

If one's visit to Jerusalem does not coincide with one of the holidays, one need not be despondent, for in Mea Shearim each Sabbath is in itself a holiday. The rushing around begins early Friday morning, but intensifies as the day continues, because all the shopping, cleaning and cooking must be completed before sunset. The objective length of the day is not a factor: last-minute is last-minute, both during the winter, when sunset is at 4 p.m., and during the summer daylight savings time, when it is at 8 p.m.

The smells of the Sabbath preparations are part and parcel of the visitor's experience. And while one cannot just walk into a house and ask for a plate of chicken soup, the fresh Sabbath challah can be bought in any bakery (just follow your nose). Forget your calorie counting, for the taste of a freshly baked challah should not be measured in carnal but rather in spiritual terms.

Mea Shearim shopping is mainly for Jewish ritual objects and several shops of this nature can

Teddy Kollek enjoying (or perhaps just enduring) a camel ride during Purim Holiday festivities.

be found on the main street and in the alleyways. There are also a few small outdoor fruit and vegetable markets, although just a fraction the size of the main market in Mahane Yehuda (see p. 138).

The experience of a Friday night traditional Sabbath dinner is often open to all comers, although mainly aimed at Jewish tourists to give them a taste of a religious Sabbath experience; the purpose is to 'convert' the Jews, not the Christians. One has merely to go to the Western Wall as the sun is setting and an invitation will be proffered. While the family which hosts you may not be proficient in your language, one can nevertheless imbibe the Sabbath spirit. *Caveat emptor*: an effort will be made to initiate the uninitiated.

For a visit to Mea Shearim on any day of the week, proper dress and proper decorum are expected, even demanded. You will encounter signs in English warning the visitor: 'Women in Immodest Dress are Strictly Forbidden to Enter our Neighbourhood'. More detailed instructions are encountered: 'Request and Warning. To Women Visiting our Vicinity. Not to Appear in our Vicinity – in short garments (not covering the knee), in short-sleeeved clothes (not covering the arm). The Torah obligates to dress in modest attire that covers the entire body.' The signatories are the 'Residents of the Vicinity'. And, in fact, modest dress is highly recommended.

Hebrew or Yiddish signs, for local consumption only, are often expressive of the anti-Zionist nature of some residents. Since by law all commercial establishments must close on Israel's Independence Day, public notices claim that these closures are a sign of mourning for the creation of the secular Jewish state. When Yigal Shilo, a young archaeologist, died after a struggle with cancer, signs indicated a day of rejoicing because this archaeologist had excavated in an area which was a source of dissension (see p. 32). He was denounced as an 'evil man'; 'so may your enemies perish', was the cry. His 'great suffering' would be completed in the hereafter. During the Israeli national elections in November 1988, banners were drawn across the road exhorting people not to vote in the Zionist elections as they were an abomination. But it was merely a handful of the ultra-Orthodox community who did not vote; the majority came out with a show of strength.

The growing strength of the *haredi* population has brought increasing focus on the conflict between religious and secular Jewry. *Haredi* – literally 'the fearful', those who fear the Lord – is a general term referring to the ultra-Orthodox community. Indeed, one should say communities, because their intramural rifts are themselves often as virulent as their struggle with the secular Jewish community.

But even that crude division is in itself misleading since it is not a division into two distinct camps but rather a continuum, and even on this continuum the distinctions are imprecise. Religiosity and intolerance are not necessarily hand-in-hand partners, but the few extremists who perpetrate this kinship are viewed by the secular community as a constant threat. Moreover, there is a real attempt by the *haredi* groups to force their ideology on the majority, whether it be the observance of the Sabbath, the permissibility of autopsies or the sale of non-kosher meats.

We do agree that Jerusalem is different, for while we are concerned with Friday night entertainment for our young people, we have no desire to compete with Tel Aviv. Some form of Sabbath peace and quiet can reign in Jerusalem without infringing on those who want to spend their Sabbath otherwise. However, ultra-Orthodox intransigence often discourages moderates from reaching a compromise with them.

While Jerusalem must be a serene and reflective city, it must not be a city that breeds religious coercion. The true spirit in Jerusalem must be such that it invites people to willingly and with full freedom of conscience engage in and be open to the vitality and depth of the spiritual quest. Yet we must not violate the integrity of the individual for the sake of the spiritual quality of the past.

What frequently astonishes the uninitiated is the fury with which each religious fight is fought – and the suddenness with which it is set aside for a new fight, for it is only the new fight which will ensure renewed publicity. One year it is autopsies (opposed by the ultra-Orthodox even for medical reasons or to gather evidence for a criminal investigation); the next year, a soccer stadium (where games take place on the Sabbath); another year a swimming-pool (where men and women swim together); followed by archaeological excavations in the City of David (charging defilement of an ancient Jewish cemetery); and then the Mormon Centre (the threat of the mass conversion of the Jewish people). But no single group, however sincere its religious convictions, can control the way that others give spiritual meaning to their lives. We cannot expect Jerusalem to claim the loyalty and love of all Jews – indeed, of Christians and Moslems as well – if the city emits a message of fanaticism, intolerance and delegitimization of the religious movements found within the Jewish world.

While much of the conflict is waged on religious battlefields, it is far more a political battle, often an internecine affair. While our municipal administration has done more for the *haredi* community than any previous administration, filling legitimate needs – building more synagogues, adding more classrooms, permitting more streets to be closed on the Sabbath in wholly religious neighbourhoods – I have personally become a symbol in the *haredi* fight against non-Orthodox Jewry,

especially because of my unswerving belief in tolerance and mutual respect. The abuse has included public notices announcing my death, somewhat prematurely, demonstrations of every ilk and even offensive calls to my home – not a complicated effort since my phone number is listed in the local directory. (When a caller identified himself as the 'Angel of Death', my wife Tamar replied that it had never occurred to her that the Angel of Death had a telephone!)

The 'names will never harm me' approach once did seriously reach the 'sticks and stones' phase. The incident took place in 1983, a few weeks before the municipal elections. It was the year when the Djanogly swimming-pool in Ramot, almost completed, was the issue of the moment taken up by the *haredi* community.

I had been invited to attend services one Sabbath in a Persian synagogue on the edge of the Bukharan Quarter. Leaving the synagogue, I was attacked by a *haredi* battalion, wielding sticks and bottles, a most inappropriate way to celebrate the Sabbath. The odds were about 100 to 1, so my chances were indeed meagre. The assailants succeeded in beating me up before the police arrived to intervene. The welts on my arms and legs were painful, but the spiritual welts far more so.

There were political analysts who contended that the attack brought me additional votes, but I can think of easier methods of appealing to the electorate. My staff claimed that the most painful of the blows were dealt by the press reports, which repeatedly decried the beating up of 'an old man'. I was only seventy-two.

The main road of Mea Shearim ends at Shivtei Yisrael Street. To the right is a building which jolts the passer-by coming from any direction, but particularly so from the world of Mea Shearim, a building which seems to have been en route to thirteenth-century Siena but lost its way. This had been an Italian hospital, again an instance of the humanitarian help of the European powers. Begun in 1911, work was interrupted by World War I and the hospital was completed only in 1920. Having housed the British air force during Mandate times, it now houses the Israeli Ministry of Education (with a huge *mezuzah*, a Jewish ritual object commonly placed on the entrances to buildings, affixed to the former hospital chapel).

We have been able to witness in Jerusalem the shadows of the nineteenth-century competition of the great European powers, the French, the Russian, the German, the British, the Italian. Each was desirous of a dominant presence in Jerusalem and thus our cityscape bears the onion-domes of the Russian Church, the spires of the Anglican Church and the towers of the Italian Hospital. The Augusta Victoria Hospital on Mount Scopus was inspired by the Hohenzollern ancestral castle and the Dormition Abbey on Mount Zion (see p. 44)

The Mandelbaum house in 1948, which marked the sole border crossing in Jerusalem at that time and was manned by the United Nations.

followed Charlemagne's palace chapel in Aix-la-Chapelle. The architectural mother tongue also aided pilgrims, who could immediately recognize and relate to the buildings where they would be welcome.

TURGEMAN POST MUSEUM

I cannot conclude a walk in this area without recommending a visit to the Turgeman Post Museum on Hel Hahandasa Street, which is left from Mea Shearim Street and left again at the main road. The crosses one passes are atop a Romanian church.

While it may be hard at times to traverse a busy intersection and visualize that it was once a desolate border area, there is no one of my generation or the next who does not have, even if one stratum below full consciousness, memories of the divided city. That there were walls, barbed wire and tank traps was a fact of life.

One day, meeting with a group of teenagers, I was asked questions which indicated that the youngsters had no concept of what a divided city implied. They could not conceive that there had been streets which simply ended. Suddenly. I felt that for these youngsters to comprehend the importance of the investment in tolerance and in

understanding they would be called on to make in order to ensure the future of the reunified city, it was esential that they have a basic understanding of the divided city. The last Israeli army post during the years of division had been in a house once owned by the Turgeman family, just beyond the Mandelbaum Gate (which adjoined a house owned by the Mandelbaum family). The Mandelbaum Gate was not a gate, but a border crossing manned by the United Nations.

Late one night I travelled around the city with a well-known German publisher, Georg von Holtzbrinck. We were project shopping and the only time mutually convenient was midnight. Our good fortune was that a full moon lit our path. I pitched a handful of proposals, but none caught his fancy as did the Turgeman Post, which would house the museum of the divided city. We set the date for the official dedication, but, as Georg was unwell, his daughter Monika came in his stead. On the morning of the dedication we received the news that he had died the night before. Before boarding the plane for home, his daughter attended the ceremony, standing tall with pride, and witnessed an everlasting memorial to her father and his love for Jerusalem.

As the original purpose of the museum was to educate Israeli schoolchildren, the texts were almost wholly in Hebrew. But the demand of tourists who were equally uncertain about this period in Jerusalem's history brought us to add English labels as well.

II
DOWNTOWN JERUSALEM

While it may have its ecological downside, there is probably no better single point to begin this walk of downtown Jerusalem than the traffic island of Kikar Tsarfat, Place de la France. Edifying it is; tranquil it is not.

The square was named in the mid-1950s, reflecting the fervent romance between Israel and France which culminated in the partnership of the Sinai Campaign. This square and assorted city names – Pierre Koenig Street, the Maison de France at the Hebrew University – are the relics of that love affair.

Romance often entails the bestowal of gifts and Jerusalem was wooed with a gift of a fountain from the city of Paris. While today a host of experts would devise the appropriate setting for a gift of this nature, Jerusalemites then, with their on-going 'save every drop' psychosis, were not adept at fountain placing. Old-timer Jerusalemites remember the War of Independence siege when water was used first for washing dishes, then for washing clothes, then for washing floors

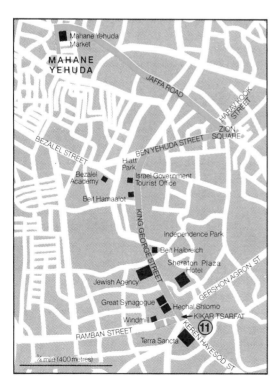

and finally for flushing toilets. The children of the besieged city believed that sinks by nature were designed with a bucket beneath an open drainpipe, so that water could be recycled. Jerusalem had never been a city of fountains.

Thus a fountain intended for a broad boulevard was installed on this puny traffic island. It is doubtful whether anyone had set the fountain in motion before its installation, and only when the fountain was placed and the switch was flipped was the predicament made clear. When operated at full force, the fountain became Jerusalem's first automated car wash, not to mention the unwanted showers bestowed on innocent pedestrians.

The immediate solution was to run the fountain on the lowest speed, and the cascading torrents envisioned by the Parisian city fathers became a pathetic trickle. As this was still Jerusalem's 'dry' period (the era before public swimming-pools), the fountain was viewed as the local fire-hydrant equivalent for make-do swimmers. But without filters or drainage, the local swimming hole became a visual and olfactory blight.

We removed it and replaced it with an unintentionally fountain-shaped light fixture, but the square continued to cry out for aesthetic improvement. The cry has now been heard across the street by the new owners of the Kings Hotel, who have taken on the beautification of what is practically their front lawn.

Since 1988, this square has become an arena for political sparring. A weekly demonstration every Friday afternoon of 'Women in Black', a group of Jewish women opposing the occupation of Arab territories, brings in its wake the attendant counter-demonstrators, and the air is often heated, irrespective of the Friday afternoon traffic jams.

The intersection is not only a traffic grid but also a cross-roads of the recent history of the city. Facing east, towards the Old City, the impressive building on our right is Terra Sancta. The design of the well-known Italian architect, Antonio Barluzzi, who designed Dominus Flevit and the Church of All Nations in Gethsemane (see p. 62), Terra Sancta was built by the Catholic Church in 1927 as an institution of higher learning. Intended mainly for Arab boys, it had a smattering of Jewish students because the Church schools were known for the fine education they provided. Beyond the common curriculum, it trained its students in commerce, as these students would eventually handle their family properties. Civic service was also taught in a period when it was not only a reputable career choice but a distinguished one.

The building, while conveying an aura of massiveness, actually covers only a fraction of the 2.75-acre plot; at least two acres are undeveloped. The building itself is underused, housing several Franciscan friars and a few offices, but basically catering for very few.

Yet, as in so many corners of Jerusalem, here too we find a unique Jerusalem personality, Father Godfrey. Beyond his religious vocation, he is an archaeology buff, who not only has become expert in the field, but has also acquired a remarkable collection of tiny archaeological items. His knowledge of Jerusalem is encyclopaedic and I can only be relieved that he has not yet written a guide to the city.

The Church is prepared to sell this site. As with all Church properties, the sale is never outright but a long-term lease. Church lands in the Holy City, as we have seen time and again, are not easily expendable. At one stage, an ultra-Orthodox Jew intended acquiring the building, but he encountered one obstacle: atop the building is a prominent statue of the Madonna, whose removal the Church would not consent to. Interest has arisen again and again among entrepreneurs of every ilk. A package-deal development is the most likely, wherein a developer would include public underground parking and public open space in the overall plans.

Our directional intentions are left along King George Street to the downtown area, but, before crossing over to the Kings Hotel, we should glimpse to the left, letting our eyes do the walking (though you may want to allow your feet to follow). We see a restored nineteenth-century windmill on Ramban Street, where boutiques and a Chinese restaurant have taken the place of a grinding mill.

This was a functioning mill in the mid-nineteenth century. The present-day Rehavia neighbourhood was then non-existent, and your imagination must conjure up the olive trees, dirt paths and empty fields of that period. This entire area was owned by the Greek Orthodox Church, then the largest landowner in the Holy City. Even today it is probably second only to the Israel Government Land Authority, which 'inherited' the lands in the state domain from the British, who inherited them from the Ottomans.

The Greeks had built this windmill in this isolated rural area, as they tended wheat fields where there were no olive groves. The flour was then distributed to the indigent of the laity, with the residue sold on the open market. It was the arrival of the Templers with their steam-driven mill (see p. 104), which tolled the death knell for the Greek windmill. The industrial age had arrived and with it a more efficient and cheaper method of grinding flour.

No longer serving as a windmill, the structure was then recycled. In the 1930s, it served as a home and office for the eminent German architect, Eric Mendelsohn, who had been invited to Jerusalem to design the Hebrew University on Mount Scopus. He lived in the windmill from 1935 to 1941, designing the University, the Hadassah Hospital on Mount Scopus and the Bank Leumi building at the beginning of Jaffa Road. From this windmill the Jerusalem strains of the international style of architecture emanated.

In the 1950s the windmill's tenant was – appropriately – the Dutch Consul. It was then sold to a local contractor, who planned to demolish it and build a five-storey house of twelve apartments, a financial windfall on this prestigious site. We tried desperately to block this, though we had no means available to compensate the contractor adequately. A proposal to dismantle the windmill and rebuild it in nearby Independence Park was panned. Achieving no practical alternative, the permit for demolition was issued – with heavy heart. Though we had conceded defeat, the seemingly hopeless battle was not yet lost. A talented young Israeli architect devised a plan wherein the site would be converted from residential use to commercial use, allowing the contractor to add additional floor space above and behind as a form of compensation. The windmill would be saved.

To the eternal credit of the contractor, he consented. But then the neighbours dissented, delaying work from 1975 to 1987. By then, the contractor was no longer interested and sold the property to a well-known Canadian real estate family. This family was willing to go a step beyond commercial considerations and raised the standard of construction as befits this historical site. The result gives truth to the adage that 'all's well that ends well', though en route to the happy ending it may have caused the city's Mayor untold anguish.

A glance to the right before we cross brings into view a tiered, multi-storeyed building, the Supersol, named for its ground-level supermarket. With the modern age fully ensconced in our lives, the excitement generated by the city's first supermarket is a vague vestige of the past, though it was as recently as 1961. Until then, food and household purchases were made at the open market or in local ma-and-pa grocery stores, with purchases limited to basic foodstuffs. Can openers did not exist in homes where today the microwave oven reigns supreme.

131

*King George Street with Hechal Shlomo on the left,
housing the Chief Rabbinate offices, and the Great
Synagogue on the right.*

The Supersol was not immediately or universally accepted as Jerusalemites then were sus-
picious of the unknown and the unfamiliar.
Today it is with difficulty, and repressed provin-
ciality, that one recalls the headlines made by a
supermarket. Jerusalem's giant step into the modern age now entails the Supersol's late-night
hours (and twenty-four-hour shopping on Wed-
nesdays and Thursdays), a new addition to the
city's social scene. The late-night shopper is not
the tense hysteric one encounters on the check-
out lines during the day and will be more prone to
explain to the tourist which package holds the
low-fat cottage cheese. For the visitor to the city
who has a late-night yen for a hot baguette and no
handy transportation across town to the all-night
Angel's Bakery, this is the address. (A favourite

joke of Tel Avivians who view Jerusalem as a
sleepy town: 'What are the three places where one
can find excitement in Jerusalem after midnight?
The Western Wall, Angel's Bakery and the hospital emergency rooms.')

I shall not make any excuses for the architectural design of the Supersol building beyond saying that in the late 1950s and early 1960s there was
a far less developed sensitivity to planning considerations and beyond adding, in true I-am-not-
to-blame style, that it was before I was Mayor. The
architect did plan the building on stilts to keep
open the vista towards the Old City, but the massive pillars block most of it. The original plan called
for an additional two floors, but the building commissions objected. Perhaps the architectural proportions were thus distorted; the elimination of
the two floors surely did not improve the design.

We begin our walk along the west side of King
George Street, passing Hechal Shlomo, housing
the Chief Rabbinate offices. In 1958, with the
tenth anniversary of the state and the confidence

that the first bridge of statehood had been successfully crossed, monumental state institutions were in vogue. With the Rabbinate included in this penchant, Sir Isaac Wolfson of London commissioned a team of architects, Dr Alexander Friedman and Meir Rubin, whose names occur again and again as we walk along King George Street. Sir Isaac, with English traditions ingrained into his being, even paid to ensure that the site opposite Hechal Shlomo would never be built up, so that this vista could not be blocked. A small museum in Sir Isaac's name displaying Jewish ceremonial art can be visited.

In the 1960s, during a period of tension between religious and secular Jews – one must not think this is an invention of the 1980s – a young secular Jew climbed on to the dome of Hechal Shlomo and, in bright red paint, outlined a traditional skullcap, marking six divisions which read in Hebrew: 'Good Jerusalem boy, Good Jerusalem boy'. The prankster's work was visible from near and far.

The next building on the left is the new Great Synagogue, built in 1982, again a design of Dr Friedman. Criticism of its grandiose nature is a local sport, but the opposition which I publicly voiced was on purely pragmatic grounds. There may have been some justification for the Great Synagogue before 1967, as a focus of pilgrimage for world Jewry, but with the accessibility of the Western Wall, this purpose lost much of its validity.

I made a quick dollars and cents calculation. The funding for this synagogue could have paid for a dozen synagogues in the new neighbourhoods of the city, where the need is pressing. And while buck-passing is a prevalent habit – the building of neighbourhood synagogues is the responsibility of the Ministry of Religious Affairs – the well-being of the city's residents cannot be passed off as easily. Thus, despite my deep respect for the Wolfson family, the major sponsor of this undertaking, I boycotted the official dedication to register my protest. But I must admit that tourists are, indeed, drawn to the synagogue and impressed by its ornate style.

While this is a walks book, it should be pointed out that this part of King George Street is closed to vehicular traffic during the time of services on the Sabbath.

The building as we reach the corner is that of the Jewish Agency, designed by Yohanan Ratner, a commander of the Haganah and a founder of the Technion University in Haifa. In 1926–7, he won a major competition sponsored by the Zionist Organization in London to enable them to centralize their offices, heretofore spread out throughout the city.

The building is horseshoe-shaped, with the Zionist Organization in the centre, the Keren Hayesod on the left and the Jewish National Fund on the right. The inner courtyard serves to set off the building from the main street. Indeed, it typifies the better architecture of Jewish public building, both modest and yet powerful.

In 1948, Arabs succeeded in planting a car loaded with explosives near the building and the death toll reached thirteen. Protective walls were then constructed creating a fortress-like enclave; these walls were taken down only in 1988, exposing once more the beauty of this building to the casual passer-by.

The Sheraton Plaza Hotel across the street occupies the site which had been intended for a new City Hall, the model for which I found awaiting me on becoming Mayor in 1965 (see p. 12). This site was not the only possibility considered. There was substantial support for a location at the present entrance to the city since it was assumed that, with no possibility of growing eastward, the city would grow westward.

The Municipality, together with the Association of Architects and Engineers, had sponsored a national competition in 1963. Both first and second prizes were won by Professor Alfred Mansfeld, who submitted a concept for a high-rise building (first prize) and for a low building (second prize). My opposition on assuming the mayoralty led to a dead-end for both these plans. (Professor Mansfeld, with architect Dora Gad, had also won the competition for the Israel Museum, and these plans had a more fortunate fate.)

I do not deny that the Plaza Hotel was a mistake. It is offensive to the horizon and to the landscape. Interestingly, while there was a major brouhaha after it was built, the proposal passed through the planning maze with little public opposition. My only consolation is that it is a good hotel.

The site adjoining the Plaza Hotel is either a run-down family hotel from the turn of the century, the Land of Israel Hotel – or a luxury hotel from the early 1990s, depending on how quickly the wheels of progress turn and when you are reading this account. The new high-rise might moderate the ugliness of its neighbour.

Passing an empty lot (or a built-up plot, again depending on the time factor), we reach a curved building serving the Yeshurun Synagogue. Established in the 1930s by a congregation considered rather liberal, the building was designed by Dr Friedman and Meir Rubin as the library of the synagogue slated for the adjacent property. This synagogue was never built, so the library building was used as the synagogue; there is now an idea to create a community facility on the unused plot. Hachal Shlomo, built thirty years later, was almost an exact replica of Dr Friedman's design for the unbuilt Yeshurun Synagogue.

The tall building opposite is Beit Halbreich,

named, as many Jerusalem buildings, for its contractor. It was famous for its height and served as a popular suicide venue. Children named it the 'municipal diving-board'.

If we cross the street, we can walk along the edge of Independence Park, developed by the British. During the War of Independence, this open area was a prime danger zone, exposed as it was to Arab sniping. As King George Street was a main thoroughfare, a concrete wall was erected to provide cover, demolished only when the city's reunification made it obsolete. The park entrance is graced by a Jean Arp sculpture.

The concept of the city as a living museum was not a traditional one for Jerusalem, even if the Hadrian bust, purported to have adorned the column at Damascus Gate, could be considered a foray into the world of outdoor sculpture. And while we had created the Billy Rose Art Garden at the Israel Museum, it was still art in a finite space. The Second Commandment forbidding 'graven images' was not conducive to representational art and even today 'horse and rider' monuments are absent from the Jerusalem landscape.

The inspiration for the placement of sculptures throughout the city came in 1968 from a couple who owned a well-known gallery in New York, Arthur and Madeleine Lejwa, refugees from Poland who had made their mark on the international art world. Their idea was not a whim, but a plan conceived to the most minute detail. They wanted to begin this programme with a major work by Jean Arp, *The Threshold of Jerusalem*.

I had to be convinced. My concerns were, as is my wont, pragmatic. We were just beginning to succeed in educating people to respect the flowers, bushes and trees of the neighbourhood parks we had created. It was not an easy lesson to teach and many flowers were uprooted before it was learned. I wondered about the wisdom of placing major art works in public places without an extensive educational effort beforehand. The Lejwas felt the educational effort would emanate from the existence of the art and their conviction was incisive enough to still my doubts. And so began a programme of 'The City as a Museum', with sculptures taking root in assorted open spaces. None has been vandalized.

The Tirat Batsheva Hotel on the western side of King George Street was built in the late 1960s for observant tourists before the larger hotels began catering specifically for the needs of this community. The adjacent parking lot is owned by the Russian Government (not the Russian Church as elsewhere in the city) and in the 1950s, during the heyday of good relations between Russia and Israel, this was proposed as the site of the Russian Embassy. With the break in relations between Israel and Russia in 1967, there was a flurry of activity by those eager to build on this site. I was

against making irrevocable decisions and thus allowed its use only as a parking lot. In 1988, with the thaw in Israel–Soviet relations, the first Russian consular mission immediately laid claim to compensation for use of the land.

The residential house on the corner, Beit Hamaalot, also a Friedman/Rubin collaboration, was noteworthy when built in the 1930s, once again a prototype of the international architectural style of that period. It was a condominium-style house, which even boasted an elevator.

On the western side of the street, we pass the Ministry of Tourism and the Israel Government Tourist Office. If you have any unanswered queries or quests, you might seek help here.

There is nothing to indicate that the previous occupant of the building was the Knesset. When Ben-Gurion had sought premises for the young state's government in the city centre, large, empty commercial space was not plentiful, so he grasped the opportunity when this building became available. The offices were cosy, though crowded, a far cry from the comfort of today's office, which elicits far more complaints.

The vicinity of the Knesset was closed by the police when Parliament was in session, which made the street open prey for major demonstrations of one kind or another. There were demonstrations on trivialities and demonstrations on matters of import, perhaps the most notable that led by opposition member Menachem Begin in 1952, when the question of accepting German reparations was being weighed.

The stores in the building opposite the Knesset also bear no memory of the Pygmalion Café, a minuscule space which was frequented by Members of Parliament. Without question, as much government business took place at the little tables here as in the plenary hall of the Knesset itself.

The Hiatt Park on the left side of the street, where the Knesset Menorah once stood, is often filled with day-time strollers. The Miró sculpture, *Tête*, was a gift of Muriel and Phil Berman, who have spread the word of sculpture both in Allentown, Pennsylvania, as well as in Jerusalem, taking up as they did the gauntlet of the Lejwas.

The Hiatt Park seems to descend into a pit-like formation. Geology buffs should not delve into scientific journals to seek explanations for this phenomenon, for the explanation is a simple one. In the 1930s, the site had been bought by a Jewish family, who excavated the foundations of a hotel – and ran out of money. An Arab contractor and engineer, George Schieber, bought the site but never built on it, but his ownership explains why this is known as the 'Schieber Pit'.

Today's plans call for the construction of a vast

Ben Yehuda Pedestrian Mall.

underground parking lot, which carries our commitment to re-landscape the park when the work is completed. I can only hope that these plans reach fruition; I am loath to think of the 'Schieber Pit' being renamed the 'Kollek Pit'.

BEN YEHUDA PEDESTRIAN MALL

At the junction, we walk to the right, to the Ben Yehuda Pedestrian Mall, one arm of Jerusalem's downtown 'triangle' – Ben Yehuda Street, Jaffa Road and King George Street. For years it appeared that life in its entirety took place in this triangle; even today, this impression remains.

Until 1982, Ben Yehuda was a traffic bottleneck, with cars bumper to bumper and a generous (illegal) use of car horns. We proposed a pedestrian mall, but we faced our familiar dual stumbling blocks: financing and resident opposition. The store owners were convinced that we were signing the death warrant of downtown Jerusalem, while we contended that the stationary vehicular traffic was doing just that. We did not persuade everyone, but we obtained the necessary permits and began work. The opposition forces reconsidered even before the placement of the last paving stone; the success of the mall – the *midrachov* (a combination of the Hebrew words for sidewalk

and street) – was immediate.

In 1986, at an International Conference for the Restoration of Historic Cities, William H. Whyte, a world planning expert (and the author of *The Organization Man* and *City: Rediscovering the Center*), conducted a scientific study of the *midrachov*: he simply sat at a café and counted people. And from the head count, he pronounced the *midrachov* a success. We had sensed its success, but now it was empirically confirmed.

The walk down Ben Yehuda should be a free-fall experience, with no clutched guidebook and with no pre-planning. It is a follow-your-eyes and follow-your-instincts stroll, with a stop for coffee here and a souvenir purchase there. On summer evenings, a *midrachov* jaunt is a must, with our budding artists, artisans and musicians vying for sidewalk space. I shall let you reach the bottom of Ben Yehuda, Zion Square, unbothered.

We turn left at the corner on to Jaffa Road. Immediately across Jaffa Road is Harav Kook Street, which leads to the Ticho House and Haneviim Street (see ch. 10). Approaching the first main intersection, that of Jaffa Road and King George Street to the left, another apex of our triangle, we pass an arcaded building known as the building of the pillars. The metal bars adjutting from the roof

BELOW *Winter snow on Jaffa Road.*   RIGHT *Jaffa Road and King George Street intersection.*

seem to indicate an initial plan to build a multi-storey structure, logical for such a valuable plot of property in the city centre, but family complications were undoubtedly a barrier.

During the later years of the Mandate period, the 'Generali Building' at the lower end of Jaffa Road (two blocks from City Hall) was an office and commercial centre. When the Mandate Government established its headquarters there, it cordoned off the entire area with barbed wire, making it inaccessible to non-British. (With Stalingrad still in the forefront of people's memories, this area earned the name Bevingrad after Ernest Bevin, the Foreign Secretary.) Those evicted moved to the building of the pillars.

The traffic light at this intersection has its place in Jerusalem's history books because it was the first – and for years the city's only – traffic light. As recently as the 1960s, Jerusalemites would arrange to meet 'at *the* traffic light'. Before, traffic was controlled by a British policeman atop a colonial-style, mid-intersection platform.

The page of a telephone directory which meets the eye if you glance upwards as you cross (or, more safely, before you cross) is a work by an Israeli artist, Menashe Kadishman. The bare wall

was too reminiscent of an unused canvas for us to resist the temptation to use it as such.

We continue walking up Jaffa Road until we finally reach our goal, the Mahane Yehuda outdoor market, a medley of sights, sounds and smells, a marriage of East and West, of the pushcarts of New York's Lower East Side and the stalls of the Moroccan suq.

Its location was not by chance, but because it was on the mainstream of traffic from Jaffa Port to Jaffa Gate, the basis for the development of Jerusalem along Jaffa Road. Mahane Yehuda was the entry to the city and the logical place for the merchants to set down their goods. During the Ottoman period, the market was a mass of shacks, but the British, in the 1920s, decided to instil a bit of order. An elegant plan was drawn up by Charles Ashbee for a market area with shops around a central courtyard, but this plan reached the expanding graveyard of unused architects' plans.

The area thus grew helter-skelter, unprepared for the sudden onslaught of vehicular traffic. We have tried to help where possible, closing off the market streets to cars, adding a covered roof to ensure that purchases on rainy days are not immediately waterlogged. A planned overhaul will make working and living conditions more palatable while preserving the character which the decades have moulded.

I leave you in this wonderworld – to people-watch, to wander, to buy – and, of course, to eat!

'Bevingrad', the area of Jaffa Road cordoned off towards the end of the British Mandate period (1948), with the Generali Building in the centre background.

12
THE 99 CIRCLE BUS TOUR

No consortium of etymology and philology will prescribe or authorize the classification of the 99 Circle Bus tour as a walk. I shall thus dispense with apologies other than to say that there is no better way to circumnavigate the city for the non-marathoners among us.

Jerusalem is not a mega-city, but the starred or numbered sites on any map are geographically scattered. And while we have an excellent bus system, it is geared to the needs of the local populace rather than the visitor, tourist or pilgrim.

The 99 bus leaves, hourly, from the parking lot at the bottom of the incline opposite Jaffa Gate (9–5 Sunday–Thursday; 9–2 on Fridays). There are four specially trained drivers who ply this route and provide a running commentary, in English and in Hebrew. We had conceived the 99 bus to serve tourists, but had not anticipated its popularity with non-Jerusalemite Israelis.

You can purchase a one-time ticket and travel the route from start to finish, a ninety-minute proposition, or a one-day or two-day ticket, which lets you embark and disembark an unlimited number of times along the route. Yaacov Haziza, one of the drivers, advises that for the latter travel method it is best to map out one's route in advance and begin with the stops closest to the point of departure.

The driver will provide a brochure with a route map. If you are planning to descend en route, do not forget to ring the buzzer to give the driver ample warning of your intentions.

Traffic in Jerusalem reaches dizzying proportions on Friday afternoons, as the race against Sabbath closures reaches the finishing line. Thus, if you are taking the noon bus, allow an additional twenty minutes for the straight route.

The 99 bus 'walk' will have its own format, so I

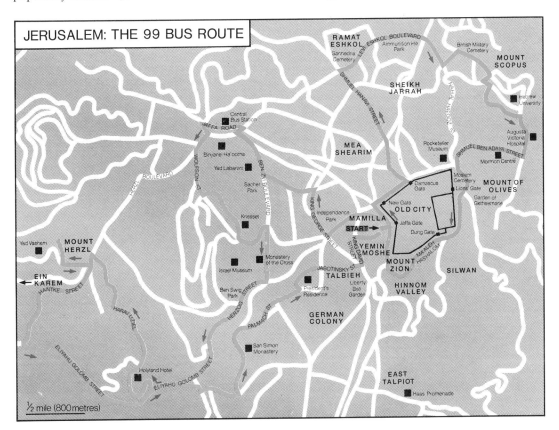

JERUSALEM: THE 99 BUS ROUTE

will just mention some of the sites not yet described in the eleven previous chapters.

Skirting the Mea Shearim and reaching the Mandelbaum Gate and the Turgeman Post Museum on the left, the bus travels along Shmuel Hanavi Street and turns right at the traffic lights at the Shmuel Hanavi Quarter. Built to house the mass immigration of the 1950s, this quarter lay within spitting distance of the frontier. Security dictated the style of architecture and thus the narrow slit windows.

The bus has probably long since made its right turn. The Sanhedria cemetery on the left includes burial tombs supposed to be those of the Sanhedrin, the supreme council and tribunal in Second Temple Judaism, as well as a twentieth-century cemetery. It is still in use, though infrequently, with the majority of burials at the Har Hamenuhot cemetery (visible from the highway to Tel Aviv) and the Mount of Olives cemetery.

On the right, just past the Alliance School, is 'Ammunition Hill' Park, an ostensible contradiction of terms. Ammunition Hill had been a Jordanian army position, where we incurred heavy losses in 1967. Finally succeeding in capturing the hill, our troops could only marvel at the arsenal and the intricate maze of trenches they found. We had envisioned removing all traces of the accoutrements of the city's division, but we decided to leave this hill, with its trench network, as a memorial to the boys who fell here. An official ceremony takes place here every spring on Jerusalem Day, the day commemorating the city's reunification.

At the main cross-roads, there is a huge, white sculpture on the far left, Lieberman's *Faith*.

The bus turns right just before the British Military Cemetery – 3,000 graves of soldiers who fell in World War I (with a special section for Jewish soldiers). There were the Highland Light Infantry, the Australian Battalion of the Imperial Camel Corps, the New Zealand Mounted Rifles and the Royal Welsh Fusiliers. In the 1920s the British Government had undertaken a commitment to maintain, in perpetuity, the open view from the cemetery to the Old City, and £125 had been collected to purchase the privately owned land to ensure this commitment. However, the funds disappeared and our attempts to trace them came to naught. In our planning commissions, we undertook to uphold this commitment. The land was allocated to the Hebrew University for sports grounds, which allowed use of the land without abusing the air space.

MOUNT SCOPUS

The Mount Scopus branch of the Hadassah Hospital is on the left. It services this entire area and almost half its patients are Arab. The Mount Scopus campus of the Hebrew University serves 10,000 students. In the euphoria of the return to Mount Scopus, a non-stop building mania covered the campus with a defence-like architecture. Passing the modern dormitory buildings on the right, we reach the Goldsmith Building, a remnant of the original 1925 campus. This building houses the Rothberg School for Overseas Students, which brings thousands of foreign students to Jerusalem during each school year and for its summer courses. For those of you interested, there is no age limit.

The driver will pass along the campus and turn into an observation path for an unobstructed view towards the Old City.

Jerusalem is a watershed, with annual rainfall of twenty-five inches on one side of the Mount Scopus ridge and three inches on the other.

The bus wends its way back to Jaffa Gate, completing its first loop, and then continues on its route, through Mamilla and King George Streets, reaching Sacher Park on Ben Zvi Boulevard. The pyramid-like structure in the park is the soldiers' memorial, *Yad Labanim*, adjacent to the Clore Soldiers' Home. The barrack-like huts we pass were built for the Ministry for Foreign Affairs in the early 1950s; it was the last government ministry to establish itself in Jerusalem. As picturesque as these huts are, they hardly qualify as appropriate office space and a proper office building is planned.

BINYANEI HA 'OOMA

As we turn, the huge building on the left is Binyanei Ha'ooma, the Jerusalem Convention Centre. (Since the Hebrew name is unpronounceable to the uninitiated, anyone trying to reach there by taxi is best off asking for the adjacent – and pronounceable – Hilton Hotel and walking a few paces.) An amazing fact of life is that this huge, modern edifice was built in 1950, with our state barely weaned. As is often the case, this centre was the product of the obsession of a single man, Yevzeroff, a friend of the Revisionist leader, Zev Jabotinsky.

Food was still being rationed and Yevzeroff dreamed of large-scale tourism, international congresses, conferences and conventions. I remember his bringing an architect's model to Moshe Sharett at the Foreign Office, still in Tel Aviv. I was then on the side of the doubting Thomases who felt this premature, but few could stand up to his powers of persuasion. He won – and he was

---

ABOVE RIGHT *The Mount Scopus campus of the Hebrew University.*

RIGHT *The Augusta Victoria Hospital, on the left of the road after the campus, has seen many different uses since its construction at the turn of the century and now houses the Lutheran World Federation.*

The Arab village of Silwan above the Kidron Valley and City of David.

right. He may have inculcated me with his maverick way of thinking.

By the late 1980s, this once-trailblazing building, also used for concerts of the Israel Philharmonic, was antiquated and deteriorating. I fought a non-ending battle with the Jewish Agency which owned the building, but I was having difficulty pleading the case for renovations and remodelling. Where was Yevzeroff when I needed him? As I sat at a concert one evening, the arm of my chair dropped precipitously into my lap. I took it home and the following day sent it off with a note, hoping that people's exhibit A would be more tangible than any circumstantial evidence. Eventually reason won out – and modernization is under way.

I cannot attest to the appropriateness of adding a paragraph about a Jerusalem event which takes place once every two years, but as it is a favourite of mine, I hope this gives it a modicum of legitimacy.

The biennial Jerusalem International Book Fair, which takes place at Binyanei Ha'ooma, was started under my precedessor, Mordechai Ish-Shalom, in 1963. It was a modest affair, but laid the basis for a growing concern. The 1989 Fair comprised 1,000 publishing houses, including publishers from Hungary, the head of the Moscow Book Fair and a representative from China. The Russians and the Yugoslavs worked out a joint publishing venture, surely inspired by the aura of Jerusalem.

From the Fair's inception, it was the occasion for the awarding of the Jerusalem Prize to an

in the business world, the Jewish world and the Zionist world. A man who imparts much warmth and love to this world, he is deeply emotional. Thus at the dedication of every project he has given in Jerusalem, he stands at the podium to speak and the tears soon interfere. 'Well, Teddy,' he shouts, 'you wanted to make me cry. You have succeeded.'

The scenario for the Swig Park dedication deviated from the set script. Some months before the park was completed, we had asked Jack to increase his gift so that we could add a work of art to the park; he readily agreed. He had not seen the work beforehand and thus at the dedication found himself facing a modern amalgam of steel girders and plating. When it was his turn at the microphone, he spoke emotionally of his links to Jerusalem and of his ties with his late partner. 'And, Teddy,' he concluded, 'about this sculpture I will talk to you later.'

He was appalled, even offended. He demanded its immediate removal. The following day he phoned my office. 'Okay, Teddy you can leave the junk in the park.' I wondered at this sudden change of heart. Had someone given him a late-night crash course in modern art? Not at all. He had revisited the park and found children rapturously climbing all over the sculpture. If the children revelled in it, it could remain.

We pass Israel Orion's sculpture, *Jacob's Ladder*, on our right, truly a stairway to heaven since it leads nowhere else. The YMHA/YWHA, a trailblazer for our network of community centres, is on our left.

HOLYLAND HOTEL MODEL OF THE SECOND TEMPLE
We turn right to the Holyland Hotel. The slow climb affords time for the panoramic view of the new city: the nearby residential quarters, the Israel Tennis Centre, the Gilo neighbourhood in the distance and the Manhat Quarter (once an Arab village as its minaret attests) on the left.

We reach the model of the Second Temple on the Holyland Hotel grounds. Mr Kroch, a German immigrant from Leipzig, had built the hotel in what was then the end of the world, showing great vision and acute business sense. He had another fantasy: to create an accurate model of the Second Temple and, together with Professor Avi-Yonah, he did so, in memory of his son who fell in the War of Independence.

Before the reunification of the city and the heyday of 'Jerusalem Revealed', this model was the key to a distant door and tourists flocked there. But its popularity has not waned; on the contrary, it serves the newly kindled interest in the history of this period. Excavations have proved the model astonishingly accurate, with only a few pieces of the puzzle missing.

author whose writings express the theme of the 'Freedom of the Individual in Society'. The recipients represent true globe-trotting: Bertrand Russell, Ignazio Silone, Jorge Luis Borges, Octavio Paz, Max Frisch, Grahame Greene, Simone de Beauvoir, V.S. Naipaul, Milan Kundera and Isaiah Berlin, to name a sampling. Their presence at the Book Fair adds a further literary glow. Since 1983, the Fair has also hosted an international forum of the Aspen Institute for Humanistic Studies on themes related to books and publishing.

A left turn brings us to the centre of the world: the Jerusalem Central Bus Station. Continuing on its route, the bus soon turns right on to Herzog Street. At the next traffic lights, the Ben Swig Park and the sculpture by the Israeli artist, Yehiel Shemi, welcome us. This park was a gift of Ben Swig's partner, Jack Weiler, a unique personality

The model of the Second Temple in the grounds of the Holyland Hotel.

MOUNT HERZL

The bus soon approaches Herzl Boulevard just opposite Mount Herzl. To our right is the military cemetery, a poignant reminder of the heavy toll paid by this state. The national Memorial Day service takes place here on the eve of Independence Day and the grief of the thousands who cover the hillside becomes a unified grief.

Mount Herzl is the burial place of Theodor Herzl, the founder of Zionism, and prominent national leaders like Levi Eshkol and Golda Meir.

Herzl had been buried in the Jewish cemetery in Vienna and, during my youth, on Herzl Day, all Zionist organizations gathered in a pilgrimage to his grave. Following the creation of the state, Gideon Ruffer, later Ambassador Rafael, went to Vienna on behalf of the Jewish Agency to negotiate the transfer of Herzl's remains with the various occupation authorities. I clearly remember the cable which arrived, announcing that 'Mr Herzl will arrive with the remains of Mr Ruffer' at such and such a time.

Soon after I was elected Mayor, the Jewish Agency proposed covering Herzl's grave with a glass dome to make it more 'prominent'. Nothing could be as prominent as the simple black stone with the name Herzl distinctly engraved on it; I fought, and prevented, the planned abomination.

Zev Jabotinsky died in the United States in 1940 and included a clause in his will stipulating his desire to be buried in the still-unborn Jewish state. Early leaders of the Labour Party objected to his being reinterred on Mount Herzl, fearing that this would add strength to the Revisionist, later the Herut, Party. I felt that this argument was tenuous and I had a share in persuading Prime Minister Levi Eshkol to disregard these sectarian and partisan considerations and carry out the terms of Jabotinsky's will.

YAD VASHEM

We turn right to Yad Vashem, the Museum of the Holocaust. It is not an easy visit but it is a must, and if you are on the start-to-finish route of the 99 bus and this is not an opportune time to stop, you can reach here by public bus or by cab.

Yad Vashem's Avenue of the Righteous Gentiles is planted with trees commemorating individual non-Jews who, throughout the Nazi period, at great personal risk, saved the lives of Jews. There have been Jews who searched for years to locate their saviours.

I have often attended these commemorative ceremonies (including that honouring Dr Willem Sandberg, the first art adviser to the Israel Museum). Each tale is a wonder in itself. Before you stands a German or Pole or Dutchman or Frenchwoman, elderly, ailing, and yet you perceive that you are in the presence of a hero. You see a family, for the one person who was saved has since multiplied, which exists because of this nobility and valour. And you sense the intangible ties binding these people.

The low building on the right is a single hall whose floor bears the names, and the weight, of the Nazi extermination camps – and a memorial candle which is perpetually lit. Nothing can add to this.

The main building is a chronological portrayal of this history. The stark simplicity of Yad Vashem is more effective than any modern, multimedia portrayal. The new addition to Yad Vashem is a Children's Memorial, commemorating the 1.5 million children who were killed. How can one fathom killing 1.5 million children?

The bus has long left Yad Vashem and returned to the intersection of Mount Herzl. The red sculpture which graces the turn is *Homage to Jerusalem – Stabile*, the last major work by Alexander Calder. Calder travelled to Jerusalem expressly for the purpose of choosing the site for this stabile and, after traversing the city as often as the 99 bus, he selected this site.

The view to the right encompasses the village of Ein Karem, where John the Baptist was born, and the Hadassah Hospital at Ein Karem, home of the Chagall windows.

The traffic lights for our left turn introduce us to the Monster, the unqualified favourite of our youngsters. It is a play sculpture by Niki de Saint Phalle called *The Golem* – the Monster. While our first inclination had been an installation in the city centre, we reconsidered and favoured one of the less privileged neighbourhoods, to give children there a source of pride that the Monster was theirs. This Monster fulfilled our expectations – as has been proved in two doctoral dissertations studying the influence of this work.

Our route back to our starting-point takes us past the San Simon neighbourhood and the San Simon monastery. In the centre of this park is a decades-old tank, which protected the southern flank of Jerusalem during the War of Independence. Eventually the familiar windmill greets us as we turn left up King David Street (see p. 90), cross Mamilla and return to square one.

You have covered a good part of Jerusalem – and, no blisters.

A sculpture by Nandor Glid at the Yad Vashem Memorial to the Holocaust.

EPILOGUE

An epilogue is defined as a closing chapter providing further comment, interpretation or information. I hope to comment, interpret and inform, an epilogue both to my thoughts and to your walks, whether done on pavement or in an armchair.

I chose the Haas Promenade for these pages of reflection, for in a city of stupendous views, this is the acme of stupendous views. The terrain of the promenade, no-man's-land in the divided city, witnessed fierce fighting at the outset of the Six Day War, following the Jordanian take-over of the nearby United Nations headquarters. The plaque commemorating the Israeli soldiers who fell in this battle attests to its intensity.

The United Nations headquarters, the fortress-like building beyond the trees, originally served the British High Commissioner, giving birth to the Hebrew name of the adjacent housing quarter, Armon Hanatziv, the Palace of the Commissioner. This quarter is beyond the ironwork sculpture by the Mexican artist Helen Escobedo. The odd-angled building visible from this work is the Saltiel Community Centre, designed by the Mexican architect Mathias Goeritz.

It took little time following the city's reunification for commercial developers to perceive this ridge as a potential goldmine. Houses could be sold for astronomical prices and a pretty penny could be made. We did not obstruct the onslaught of requests out-of-hand, but consulted the Jerusalem Committee, our international advisory council. The building proposals were reviewed and analysed and argued. The committee resolution was unanimous: no houses.

To perpetuate this decision, an alternative statement was sought. The eminent San Francisco architect Larry Halprin was the choice of the Haas family, fellow San Franciscans, to create this impressive promenade. As a member of the Jerusalem Committee, Larry Halprin was well briefed on the intricacies of this undertaking.

Walking along the promenade, a sculpted array of Jerusalem stone, I find myself astounded by human nature. Scores of cars are parallel to the main road, the inadequate parking area betraying our mistaken assessment of the promenade's success. Hundreds of visitors stroll and relax and

muse, not to mention the Saturday afternoon kite-flying contingent who take advantage of the ridge's climactic co-operation. And I wonder.

Before the existence of the promenade, one encountered a smattering of passers-by, a Bedouin with a shepherd's crook in hand or an American tourist with a Sony Walkman in hand. The stupendous view had always existed, but apparently concrete assurance was needed to ensure the stream of visitors, day and night.

Nothing inspires like success and a walk westward along the Haas Promenade intersects with the Gabriel Promenade, created in memory of a young Jerusalemite, Gabriel Sherover. Because of the steep slope, this walk is an up-and-down proposition, with a good number of steps, though there is access for the handicapped. But it is these steps which create the changing views and the nooks and crannies which provide instances of privacy. It is well worth the aerobic effort which is called for.

There is a jumble of thoughts which I would like to share and thus you might seek a comfortable spot, either on the balustrades or benches of the promenades, on the inviting lawns beneath them, or at the restaurant which will also provide sustenance.

My original game-plan for this book was a definitive approach rather than a transitory one. My intent was a guidebook, not a political treatise or journalistic up-date. But current events have necessitated an intrusion of the latter, even for the casual tourist, though the state of flux of the present reality may induce obsolescence even before publication date.

The year 1988 brought a new word into the general lexicon of the world: 'intifada', the Arab uprising. Beginning in Gaza, it rapidly spread to the West Bank and then to Jerusalem. But the dissimilarity between what took place in Gaza and the West Bank and what took place in Jerusalem is in itself a revealing insight into the nature of our city.

While we have had difficult days, none have resembled the reporting of the international media. We long ago learned that we are under the microscope of the world, but the lesson often has to be relearned. We watch as a single stone thrown in

Jerusalem receives wider news coverage than 5,000 Moslem Kurds gassed in Iraq or 20,000 anti-government rebels killed in Syria, thereby magnifying the ramifications of this single stone.

It was not only the intensity of the disturbances which was less in Jerusalem but their nature. It is not to say that stones were not thrown by the Arab youth of Jebel Mukabar, breaking windows in the nearby Jewish neighbourhood of Armon Hanatziv. These two neighbourhoods have lived peacefully side-by-side and yet both became the victims of the intifada.

Pressures on the Arab population in Jerusalem to intensify the uprising were unremitting. The Arab political and journalistic leadership is concentrated in Jerusalem as here they function under civil law rather than under military law as in Gaza and the West Bank, thus ensuring equal rights. Both Arabs and Jews enjoy a free press, though both are subject to mild military censorship. Complaints do arise, often justified, that the censorship of the Arab press is harsher, even though there remains no freer Arab press anywhere in the Middle East.

The uprising in Jerusalem, even with its limited nature, carried an element of surprise. Even I was surprised, despite my frequent warnings against complacence. We had succeeded in fostering tolerance and harmonious co-existence, but it remained a delicate balance. The events in Gaza and the West Bank jolted this balance.

While all 1,500 Arab municipal workers came to work despite daily pressures to strike, and while the Arab Health Centre and similar institutions continued their activities – Arab art teachers from Gaza came regularly to a weekly course at the Israel Museum's Ruth Youth Wing – it was not business as usual.

Those most shocked were those who did not comprehend the powerful patriotism of the Arabs of Jerusalem, which we had never discouraged. In 1967, we followed a course rare in modern history. Changes in frontier had always entailed citizenship changes or forced migration as in Alsace-Lorraine, the Sudetenland or Silesia. While offering Arabs the possibility of Israeli citizenship, we allowed them the option of retaining Jordanian citizenship. We authorized the Arab League curriculum in city schools, enabling students to continue their studies in Arab universities abroad. We sanctioned open bridges with Jordan, permitting mutual access for both East and West Bank populations. A little known fact is that over 100,000 visitors from countries which at least nominally are at war with Israel – Jordan, Iraq, Saudi Arabia, etc. – have entered Israel over these two decades for family visits or pilgrimage.

I cannot prophesy what the visitor to Jerusalem will find next week or next month or next year, but I can relate what is happening today. All Arab-owned shops in East Jerusalem and in the Old City have been on partial strike imposed by the PLO and are open only from 9 a.m. to noon. On days when full strikes are called, the closures include the morning hours as well.

During the early days of the unrest, when spur-of-the-moment decisions were all too common, the police decided to press the Arab shopkeepers to counter the demands of the uprising by forcing them to open their shops in the afternoon hours as well. A delegation of shopkeepers explained to me simply why the situation would remain unchanged: 'If we counter the police orders, we will be fined or gaoled; if we counter the orders of the intifada, our shops will be burned, our cars will be smashed, our children's lives endangered.' The balance of fear was clearly on the other side and the police order was rescinded.

Most days are quiet, though any incident has the potential of immediate escalation. Restraint is imperative and the burden of this restraint falls more and more heavily on the moderates of all sides who must struggle to contain extremism.

Despite the Sisyphean nature of this task, it does not compare to the sadness of the divided city. Arab Jerusalem during that period was neglected in favour of the Jordanian capital, Amman: no government offices were located here; economic development ceased as investments were diverted to Transjordan; the establishment of educational and cultural institutions were blocked for internal political reasons. Consequently, East Jerusalem was partially drained of its educated and business elite which emigrated to Amman, to the Arab world and to the non-Arab world. The population remained stagnant at 65,000 during the entire period, while Amman increased from 45,000 in 1947 to 300,000 in 1967.

In contrast, during the two decades under Israeli governance, Jerusalem's Moslem population doubled to 130,000. For those who try to accuse us of seeking to obliterate the Arab presence in the city, the numbers speak for themselves.

The Israeli sector of the divided city also faced hardships, including the absorption of tens of thousands of Jewish refugees (see p. 106). The population increased from 84,000 in 1949 to 123,000 in 1951 and to 195,000 in 1966. Few immigrants were conversant in Hebrew and many were lacking in basic work skills. We had to obtain means to house and to educate – in some cases, even to clothe – this mass influx.

The reunification of the city was sudden and unplanned. Thus improvisation became the methodology of decision-making. Few precedents could be extrapolated. Each new step had to follow the preceding one.

We faced two overriding challenges: to foster tolerance and understanding between two

*The Haas Promenade in East Talpiot – and the view to
the Old City and beyond.*

peoples who had lived in enmity and war and to provide the neglected East Jerusalem community with services as similar as possible to those available in West Jerusalem. Both were formidable challenges in and of themselves; both entailed, besides formidable budgets, countering extremist forces pulling away from the centre.

We cannot solve the complex issues of the Middle East in the Jerusalem City Hall, but we can strive to strengthen the foundations of mutual tolerance. It must be clear that safe national borders can neither be based on the promises of the scriptures nor guaranteed by military strength alone. Ultimately peace and secure borders must be built in the minds of people and the schoolbooks of children.

Internationalization is an idea which crops up sporadically despite its evident impracticality. The Moslems will never accept an infidel as the authority over their holy mosques and the United Nations is as much an infidel in Arab eyes as the Israeli Government. Even the Jewish leaders who agreed to the internationalization clause in the 1947 partition plan, pressed as they were to achieve a Jewish state and provide a home for Jewish refugees from Islamic countries and displaced persons who had survived the Nazi concentration camps, would not be able to acquiesce today.

Dual sovereignty has been mooted, suggesting an Arab capital alongside a Jewish capital. Dual sovereignty is not a viable solution. Two sets of laws? Two police forces? A customs barrier? How long before the walls would reappear? The barbed wire and the mines?

Jerusalem's spiritual singularity is obvious, as the birthplace of monotheism. Jerusalem is mentioned 667 times in the Bible. For Jews, it is the only source of spirituality. During three millennia, since the time of King David, Jerusalem was the chosen capital. And when no Jewish entity existed, Jerusalem remained the emotional focus of the scattered Jewish people, whose longings were expressed in their daily prayers: 'On the shores of Babylon, there we sat and also wept, when we remembered Zion.'

For Christians, though there are other sites of reverence, whether Rome, Constantinople, Lourdes or even Bethlehem, the history of Jesus unfolds in this city. And for Moslems, though Mecca and Medina are imbued with higher degrees of holiness, Jerusalem bears a weighty role.

Yet note should be made that through centuries of Moslem rule – Omayyad, Ayyubid, Mameluke, Ottoman and, most recently, Jordanian – there was never an Arab ruler who chose Jerusalem as his capital. And it was there for the taking. Moreover, as neither Mecca nor Medina was designated the capital of Saudi Arabia but Riyadh, the holiness of a city in Islam is not the *sine qua non* for establishing a capital.

I am convinced that a solution is possible, though equally convinced that it will have to be a wholly original notion. The impasse we face in explaining our problems is that there are no similar situations and people tend to seek familiar comparisons. Creativity will have to replace precedents.

Perhaps a new concept, functional sovereignty, will have to replace geographical sovereignty. In recent years we have created neighbourhood councils called '*minhalot*' to encourage citizens' participation in local governance. The *minhalot* do not yet have legal authority, though this bears the advantage of acceptability for the Arab population as they are not subject to objection on grounds of sovereignty or nationalism. Similarly, they are acceptable to our right-wing politicians who might be loath to endorse the word borough as they suspect us of a readiness to give 'too much' independence to the Arab population. An expanded system of *minhalot* might eventually play a role in a permanent arrangement by evolving into a framework for self-administration by autonomous communities.

In 1977, I wrote an article in *Foreign Affairs*, a periodical published in the United States. I talked of the four principles guiding us in Jerusalem, principles which continue to dictate our decisions and actions:

1. There will be free access to all the holy places (irrespective of nationality) and they shall be administered by their adherents.

   This principle includes the obligation to prevent religious assembly from being hijacked for political purposes, whether by Jews, Christians or Moslems.
2. Everything possible shall be done to ensure unhindered development of the Arab way of life among Arabs in the city and ensure Moslems and Christians a practical, religious, cultural and commercial governance over their own daily lives.
3. Everything possible should be done to ensure equal governmental, municipal and social services in all parts of the city.

We are at times berated that a gap still exists between services available in East and West Jerusalem, but unfortunately it takes more than nineteen years to undo the neglect of centuries. Moreover, while there are Jewish donors to the Jerusalem Foundation who comprehend the importance of financing projects for the Arab community, this understanding is not widespread. Thus there is a differential in philanthropic moneys available for public projects in spite of some generous Christian donations.

We once strove to enlist the help of wealthy

Arabs living abroad, as we had enlisted the help of Jews, but with little success. In one instance a former Jerusalem Arab living in Washington offered to support an Arab day-care centre, but he was subsequently threatened and ceased his donations.

The Arabs know that City Hall fights each day for their needs, for their dignity. Sadly it is still often swimming against the stream, even more so since the unrest. I am sorry that the Arabs do not join in the democratic political fray as they could fight even more effectively than I for their needs. The Arab population, like Jewish non-citizens, have the right to vote in municipal elections. Until the uprising, many took advantage of this right, but they always feared presenting a candidate for the City Council because of internal threats.

4. Continuing efforts should be made to increase cultural, social and economic contacts among the various elements of Jerusalem's population, while preserving the cultural and even the national identity of each group.

Jerusalem is not a melting-pot like America where all immigrants strive to be Americans. Jerusalem is a mosaic where national identities like Greek, Armenian and Arab have been preserved and nurtured for centuries.

The unceasing scrutiny of the world which places Jerusalem under a powerful microscope makes a formidable task even more so. We are frequently vexed by the lack of fairness in how the world judges Israel, but we must judge ourselves, and expect to be judged, by our own standards no matter what the standards of others may be or how the world judges them.

I am convinced that the era of investigative reporting makes any step that much harder to take. I often jest with American friends that were there television in the eighteenth-century, the Constitution would never have achieved consensus.

The hardest lesson we have learned is that it is easier to declare a state or a capital than to build one. Nevertheless, I am convinced that in this century of failed liberalism, socialism, fascism and communism, the return of the Jewish people to Zion after 2,000 years will be judged as a singular historical event, one of the most successful socio-political movements of the twentieth-century.

We know that history does not move in a straight line, and it is often hard to know where you are when you are caught in its zigs and zags. History is a slow process and we must understand that, despite the fast lanes of our era. Some problems have taken and will take generations to resolve, as is the case with the Irish or the Basques or the Walloons. If we learn to be patient with a more deliberate speed, perhaps others will.

A further handicap is the lack of democratic traditions among Jerusalemites. The 100,000 members of the ultra-Orthodox Jewish communities live in small theocracies, often under hereditary rabbis; the 200,000 Jerusalemites who are immigrants from Moslem countries or Eastern Europe brought no tradition of involvement in public affairs or democratic decision-making; the Christians live in communities ruled by their elders and clergy; and the Moslems have no democratic tradition or state anywhere. In Jerusalem, the Moslems have been ruled by Turkish tyranny, British paternalism and Jordanian discrimination, none conducive to the evolution of democratic traditions.

The city has little authority to make formal and lasting arrangements because we still function under the colonial code inherited from the British. The city's communities rightly feel insecure with the informal arrangements we have instituted since future municipal or central governments might not feel bound by them; if we could legalize these arrangements, we could eliminate this insecurity and ease tensions.

The formal guarantee of each group's rights will help ensure that one day the passive habit of non-violence and tolerance may become a conscious pride in the peace of Jerusalem and in the acceptance of others. Practical and unglamorous efforts are needed to further this process.

Perhaps the significance of the uprising is the feeling of pride it instills in the Palestinian population, similar to that instilled in the Egyptian people with their crossing of the Suez Canal in the 1973 war. It is commonly postulated that Sadat could not have reached an agreement with Israel without the pride of this initial success. That subsequently the Israeli army recrossed the Suez, surrounded the Egyptian Third Army and was in sight of Cairo was inconsequential.

It may take several generations to eradicate fear, resentment and religious fanaticism. But only a united city can ensure that Jerusalem, too often the battleground of holy wars, will be a city of peace, a city with sufficient spiritual space to embrace its multiplicity of faiths and ideologies.

CHRONOLOGY

20th century BC	Canaanite Jerusalem
	First mention on Egyptian clay figurines (execration texts)
	Abraham meets Melchizedek, King of Salem
1004 BC	King David establishes Jerusalem as capital of United Kingdom of Israel
967 BC	King Solomon builds First Temple
586 BC	Destruction of Jerusalem and of Temple by Nebuchadnezzar and exile of Jews to Babylon
537 BC	Return of Jews from Babylon
515 BC	Completion of Second Temple
332 BC	Alexander the Great conquers the land
	End of Persian period; beginning of Hellenistic period
169 BC	Seleucid king, Antiochus IV Epiphanes, plunders Temple
167–141 BC	Hasmonean War of Liberation
164 BC	Reconquest of Temple Mount and rededication of Temple
63 BC	Pompeii captures Jerusalem
	Beginning of Roman period
37–34 BC	Reign of King Herod the Great
AD 26–36	Pontius Pilate, Roman procurator of Judea
c. 33	Crucifixion of Jesus
66–70	The Great Revolt – the War of the Jews against the Romans
70	Fall of Jerusalem and destruction of the Second Temple by Titus
132–5	Bar Kochba's Revolt
135	Emperor Hadrian's total destruction of Jerusalem
324	Beginning of Byzantine period
326	Visit of Queen Helena, mother of Emperor Constantine the Great, who determines the location of events associated with the last days of Jesus and initiates churches to commemorate these events
end of 6th century	Madaba map of Jerusalem
614	Persian conquest
629	Recapture by Byzantines
c. 638	The Caliph Omar enters Jerusalem
691	Completion of the Dome of the Rock
1099	Crusader capture of Jerusalem
1187	Saladin captures Jerusalem from Crusaders
1250–1517	The Mameluke period
1517	Ottoman conquest of Jerusalem
1538–40	Sultan Suleiman the Magnificent rebuilds the city walls
1860	First Jewish settlement outside city walls
1917	General Allenby's entry into Jerusalem
	Beginning of British Mandate period
1947	United Nations Resolution partitioning Palestine into Jewish and Arab states and designating Jerusalem as an international city
14 May 1948	End of British Mandate
	State of Israel proclaimed
	Attack on Israel by five Arab armies
28 May 1948	Jewish Quarter in Old City falls
April 1949	Armistice Agreement signed
	Jerusalem divided between Israel and Jordan
13 December 1949	Jerusalem declared capital of the State of Israel
5 June 1967	Attack of Jordanians on West Jerusalem
	Beginning of Six Day War
7 June 1967	Israeli troops capture Old City
	Jerusalem reunited

GAZETTEER

Note: Tourist offices are listed separately at the beginning of the gazetteer. Otherwise all places are listed alphabetically, and under their names rather than under their titles or designations – thus the Basilica of Ecce Homo will be found under 'E' for Ecce Homo.

Please also note that, while every effort has been made to check the accuracy of the information given here, it is subject to constant change. Visitors are therefore advised to check before setting out.

Government Tourist Information Offices
24 King George Street – Tel. 241281
Jaffa Gate – Tel. 282295/6
    Sun.–Thurs.: 8.30 a.m.–5 p.m.
    Fri.: 8.30 a.m.–2 p.m.

Municipal Information Office for Tourists
17 Jaffa Road – Tel. 228844
    Sun.–Thurs.: 9 a.m.–1 p.m.

Christian Information Centre
Inside Jaffa Gate – Tel. 287647
    Mon.–Fri.: 8.30 a.m.–12.30 p.m.; 3 p.m.–
        6 p.m. (5.30 p.m. in winter)
    Sat.: 8.30 a.m.–12.30 p.m.

Al Aqsa Mosque, Dome of the Rock
Haram al Sharif (entry inside Dung Gate) –
Tel. 283313, 272358
    Sat.–Thurs.: 8 a.m.–3 p.m.
    During Ramadan: 8 a.m.–11 a.m.
    Closed Moslem holidays
    Entrance fee to mosques and museum

Church of All Nations, see *Basilica of Gethsemane*

Ammunition Hill Museum (Givat Hatachmoshet)
Eshkol Boulevard – Tel. 828442
    Sun.–Thurs.: 9 a.m.–5 p.m. (4 p.m. in winter)
    Fri.: 9 a.m.–1 p.m.

Archaeological Seminars
36 Chabad Street, Jewish Quarter – Tel. 282221

Armenian Cathedral of St James
Armenian Quarter – Tel. 282331
    Mon.–Fri.: 3 p.m.–3.30 p.m.
    Sat., Sun.: 2.30 p.m.–3.15 p.m.

Armenian Cemetery
Mount Zion
    Daily: 8 a.m.–5 p.m.

Armenian Museum
Armenian Quarter
    Mon.–Sat.: 10 a.m.–4.30 p.m.
    Closed Sundays
    Entrance fee

Pool of Bethesda, see *St Anne's Church*

Botanical Gardens see *Hebrew University*

Burnt House
Jewish Quarter – Tel. 287211
    Sun.–Thurs.: 9 a.m.–5 p.m.
    Fri.: 9 a.m.–1 p.m.
    Entrance fee
    Check for times of Sight and Sound
        presentation

Bus 99
Parking area below Jaffa Gate – Tel. 551868,
534596, 247783
    Departure every hour on the hour
    Sun.–Thurs.: 9 a.m.–5 p.m.
    Fri.: 9 a.m.–2 p.m.
    Fee

Chaba Museum of Jewish Micrography
43 Haneviim Street – Tel. 244242
    Sun.–Thurs.: 9 a.m.–noon

Citadel (Tower of David)
Inside Jaffa Gate – Tel. 283273
Museum of the History of Jerusalem
    Sat.–Thurs.: 10 a.m.–5 p.m. (7 p.m. in
        summer)
    Fri.: 10 a.m.–2 p.m.
Sound and Light Show
    English – nightly at 9.30 p.m.
    Hebrew – nightly at 8.30 p.m.
    French – Mon., Wed., Sat. at 10.30 p.m.
    German – Sun., Tues., Thurs. at 10.30 p.m.
    No performances on Fridays
    Above hours are for summer time; otherwise,
        all performances are an hour earlier
    Dress warmly

Coenaculum (Room of the Last Supper)
Mount Zion
    Daily: 8.30 a.m.–sunset
    Closed Friday afternoons

Monastery of the Cross
Valley of the Cross, below Israel Museum –
Tel. 667121
    Mon.–Thurs., Sat.: 9 a.m.–5 p.m.
    Fri.: 9 a.m.–1.30 p.m.

Damascus Gate Roman Plaza
Sultan Suleiman Street – Tel. 224403/4
  Sat.–Thurs.: 9 a.m.–5 p.m.
  Fri.: 9 a.m.–2 p.m.
  Entrance fee

City of David Archaeological Excavations
Below Dung Gate, outside City Wall –
Tel. 224403/4
  Sat.–Thurs.: 9 a.m.–4 p.m.
  Fri.: 9 a.m.–2 p.m.
  Entrance fee

Tomb of King David
Mount Zion – Tel. 719767
  Sun.–Thurs.: 8 a.m.–sunset
  Fri.: 8 a.m.–1 p.m.

Tower of David, see *Citadel*

Museum of the Divided City, see *Turgeman Post Museum*

Church of Dominus Flevit
Gethsemane – Tel. 285837
  Daily: 8 a.m.–11.30 a.m.; 3 p.m.–5 p.m.

Dormition Abbey
Mount Zion – Tel. 719927
  Mon.–Sat.: 8 a.m.–noon; 2 p.m.–6 p.m.
  Sun.: 9 a.m.–noon; 2 p.m.–6 p.m.

Basilica of Ecce Homo (Sisters of Zion Convent)
Via Dolorosa – Tel. 282445
  Mon.–Sat.: 8.30 a.m.–12.30 p.m.;
    2 p.m.–5 p.m.

Church of Eleona, see *Pater Noster*

Model of the First Temple
Jewish Quarter – Tel. 286288
  Sun.–Thurs.: 9 a.m.–5 p.m.
  Fri.: 9 a.m.–1 p.m.
  Entrance fee

Chapel of the Flagellation
Via Dolorosa – Tel. 282936
  Daily: 8 a.m.–noon; 2 p.m.–6 p.m.
    (1 p.m.–5 p.m. in winter)

Garden Tomb
Conrad Schick Lane, off Shechem (Nablus)
Road – Tel. 283402
  Mon.–Sat.: 8 a.m.–12.15 p.m.;
    2.30 p.m.–5.15 p.m.

Germany Colony Pool
Emek Refaim Street
  Entrance fee

Basilica of Gethsemane (Church of all Nations)
Gethsemane – Tel. 283264
  Daily: 8 a.m.–noon; 2.30 p.m.–6 p.m.
    (5 p.m. in winter)

Grotto of Gethsemane
Gethsemane – Tel. 283264
  Mon.–Wed., Fri., Sat.: 8.30 a.m.–11.45 a.m.;
    2.30 p.m.–5 p.m. (4 p.m. in winter)
  Sun., Thurs.: 2.30 p.m.–3.30 p.m.

Great Synagogue
58 King George Street – Tel. 247112
  Sun.–Thurs.: 9 a.m.–1 p.m.
  Fri.: 9 a.m.–11 a.m.

Greek Orthodox Patriarchate Museum
Christian Quarter – Tel. 284006
  Mon.–Fri.: 9 a.m.–1 p.m.; 3 p.m.–5 p.m.
  Sat.: 9 a.m.–1 p.m.

Hebrew Union College
13 King David Street – Tel. 203333
  Sun.–Thurs.: 10 a.m.–4 p.m.
  Fri., Sat.: 10 a.m.–2 p.m.

Hebrew University, Botanical Gardens
Givat Ram Campus, Ruppin Street – Tel. 585111
  Sun.–Thurs.: guided tour at 10 a.m.
Botanical Gardens
  Always open

Hechal Shlomo (Chief Rabbinate), Wolfson Museum
58 King George Street – Tel. 247112
  Sun.–Thurs.: 9 a.m.–1 p.m.
  Fri.: 9 a.m.–noon

Herodian Mansions, see *Wohl Archaeological Museum*

Herzl Museum
Mount Herzl – Tel. 531108
  Sun.–Thurs.: 9 a.m.–5 p.m.
  Fri.: 9 a.m.–1 p.m.

Chamber of the Holocaust
Mount Zion – Tel. 716841, 719767
  Sun.–Thurs.: 9 a.m.–6 p.m.
  Fri.: 9 a.m.–1.30 p.m.
  Nominal fee

Museum of the Holocaust, see *Yad Vashem*

Holyland Hotel Model of Ancient Jerusalem
Bayit Vegan, at Holyland Hotel – Tel. 788118
  Daily: 8 a.m.–5 p.m.
  Entrance fee
  For visits on Saturday, purchase tickets in
    advance

Church of the Holy Sepulchre
Christian Quarter – Tel. 284213
  Daily: 4.30 a.m.–8 p.m. (7 p.m. in winter)

Hurva Synagogue Site
Jewish Quarter Road – Tel. 288141
  Sun.–Thurs.: 9 a.m.–5 p.m.
  Fri.: 9 a.m.–1 p.m.

Islamic Art Museum
2 Palmach Street – Tel. 661291/2
  Sun.–Thurs.: 10 a.m.–5 p.m.
  Sat.: 10 a.m.–1 p.m.
  Entrance fee

Israel Museum, Shrine of the Book, Billy Rose Art Garden
Ruppin Street, Hakirya – Tel. 698211
  Sun.–Thurs.: 10 a.m.–5 p.m.
  Tues.: 4 p.m.–10 p.m. (10 a.m.–10 p.m. in
    summer); Shrine of the Book 10 a.m.–10
    p.m. (year-round)
  Fri., Sat.: 10 a.m.–2 p.m.
  Entrance fee

Israelite Tower
Jewish Quarter – Tel. 286288
  Sun.–Thurs.: 9 a.m.–5 p.m.
  Fri.: 9 a.m.–1 p.m.
  Entrance fee

Jewish Quarter Memorial Site
Jewish Quarter Road – Tel. 288141
  Sun.–Thurs.: 9 a.m.–5 p.m.
  Fri.: 9 a.m.–1 p.m.

Jewish National and University Library
Hebrew University, Givat Ram Campus –
Tel. 585026
  Sun.–Wed.: 9 a.m.–7 p.m.
  Thurs.: 9 a.m.–3 p.m.
  Fri.: 9 a.m.–1 p.m.
  Closed on all holidays

Knesset (Parliament)
James de Rothschild Boulevard, Hakirya –
Tel. 554111
  Sun. and Thurs. only: 8.30 a.m.–2.30 p.m.
    (bring passports)

Room of the Last Supper see *Coenaculum*

Tomb of Mary
Gethsemane
  Daily: 6.30 a.m.–noon; 2 p.m.–5 p.m.

Windmill and Museum of Sir Moses Montefiore, see
Yemin Moshe

Old Yishuv Court Museum
6 Or Hahayim Street – Tel. 284636
  Sun.–Thurs.: 9 a.m.–2 p.m.
  Entrance fee

Ophel Archaeological Excavations
Inside Dung Gate, south of Western Wall –
Tel. 224403/4
  Sun.–Thurs.: 9 a.m.–4 p.m.
  Fri.: 9 a.m.–2 p.m.
  Entrance fee

Pater Noster (Church of Eleona)
Mount of Olives – Tel. 283143
  Mon.–Sat.: 9 a.m.–11.45 a.m.;
    3 p.m.–4.30 p.m.

Pontifical Institute Museum and Library
3 Emile Botta Street – Tel. 222843
  Mon., Wed., Fri.: 9 a.m.–noon

Ramparts Walk
Entry at Damascus Gate (and Jaffa Gate) –
Tel. 224403/4
  Sat.–Thurs.: 9 a.m.–4 p.m.
  Fri.: 9 a.m.–2 p.m.
  Entrance fee

Church of the Redeemer (Lutheran)
Muristan Street – Tel. 282543
  Mon.: 9 a.m.–1 p.m.
  Tues.–Sat.: 9 a.m.–1 p.m.; 2 p.m.–5 p.m.

Dome of the Rock, see *Al Aqsa Mosque*

Rockefeller Archaeological Museum
Sultan Suleiman Street – Tel. 283151, 282251
  Sun.–Thurs.: 10 a.m.–5 p.m.
  Fri., Sat.: 10 a.m.–2 p.m.
  Entrance fee

St Alexander's Chapel
25 Dabbagha Street, Old City – Tel. 284580
  Daily: 9 a.m.–3 p.m. (ring bell)

St Andrew's Church of Scotland
Opposite Railway Station – Tel. 714659

St Anne's Church, Pool of Bethesda
Via Dolorosa – Tel. 283285
  Mon.–Sat.: 8 a.m.–noon; 2.30 p.m.–6 p.m.
    (2 p.m.–5 p.m. in winter)

St Mary Magdalene Church
Gethsemane – Tel. 282897
  Tues., Thurs.: 10 a.m.–11.30 a.m.

St Peter in Gallicantu Church
East of Mount Zion – Tel. 283332
  Mon.–Sat.: 8.30 a.m.–11.45 a.m.;
    2 p.m.–5.30 p.m. (5 p.m. in winter)

Sephardi Synagogues
Entry to Jewish Quarter – Tel. 224371
  Sun.–Thurs.: 9 a.m.–3 p.m.
  Fri.: 9 a.m.–1 p.m.
  Entrance fee

Solomon's Quarries (Zedekiah's Cave)
Sultan Suleiman Street, between Damascus Gate
and Herod's Gate – Tel. 224403/4
  Daily: 9 a.m.–2 p.m.
  Entrance fee

Museum of Taxes
32 Agron Street – Tel. 703333
  Sun., Tues., Thurs.: 1 p.m.–4 p.m.
  Mon., Wed., Fri.: 10 a.m.–noon

Ticho House Museum
7–9 Harav Kook Street, City Centre – Tel. 245068,
244186
Museum
  Sun., Mon., Wed., Thurs.: 10 a.m.–5 p.m.
  Tues.: 10 a.m.–10 p.m.
Café and light meals
  Sun.–Thurs.: 10 a.m.–11.45 p.m.
  Fri.: 10 a.m.–2.45 p.m.
  Sat.: Hour after sunset – 11.45 p.m.

*Turgeman Post Museum (Museum of the Divided
City)*
1 Hel Hahandasa Street (corner Shivtei
Yisrael) – Tel. 281278
  Sun.–Thurs.: 9 a.m.–4 p.m.
  Fri.: 9 a.m.–1 p.m.
  Entrance fee

Wilson's Arch
Western Wall
  Sun., Tues., Wed.: 8.30 a.m.–3 p.m.
  Mon., Thurs.: 12.30 p.m.–3 p.m.
  Fri.: 8.30 a.m.–noon

Wohl Archaeological Museum (Herodian Mansions)
Off Hurva Square, Jewish Quarter – Tel. 288141
  Sun.–Thurs.: 9 a.m.–5 p.m.
  Fri.: 9 a.m.–1 p.m.
  Entrance fee

Wolfson Museum, see *Hechal Shlomo*

Yad Vashem (Museum of the Holocaust)
Mount Herzl – Tel. 531202
  Sun.–Thurs.: 9 a.m.–4.45 p.m.
  Fri.: 9 a.m.–1.45 p.m.

*Yemin Moshe Windmill and Museum of Sir Moses
Montefiore*
Yemin Moshe, off King David Street
  Sun.–Thurs.: 9 a.m.–4 p.m.
  Fri.: 9 a.m.–1 p.m.

Zedekiah's Cave, see *Solomon's Quarries*

INDEX

Page numbers in *italics* denote illustrations